I took all the stories, my own and those of my family's, and wove them into one story—this story. I placed it in the Ozarks because that's where my people lived and where they left. Some of the names I swapped; others I borrowed. The stories changed in the weaving, but the love and the loss, the hope and heartache, the glory and the shame are all flesh and blood true.

To my wonderful neighbors! Janet

Copyright © 2011 Janet Smith Post

All rights reserved. No part of this book may be reproduced, transmitted, or stored in an information retrieval system in any form or by any means, graphic, electronic, or mechanical, including photocopying, taping, and recording except as may be expressly permitted by the 1976 Copyright Act or in writing by the publisher.

Requests for permissions should be addressed to:

Natural Way Publishing
P. O. Box 2242
Cupertino, CA 95015
Fax: 408 564 5685

Distributed by: Natural Way Publishing

www.writingthenaturalway.com

The Ingram Group

First U.S. edition 2011
Library of Congress Control Number 20011936102
Post, Janet Smith
Cotton Rock
p. cm
ISBN   978-0-9832524-1-2
1. biographical fiction   2. mystery

Cover design: Jeanne Bullard, JB's GraphicWorks
White River photos courtesy of Kim Irby.
www.artistrising.com/galleries/KimIrbysGallery

Printed by: Lightning Source, printing division of the Ingram Group.
www.lightningsource.com

For my husband, Jim,
and my sister, Gayle,

who always believed…

Based on the White River of the Ozarks
(The names of people, places, towns, and dams are fictitious.)

My grateful appreciation to Gabriele Rico who willed my manuscript from a forgotten drawer, gave it life and wings; to Jeanne Bullard, without whose daily help and patience, this work would not be dressed and ready to meet the reader; a special thanks to Georgia Thurman, Joan Klaus, Carol Poston and Meta Mazur. Thank you to my darling husband, Jim Post, who never tired of listening, and thanks upon thanks to all my children and my friends—it takes many hands to circle our dreams.

Thoughts from the Back Porch   October 1996

In times past when Ozark women made vinegar, they added five kernels of corn. Each of the kernels was named for a man or woman noted for meanness, and they were dropped into the fermenting liquid, one at a time as the names were recited. While the kernels steeped with the esters of cider, they instilled the stinging bite required of good, stout vinegar—or so it was said.

When the women baked a wild berry pie, they added three spoons of rich cream to its center. Each of the three spoonfuls was named in honor of a woman noted for kindness. It was said you could guess the women from the sweetness of the pie.

But when the hill-taught apothecaries searched pockets of woodland shade for wild ginseng and goldenseal, selecting only the most mature plants, sometimes waiting years before harvesting their healing medicine they chose a single name. As they crushed the herbs beneath their pestles, they whispered only one name—someone known for a deep sense of purpose, without which a person never fully recovers. I would have whispered the name of Anna McKerry. Anna was a student in my writing class. To think of Anna is to think of the river. In one of her notebooks she wrote:

"Whether folks love the river or whether they never give it a thought, it goes right on doing its work, day after day, year after year, running along between its banks, picking up its bed and moving it downstream, then picking it up and moving it again. Day and night, never resting. A piece of eternity sliding by."

To think of Anna was also to think of her struggle. She was a soul-searcher in need of relief, a woman who grappled with guilt and with God. It echoed in the lines she wrote describing the river's catastrophic change:

"Sometimes without warning things can change the whole course of a river. Up at New Madrid, an earthquake lifted the Mississippi right out of its channel and shifted its bed forever. The air, chock full of sulfur, turned dark as a cave. Whole river banks collapsed into the churning water."

I suppose many people can point to a day their lives were forever altered. For me, it was the day a loaded gravel truck failed to stop at a stop sign. For Anna it was the day Rayley Larkin forgot to sound the warning whistle, and the White River sent down a savage and unforeseen wall of water. There are also small catastrophes far less galvanizing, tragedies quiet and unnoticed, where hope dies silently, and love shifts to an altered and unrequited course. Anna wrote about this in her first notebook:

Anna's First Notebook

Like I said, Mr. Sinclair, I'll be putting my life down in a notebook and bringing it to your writing class. I think writing it down will put it to rest, free me from thinking till my head is sore, keep me from traveling down worn paths that lead into old, sad hollows, up to new ridges where there are things I didn't know, down into sloughs so deep and dark, it feels like I'll never find my way out.

It was 1958 and it was spring, a time when the bee carries pollen on its wing, the female moth spreads her perfume on the night air, and young blood runs under skin the color of ripe peaches. I don't think we ever love like we loved the first time. First love doesn't calculate. It opens every petal wide, lifts itself up to nature's warm, sweet prodding. I was seventeen, and I fell in love with Jake Kenaway.

When Jake walked into the room, things woke up and danced. He would slide onto a stool at the Sugar Gum Cafe, with his dimples and happy blue eyes and say, "Honey Girl, bring me a cup of Joe and a piece of Ozark pie."

Jake came into the Sugar Gum Café with the crew who worked on Marble Head Dam, up on the White River. I waited tables after school and weekends and saved my money for tuition in Springville. It wasn't that my college plans weren't as real as the moonlight. It was that I didn't know love and hormones could put a sleeper-hold on common sense. I didn't know then that we can be our own worst traitor.

The night finally came when I waited in the moonlight on the banks of the Sugar Gum River, and Jake stepped out of a johnboat and dropped down on my blanket.

"I don't know how to kiss," I told him, "You'll have to teach me."

He said, "Just take all the love you have, Honey Girl, and put it in your mouth."

A young man's chest is a wondrous surprise. Underneath a young man's shirt, his chest is solid as an ironing board. It's the finest place to lay your head. Feels like coming home. But it's a man's hands that I never considered. I'd seen men's hands laboring in the field, veins standing up in knots, men's hands gripping an ax handle, swinging down hard on a block of wood or prying a tire off its drum. I'd seen angry hands: My step-father's hand balled into a fist pounding the table. I'd even been slapped by his hand when his blood rose up with temper.

I didn't know that a man's hands could touch soft as corn silk, or that they knew how to slide along the skin, slow and careful, knew just where to stop and wait to read the tremble of a young girl's surprise. I walked home by moonlight through the cane fields, my cotton dress wrinkled by love.

Love doesn't know how to give anything less than everything. When I had turned twelve I took flowers to my sixth grade teacher, Mrs. Bedford. I put them in Momma's best vase, handed down from Grandma Effie. Momma would never have wanted that vase to leave the house, but I was willing to believe Mrs. Bedford would return it unharmed. The flowers looked beautiful in the girlish pink of the china. Mrs. Bedford loved the vase. I don't even know if she liked the flowers. She figured the vase was hers, and I didn't know how to tell her it wasn't.

Sugar Gum wasn't forgiving of a baby born from the moonlight. Old French miners and trappers who came to dig for lead and set traps for beaver and fox sometimes left behind a "pack saddle baby," a baby conceived on a saddle used as a makeshift bed. A baby born on a love blanket in 1959 in Sugar Gum got labeled "pack saddle" for life.

Grandma Poinselot had warned me often enough. "When a man gets through making love, honey, all he has to do is zip up his britches. A woman is left with a baby in her belly and the world's judgment on her back."

A young girl in love doesn't believe those words, though they've been recited for generations. A young girl in love is more than willing to tell herself a lie. Grandma Poinselot proved right. I was left with a baby growing under my Sugar Gum Cafe apron, and Jake was in Kalispell, Montana, waiting to be sent to the next new dam.

"Reckon you'll be going off to Springville. Learn to be a teacher like your sister, Zoe." That's what I heard each day at the Sugar Gum Cafe. Everyone knew that Jake had left with the crew. I was the only one who knew he'd left without saying good-bye. Mrs. Bedford took a teaching job in Duluth, Minnesota. I guess she took Momma's vase with her. I never saw her or Jake Kenaway again.

The day came when folks began whispering. Folks in Sugar Gum are no different from most. They call a thing what it is. "Looks like Anna McKerry's gonna have herself a baby born on the wrong side of the blanket." Each whisper felt sharp as a thrown rock. Something inside me fell under the weight. It's been laying low ever since.

There are many vulgar names for sex. The Sugar Gum girls knew some of them. We knew the boys whispered about getting their first "piece." For them it meant their first helping of sex; but for a girl in love it's about a piece cut straight through her heart, like a cored apple. My beginning is lying dead at the bottom of Pearl Harbor. Most of my future drowned in the White River. My childhood is buried under Marble Head Lake, and my turn at love is laying low under an unnamed swamp. I figure when I get a name for that swamp I'll be climbing out. That's why I'm writing these notebooks.

Thoughts from the Back Porch   October 1996

There are fourteen more of Anna's notebooks stacked on the little table beside me. The Grand Jury subpoenaed them a few days ago and returned them to me today. Anna called to ask, "All right if I come in the morning to pick up my notebooks, Mr. Sinclair?" She never learned to call me John, though she was nearly old enough to be my mother. "Respect," she said. "Professors don't usually put down roots in the Ozarks. Soil's too thin."

But it wasn't the limits of the soil that restricted my stay. I came down on a sixth-month leave of absence granted by the college in Springville, time I planned to spend at the cabin my granddad Rowden built—my cabin now. I agreed to teach a writing class as a community service for the little town of Cotton Rock, but the majority of my time would be spent writing my novel and following Granddad's admonition, "Drop your line in the river, Johnnie boy. Eat fish fresh from the bone of heaven."

I've used up two-thirds of my sabbatical; the summer has come and gone. The brown trout will be moving up river. The evenings have grown cool, and the dogwood trees along the bank are turning scarlet. The water, mirroring the hillsides of oak, maple, and sweet gum holds wrinkled pools of red and copper. The shagbark hickory tree at the corner of the porch has turned gold. "Not just yellow," Grandma Rowden always clarified, "but true gold."

The horn blew sometime ago. The generators opened up at the dam, and the river's rising. Granddad's boat, *Rosalee*, is bumping against the side of the dock asking to be set free of her tether, but I won't be taking her out today. October's nearly over; there's a hint of approaching winter on the air. Time for a decision. Granddad used to say, "When you go fishing, boy, you gotta know what kind of fish you're after. Then when you drop the bait into the water, you got to learn to trust the nibble. No shilly-shallying hesitation, or you'll wind up missing the take." Sometimes he'd add, "When it comes to love, boy, and especially the right woman don't shilly-shally." On this day of decision I needed to admit two things to myself: Leah was the right woman, and I didn't take Granddad's advice.

I first met Leah through the pages of Anna's notebooks. Anna attended my writing class that met Monday evenings at the Cotton Rock Library in a back room with stout oak tables, the heavy smell of Manila paper, old cloth bindings and walls lined with book shelves.

Several people signed up for the class—most of them recently retired from Kansas City or St. Louis. But as I had hoped, some of them were Ozark natives: Anna, whose last name was McKerry, Lucy Freeman, and Emmett McDougal.

Lucy was, as she wrote in her notebook, "old as dirt and freckled as a turkey egg." She wrote little tales she believed had been witnessed by guardian angels and which she titled "Angel Gossip." Emmett never ventured far from a fishing pole and the river bank. He signed up for the class because the Osage Fish Hatchery hired him to publish a column in their news letter, titled simply "Emmett's Fishing Report." According to Emmett they'd pay him enough to buy his fishing license and keep his tackle box full, and he needed someone to help him with his writing—hopefully me.

I'm used to teaching college students, and I looked forward to teaching older adults, people who had lived long enough to accumulate a story, though even the smallest child has a story. The trick is to know what is not the story, so that only the purest essence is skimmed from a life and rendered to the paper. That takes talent. I try to warn students from the start that I can't teach talent, though many of them arrive expecting to receive that very gift.

Nevertheless I can offer some helpful suggestions and maintain a gentle pressure that keeps the natural writer writing, the person compelled to distill life into words. Of course there's usually one student whose soul is tone deaf to the sound of life, who has absolutely no idea what another human being might like to find in print, who stays after class to ask painful questions, never hesitates to volunteer to read, has the constitution of a John Deere tractor and would never consider being absent, let alone sick.

Conversely in nearly every class, there's at least one compelling writer who rewards my efforts and reminds me why I wanted to teach. Anna was that writer. Good writers can inspire the class. They can also evoke certain resentment. Cora Eckert was a woman who resented most everything. It wasn't surprising that Cora's rancor would eventually take her to the Grand Jury where she reported that Anna's notebooks contained information vital to their investigation.

I had required my students to keep the notebooks, and for Anna her notebooks became her primary mode of writing. In fact they became a kind of memoir. On the night of the first class she waited until everyone had gone before walking to my desk. She wore her usual cotton dress, which appeared to have been washed often and ironed by a determined hand. Her once-dark hair, now lined with gray, caught up at the back of her head in a fixed knot. She wore no visible sign of jewelry or ornamentation, as though she had long ago reduced her life to a singular sense of mission. Her eyes were dark and intense.

"Will we be expected to read each week?" Her voice proved equally intense.

"Writers usually want to share their work," I said.

"I'm writing my way to the truth, Mr. Sinclair. I'm ready to peel off all my excuses. See what's underneath. That will take some privacy."

I suggested she read aloud only selected portions she felt would not be invasive. She agreed and held out her notebook. Although she was a quiet, almost shy woman, her unflinching determination soon dismissed any thought of weakness. She released the notebook into my hand but kept her eyes fastened on me as though she were judging the ripeness of a tomato or melon from her garden. I half expected she might reach out and take the notebook back.

"Okay then," she said and left the notebook to my care.

But for all her spunk, she carried with her an almost perpetual self-doubt. And beneath that fiercely ironed dress, she wore a buckeye on a chain around her neck to thwart bad luck. Her mother, she would write in one of her notebooks, had failed to wrap her in her father's shirt as soon as she was born, and a charm once neglected could require a lifetime of remedy.

She proved to be relentless in her pursuit of the truth and produced substantial writing in her weekly notebooks. Her writing inspired me to do some journaling of my own here on the back porch—notebooks I titled, "Thoughts from the Back Porch."

If I should be given a second chance, I don't want to be foolish enough to repeat old mistakes. So I'm taking the day to ask myself some hard questions. Like Anna I'm also ready to peel off all the excuses and see what's left. That requires looking back over the past summer and its story. It's a story of several lives, how they intertwine and influence one another, as the river carves the land and the land shapes the river's course—a communal reciprocity, traced most clearly in a small town like Cotton Rock.

The notebooks—Anna's and mine—tell the story, so I've decided to sit here on the back porch and read them aloud to the White River and to

Grandma's true-gold hickory tree, which seems to lean in now and then to listen.

From time to time I'll read a bit of Lucy Freeman's "Angel Gossip," or Emmett McDougall's "Fishing Report" and allow some Ozark humor to spread across the porch like one of the breezes that occasionally swells up from the river. Grandma used to stand in the midst of those breezes, her eyes closed and her arms held out and order me: "Fluff your lungs, John Sinclair. We may need to laugh!"

Anna's Second Notebook

They say the Scotch-Irish can't settle down till they've moved at least twice. Maybe that's why my folks had to leave the Appalachians and travel hundreds of miles west, before they could find land as lovely and desperate as the land they left behind, before they could put down roots in the Ozarks and be no better off.

Maybe they didn't feel at home till they saw the possibility of suffering and chose to carry their dreams along the path the Cherokee called the "trail of tears." Maybe that's why they decided to plant their corn and barley seeds on the limestone table where most any farmer would see only hard-scrabble, mountain land. It could have been the outright name "Desperation Mountains" that stopped the wheels on their wagons, even spoke to their Scottish humor or their talent for a good fight.

Then again it might have been their love of poetry that made them forget the thin, rocky soil, caused them to see only the promising streams of sweet water crisscrossing the hills, streams so clear you could see the rocks shining up from the bottom like cobblestone rainbows. Perhaps it was the woods, thick with pine, oak, black gum and hickory, and the hillsides so heavy with berries that in the spring when the white blossoms covered everything, it would be called blackberry winter. Or it might have been the thought that a cabin could hide like a bear in the deep woods, where quiet hung over everything like the thick, white fog that lays on the hills in the early mornings, made them think they could hide from past regrets.

But judging from the fact that Scots are just naturally against any kind of authority, it was likely the promise that a man could throw off a king and wear his own crown, ruling a forgotten little valley or the backside of a sheltered hill, where the nearest neighbor was a good walk, and a person didn't have to get along with anybody, could do things his own way. Whatever the reasons they stopped their wagons, unpacked their dreams and dug in.

The Ozark Mountains were home to more than the Scotch-Irish. They were home to the English and French. By the time my Grandma Effie was born the blood got well-mixed. I think mixing the blood of such long-standing enemies heated their hankering to choose against themselves whenever they could. Long years of living hunkered down in the hills made for loneliness and lingering sadness. The sound of fiddle music, the smell of corn liquor and the Sunday ring of a church bell coaxed them from their hiding. In between dancing and praying, necessity did the rest.

Like a tooth that wants pulling, need pried them out of the hills. Sooner or later they had to have a doctor or a preacher. Sooner or later they had to have someone help with birthing or dying and schooling in between. No matter how many vegetables they buried under straw in their root cellars, or how much side meat hung in their smoke houses, they still needed someone to grind their sorghum into molasses and their wheat into flour. Need makes for neighboring, and neighboring builds itself into a town like Sugar Gum, built on a fine river like the Sugar Gum River. Course the Sugar Gum got swallowed up by the White River when the Dam came, and life as we knew it got buried under fifty-thousand acres of Marble Head Lake.

But before the dam came, Sugar Gum was my home. My Grandma Effie McKerry lived fifty miles away in Walnut Hill where my daddy was born. My Grandma and Grandpa Poinselot lived in Sugar Gum, where my momma was born, where I was child and where I stopped being a child.

When my Momma, Mayta Poinselot, was eighteen, she went to Springville to live with her sister, my Aunt Nellie, and her brother-in-law, my Uncle Martin. She got a job at the Dosha Tomato Cannery. My daddy, Tom McKerry, first saw her at the corner of Twelfth and Grand.

He was reading his newspaper and waiting for the streetcar. She must be waiting too he thought. She had on her blue factory dress, her apron folded over her arm. Her hair was as black as the polish on his sailor boots.

She noticed that he noticed her. She smoothed her hair. It must be in need of something—eight hours of being tied in a bandana while she put tomatoes into cans. The yellow streetcar came up the street, sliding on its smooth rails, ringing its little bell. Daddy stepped back so Momma could get on first. She took the last empty seat, but there was room for him. ("It was a sign," he would say later.)

He took his sailor hat off to be respectful and asked, "Do you mind if I sit here?"

She shook her head.

He sat down and opened his paper to the back page. The headline read, "Humphrey Bogart plays Duke Mantee in *Petrified Forest*." A sailor on leave has no time to waste. So he spoke right out, though his face went red, "Do you like Humphrey Bogart?"

"I love Humphrey Bogart," she said, and her face went red too. In spite of herself she added, "I've seen *Petrified Forest* twice."

"I've seen it three times!" he said. (She would later say it was the second sign.)

He found out her name soon as he could.

"Mayta Poinselot. My folks are mostly French and English."

He said he could have guessed that much. He knew her pretty dark eyes were French soon as he saw them.

And she said, "Tom McKerry? I knew you's Scotch-Irish. Sandy red hair and those hazel eyes. Sure sign. Can't decide if they're green or brown. Neither color willing to give up the fight." But she was smiling big when she said it.

He said, "How 'bout that great line when Bogart says to Bette Davis, 'Looks like I'll spend the rest of my life dead.'" Later, she would tell Aunt Nellie she should have known it was a "death tick." (That's what hill people say when death gives a small warning it's coming near.)

Anyway, he was saying how they really ought to get off the streetcar and see *The Petrified Forest* one more time. Then between them they'd have seen it six times, a nice even number. Now that he knew her name and all. He confessed later that it was a mighty rickety argument, and he didn't expect it to hold up. He sat waiting for her answer, turning his sailor hat round in his hands, listening to the clack of the wheels on the track and the soft chime of the street car bell. His hat made the round six times before she said, "Okay, but you mustn't think I'm always so rash."

When the movie ended she took the street car to my Aunt Nellie's house, and he took a bus to the naval base in Norfolk, Virginia, with Momma's address in his pocket. They wrote letters nearly every day. He came to Springville six months later. Got right off the bus and kissed Momma in front of God and the whole town without so much as asking. Momma said he was going to whittle her morals down to such a sliver you wouldn't know her from a Drinkwater, and those Drinkwaters were all in jail or on their way.

But Daddy said she enjoyed that kiss, and Aunt Nellie said Momma was in no hurry to deny it. They were married a week later in Aunt Nellie's living room. Pastor Whiting married them for free, because Momma played piano every Sunday at the Riverside Tabernacle. Aunt Nellie would later say, "Bad luck came because they stood with their feet cross-ways on the floor boards, instead of running with the planks. Everyone in the Ozarks knows when you marry, it matters that your feet run in harmony with the place where you're standing."

Daddy left for California two days later, and Momma kept putting tomatoes in cans until my sister Zoe arrived nine months later. Momma paid Aunt Nellie to watch Zoe and went back to work at the tomato cannery. When Momma had saved up enough money, she took baby Zoe to San Diego where Daddy got stationed. She and Daddy had a whole year together, having picnics on the Pacific beach and catching every Humphrey Bogart movie that came to town.

By the following November Momma was four-months pregnant with me, and Daddy was aboard a ship in Pearl Harbor. Daddy wrote to her from the deck of the U.S.S. *Arizona* how he would finish up his hitch and take her back to Missouri, start up a regular life in Springville. His letter went out on the last mail plane. The Japanese bombed Pearl Harbor, and Daddy never came home again. He's still aboard the U.S.S. *Arizona*, lying at the bottom of Pearl Harbor along with 1,177 other men.

Momma got a telegram bearing out the truth of his death. She took the train home, cried all the way from San Diego to Springville. Uncle Martin and Aunt Nellie met her at the station and took her straight home. They thought that by nightfall Momma would be able to stop her crying and maybe sleep a little. But not long after the lights were turned out, Momma crept up the stairs, climbed into bed right between Uncle Martin and Aunt Nellie and cried like a broken child the whole long night.

The next morning she went home to Sugar Gum and moved in with Grandma and Grandpa Poinselot. I was born five months later. Momma got a job selling Radio Girl Perfume at the Sugar Gum Five-and-Dime, but the best part of Momma stayed behind in San Diego with Daddy and Humphrey Bogart.

Grandma and Grandpa Poinselot looked after Zoe and me. They had already raised five kids and should have been left alone. Grandma Poinselot was ten years younger than Granddad, and her dark hair, nearly absent of gray, made her look even younger. She spent her days in the woods, filling her apron pockets with leaves or roots for a neighbor's malady: the inside bark of a willow tree for easing pain or reducing a fever, elderberry leaves to stop bleeding, or red clover blossoms for cooking up cough syrup. When she wasn't in the woods, you could find her in the kitchen making butter from persimmons turned sweet by the frost, or picking black walnuts from their shells. On the days when the last handful emptied a feed sack, she'd be pedaling the foot feed of her sewing machine, making a dress for me or Zoe.

Long as I could remember, Granddad was nearly bald. "Good thing I have ears big as flapjacks," he'd say, "Cause they're holding on to the only hair I've got left." Granddad sat on the porch reading the *Old Farmer's Almanac* or arguing with Mr. Tillman about politics.

Granddad would talk about how good we had it with the Democratic Party, and when it came Mr. Tillman's turn to have a word for the Republicans, Granddad would turn off his hearing-aid. Mr. Tillman would just be filling up his lungs, ready to spout when Granddad would hold out his hearing aid and say, "She's turned off—can't hear a word." With all that air and argument backed up in him with no place to go, Tillman threatened to blow like a puff ball. You'd have thought it would come to him to have his say first, before Granddad flipped the switch, but it never did. Grandma always said, "Tillman was behind the door when the brains got passed out."

Grandma and Granddad touched hands. That's what hill people say when folks join together on a piece of work. And they went to raising kids all over again—Zoe and me. They were good to us, and theirs was the only happy marriage I ever saw first-hand. Grandma and Granddad loved to tell stories about the past. An old person wanting to tell a story is like a woman ready to birth. There's no holding it back. Most of their stories were handed out with something to eat. "Sit right down here, honey. We'll get you fixed up quick as pouring skim milk through a tow sack." Usually johnnycake spread with butter fresh off a cedar paddle.

I heard about the shouting Methodists who sang from a lukewarm-hymn book and the Landmark Baptists who only read their bibles so they could argue. I heard about the boy let down in a well that had damps and how he died before they could get him out—though I never thought to ask what "damps" were. I heard about Liege Brown who took his horse and buggy to Springville, where the horse got spooked by a fire whistle and ran away with Liege standing up yelling, "Stop or I'll kill you!" But he could have saved his breath 'cause the horse ran straight into a street car and both of them died on the spot.

The Ozark folks have been accused of being backwards on purpose, and I suppose that's true. Living in a place where change takes as long as growing up is both good and bad. It makes for a helping of wisdom and a helping of ignorance. So, I have a helping of both.

The thing is, God shot a hole in my heart, and I'm trying to write my way to figuring out my part and God's part. I'm going to write my way to a piece of solid ground, write about watching my Momma fade away with Alzheimers, about my little Mary whose body lies in the Cotton Rock Cemetery, about my son Sam, whose body never was found and about my beautiful Leah and her little Harlo. I'm going to write about turning over the pieces of time till they look like something I can recognize. It means pulling the scabs off old wounds.

The hill folks cover their clocks and stop their watches when a loved-one dies. They put cloths over all the mirrors, put cats under baskets, and life stops. Time stops until the last shovel of dirt covers the loved-one's grave. I'm caught somewhere between the death of my dreams and the last shovel of dirt. I've failed at most everything I tried to do. So, I have two final things I'm seeing through. I'm taking care of my Momma while there's still some of her left, and I'm giving my Leah and little Harlo a place to live till Leah gets her courage back.

I need to put my hand to something and see it turn out. If that doesn't happen I reckon I'll be all done with hoping. A coffin is what they use to box up the dead. I don't know what they use to box up hope that doesn't believe its own argument, but will not cover up the cat or stop its watch.

Thoughts from the Back Porch   June 1996

I skimmed along River Drive, headed for Lushbaugh's Grocery. I liked the way the road traced the river's edge, the way my jeep handled on the curves, my hand resting easy on the soft leather of the steering wheel and the radio playing an old favorite song. It was good to get away from the demands of the college.

In time the road left the river and yielded to the newly developed River Walk. Both sides of the road were lined with boutiques and souvenir shops. I turned onto Main Street and parked in front of Lushbaugh's.

Lushbaugh's is the only grocery store in town, and sooner or later you meet everyone in Cotton Rock at Lushbaugh's. Today, I met Anna's five-year-old granddaughter. She was sitting in a grocery cart, legs swinging. Her hair was parted into two blond pony tails, one on either side of her head, and her large, blue eyes were red from what must have been a recent cry. She tapped her heels against the metal cart in rhythm with the words she pretended to read from a chocolate chip coupon, "Put the cookies in the oven. Go out and play. When you come back, the cookies will be done." She looked up from her coupon and studied me with sober, red eyes.

"Hello," I said.

"Hello. I'm Harlo." Her little brows furrowed in thought, "Are you looking for chocolate chips?"

"No, I'm after a box of oatmeal," I said, reaching just above her head.

"Do you need an oatmeal coupon?" she asked.

"Why I suppose I do."

She placed the coupons in a careful row on her lap. Once again, her forehead wrinkled in deliberation. She seemed an ancient, little spirit caught in a child's body. In time, she produced a coupon with the picture of an oatmeal box and handed it to me.

"Thank you," I said. "I never expected to meet the coupon fairy."

She giggled, and I felt relieved to see she could laugh.

"Grandma Mayta cuts our coupons. She speaks Alzheimers. And I had to sit in time-out." The memory brought back her sadness, and I was afraid she might start to cry again. She touched her hair and said, "My pony tails are crooked. They don't match."

"I hate when that happens to me," I said.

"You don't have ponytails!" she shrieked.

"Oh, no!" I said, grabbing my head, "did I forget them again?"

She giggled once more.

Anna came round the corner just then, carrying a box of crackers. "Mr. Sinclair—I see you've met my granddaughter Harlo."

We talked about the growing number of summer tourists and the forecast of rain for the weekend, then resumed our shopping.

Anna had reached the checkout line when I arrived. Harlo stood beside her, stacking cans on the conveyor belt with the same intensity of the coupon fairy. She slid cans of green beans into one careful row and peaches into another. Anna absently set a can of peaches with the green beans, and Harlo yelped, correcting the insult.

When Harlo had finished with the cans, she took up a doll that lay in the cart, a boy doll with bright red hair, which struck out in all directions. It must have been carried on numerous trips. The soft cotton body sagged from neck to knees. It too, wore a worried look that matched Harlo's.

She saw me studying the doll. "This is Bill," she said, holding out the doll for my inspection.

"Hello Bill," I said and shook hands with the doll, whose arm proved to be as limp as its body.

Harlo turned to locate Anna. Satisfied that Anna was busy writing a check, Harlo came close beside me and whispered gravely, "Are you married?"

"No," I whispered. "Are you?"

She gasped. "I'm only five!" She turned once more to look at Anna, who was talking to the cashier. She drew close once again and whispered, "Want to know a secret?"

I nodded.

"My momma's lost her courage."

I was surprised at her precociousness. She mistook my surprise to be an endorsement of her concern and nodded her little head gravely—as if to say, "Yes think of that—lost her courage!" She continued in a whisper, "Grandma Anna said so. She said she's talking to the bread dough. But I heard."

I had no idea what I should say and felt relieved when Anna finished paying her bill and turned back to get Harlo. The two of them followed the carry-out boy to the door, but Harlo looked back at me with an urgent little face, till she could no longer see me. It occurred to me that she was a miniature version of Anna, the same unmistakable sense of mission.

They were actually my neighbors; their house was located about a mile down river from my cabin. There must be four of them living there: Harlo, with her little obsessive ways; her mother, Leah, who'd lost her courage; her great-grandmother, Mayta, who spoke Alzheimers; and her grandmother, Anna, with the hole in her heart that God shot.

Anna's notebooks required me to be something of a confidant to confessions, which made me uncomfortable. I didn't want the journals to become an avenue to informality. I didn't want to develop friendships with my students here in Cotton Rock. I, like Anna, had a hole shot through my own heart. I wanted to be left alone—to fish, to heal and hopefully to be able to write once more.

I determined to keep my involvement limited to the classroom, though the truth was that Anna had become more important to my writing than I was to hers. Her notebooks had begun to serve as a kind of muse. Each morning when I sat on the back porch with a cup of coffee, the river and Anna's writing, her memories stirred my own, and I found myself able to put words into a notebook, myself—the first writing I'd done in a very long time, a secret I intended to keep from my writing class. I would naturally have to meet Anna in the grocery aisle now and then, but her journals would be my only connection with her family—or so I thought.

Cotton Rock is a small town, and a small town writes its own memoirs on the telephone, in the grocery aisle, at the post office window. Like a collective scribe, it recites its past into today's news and tomorrow's speculation—a living palimpsest.

On this particular day, the town reporter was Dee Lushbaugh. She stood at her cash register wearing a button that said "Lushbaugh's is best"—a declaration that would remain virtually unchallenged. Lushbaugh's was the only grocery in Cotton Rock.

"I'm glad to see lights in your Granddad's cabin again," Dee was saying. "Sad to see it sitting empty. I miss him. Course you do, too." And then as people like to do when they've witnessed your childhood, she said, "I remember when you were just a little feller coming in here summers."

I remembered her too, particularly her hair, which had remained the same orange every summer since I turned nine—differing little on this day from the bag of carrots in my basket. It must have been this color in her childhood, though she was far past youth. "I'll be seventy-seven the twenty-ninth day of July," she told me proudly. Despite the fact that Lushbaugh's grocery dedicated an entire aisle to various boxes of hair color, Dee had chosen orange, which perched on her head like a flaming anachronism—the one property of youth she could reproduce.

Next to being number one in the grocery business, Dee loved to fish. The wall behind the register paraded with pictures of fishing: Dee and her husband Charlie holding up a walleye; Dee sitting in the boat holding a string of carp; an article announcing that Charlie had landed a twenty-two-pound brown trout.

They often passed by my dock in their boat, rods in hand. They were never hard to spot—Charlie hunched over the motor and Dee's hair shining in the sun like the orange glint from a hunter's vest. But Dee had a good heart and never failed to call out to customers as they left, "Ya'll come on back now. We'll treat you in so many ways, you can't help but like some of 'em."

Dee made it a point to keep up with the news. "Saw you talking to Anna McKerry." She reached for the box of oatmeal, and I handed her Harlo's coupon. "She had two children drowned, you know, fifteen, sixteen years ago. That little Mary loved to fish. Course, she was only ten, but Sam was eighteen. He's a good swimmer. But nobody's gonna swim long in fifty degree water! When those generators rev up, they send down a swell of water."

"Yes sir. You got to step lively when those generators rev up." She rang up the total, jabbing a register key with each word, "Yes sir! Step lively!"

I handed her my money, and she put the bills into the cash drawer.

"As a rule, children don't swim in the river—too cold," she continued. "Course, you'd know that. But that July brought a scorcher. River had been dead low for a couple days. Left nice pockets of water, warm enough to tolerate a swim. When they turned on the generators, they ramped them up. Sent down a real swell of water. Found the little girl down river, laid out like an angel on a gravel bar. A beautiful blue-sky day. Just like today," she nodded her orange hair toward the front window. "Never found Sam. Thunderstorm moved in that evening. Spring rains set in for two weeks straight. Flooded all the way to the delta. But Sam's not the only one they never found. Had a boy drown up by Cedar Shoals. Never found him either."

Then came the question I had dreaded. "Did Susan come down with you? I know she don't care much for fishing."

"Susan, was killed—last summer," I said, "in a car accident."

"Ohhh. I'm sure sorry, honey. Didn't know nothing about it."

"It happened in Springville," I said.

She leaned close to me, her face intent. "Sure sorry, honey," she said again. I knew she hoped for more details.

I thanked her, picked up my sack of groceries and headed outside. Dee was right about the day. It was a beautiful afternoon—white clouds, blue sky. But people can die on a blue-sky day, at age ten or eighteen. A wife can die at thirty-one. I started the jeep and headed home. After Susan's funeral I went to see her car—savage twisted metal against the background of another blue-sky day with its clouds, soft and white and reasonable.

Anna had written that the hill people stopped the hands of their clocks after a death. I had empathy for the practice of such a ritual. Some Ozark man or woman in another lifetime heard the stolid, rote ticking of a clock, had cried out against its blasphemy, had stopped the hands and passed down a tradition, had forced the clock to acknowledge the truth. Someone died! Someone had no more time! And when the last shovel of dirt fell upon the grave, the clocks were allowed to begin ticking again. But this ticking sounded for the living, for those who must agree to walk with the forward-insistence of life.

Something in my gut had its own clock, one that stopped by itself. It didn't prevent me from climbing out of bed each morning and getting to work, but inside I was only treading water. I hoped that being here might restore some solid ground.

I carried the groceries into the cabin, put them away, opened a beer and went to the back porch. From my chair I had an open view of the White River, not more than a hundred feet below the cabin—750 miles of river running through the heart of Ozark country. On the far shore the thickly wooded hills rolled away to the darker lines of distant hills.

On my side of the river, moss-covered chunks of rock the size of wash tubs, flanked the right side of the boat dock, and on the left, Granddad's smooth beach ran several yards before meeting the tangle of reed grass and chinquapin trees. Granddad cleared the shoreline and dumped pickup loads of sand. "You weren't much taller than my hammer when I built the cabin," he said. You needed a place to get your river legs under you. Learn to feel the muscle of the current."

Granddad and I screened the porch the summer I turned twelve. It proved to be the only way to keep Grandma at the little table for another hand of cards. "If you two want to stay out here and donate your last pint of blood to the mosquitoes," she'd say, "you can die without me."

"How 'bout it, son?" Granddad would ask me, "Got enough blood left to try for one more rummy?" I would nod yes.

Coming back here had seemed like coming home—as much as anyone can ever go home. Perhaps I believed that returning to the place where life had once seemed certain would give me direction—point true North. I hadn't added a single sentence to my novel since Susan's death. I'd been granted a six-month leave of absence to finish my novel and perhaps by the following spring have an offer of publication. A promise of being published might convince the faculty I could teach a creative writing class at the college. So far I hadn't found the courage to lift the novel from its tomb in the bottom drawer. Is a man who does not write a writer? Granddad used to say, "When a river stops moving—it's no longer a river. Turns to a lake or a pond. Maybe a dead oxbow, but it's no longer a river."

Granddad hated the death of a river. Matter of fact, the turning of the White River into a lake was Granddad's most heated subject. Over the course of Granddad's life the White had been impounded by five dams and mutated to a chain of lakes.

"They filled the very heart of the river with concrete," Granddad said. "Gave it a whole passel of names: Chinquapin Lake, Mussel Springs, Marble Head Lake, Cedar Shoals—got more names than a bank robber."

Granddad would talk about the changes brought by the dams nearly every time he got into the boat. "Some of those dams are two hundred feet high. Those lake beds are deep. Turned that whole stretch of river into a cold-water fishery. But there's two sides to every flap jack. The Feds put up those dams. So they had to come down here and stock the lakes. Filled them full of the finest trout in the whole damned country." Yet in spite of the trout Granddad never forgave the government for altering his river.

As though it had a premonition of its future, the White River had trouble deciding which way to go. Its head waters begin in the Boston Mountains in Arkansas, wander west, then turn north over the state line, heading east along the Missouri border before retreating back to Arkansas and flowing decidedly south all the way to the Mississippi.

Granddad loved the river for more reasons than its fishing. To him, the White River was 750 miles of final triumph. "It starts out wandering and uncertain like we do when we're young," he'd say. "Just like the river we get trapped by some kind of dam before we've figured out which way we're headed. We have our middle years—like those lakes—that drain off our energy and hope. Yet, that old river in the last few hundred miles of its flow manages to rise again. Reclaims its name and its nature—even its native fish—before it empties into the Mississippi. And that's why I bought land over-looking the White. I wanted to build a cabin and look out at victory rolling by." I lifted my beer to the river. "To victory," I said.

Maybe, if I sat here watching the river's triumph, the day would come when I could—to quote Granddad—"rise again" and reclaim my nature as a writer. Maybe I could overcome writer's block—cliché expression, but it certainly described my struggle against an unseen barrier no less formidable than the concrete dams blocking the White River.

I finished my beer and checked my watch. I had just enough time for a run down river to catch the sunset. I passed Anna's house and continued on to Crooked Creek. I anchored the boat alongside a stretch of willows and watched the sun melt into the clouds of yellow and pink above the rim of distant hills. The wind had come up, and the air smelled of approaching rain. I started the motor and headed toward home.

The residents of Cotton Rock were as varied as their houses. To my left a string of small cabins nestled half-hidden in the woods, probably inhabited by some of the many hippies who had arrived in Cotton Rock in the sixties, perhaps following Thoreau's example because they "wished to live deliberately" and did not want to arrive at death only to discover they "had not lived." The last wave of newcomers was entrepreneurs who knew the promise of tourism when they saw it.

The tourists rewarded their enterprise and came by droves to play on the chain of lakes or to retire and watch the river from well-built, secluded decks. Although the primary tourist activity occurred at Marble Head or Cedar Shoals, Cotton Rock managed to receive its own wave of tourists, and its winter population of four thousand doubled in the summer.

The engine whined against the force of the wind. A gust shoved a scurry of waves into the prow and sent a spray of mist against my face. The wind, steadily flapping the tail of my shirt like an imperceptible hand caught my hat and nearly sent it into the water. The old masters like Virgil and Homer believed the wind was a metaphor for the breath of a muse, bringing them the gift of inspiration. Glorious thought—that this unseen force exciting the surface of the river could also excite the neurons of the mind with the energy of creativity.

Perhaps it was the ethereal wind carrying the sweet smell of lavender down from the hillsides and chiming garden bells from some unseen deck, the wind, rousing the surface of the water, lifting it away from its natural downward pull and sending it up to spray against my face, that drew my attention to the woman on the dock ahead of me—the playful wind, ruffling her long, dark hair, shifting it about her face like a dancing scarf.

The dock belonged to Anna, and so I decided it must be Anna who had untangled the perpetual knot of her hair to allow it to fall free in the wind. She stood transfixed as a statue, staring out into the river, motionless except for the waves of her hair, lifting on the wind. I arrived nearly parallel with her before she turned, startled by the sound of the motor as though she had come back from some distant place. For a moment she looked directly at me, a face very much like Anna's but a great deal younger, and I realized it must be Leah.

I raised a hand to wave. Perhaps she hadn't noticed. She turned away and walked back toward the house. Suddenly the old loneliness returned, as if the turning of her back had been carried on the wind and brought to fill my boat with heaviness and the apprehension of heading home to the waiting novel.

Emmett's Fishing Report

    I said I'd write down some fishing stories for them boys over at the Cotton Rock Hatchery. They're going to pay me, and all I got to do is talk fishing. Lottie my wife says they may as well pay me for breathing. They'd save money. Anyway, that's why I enrolled in your writing class.
    Right now the news is the May fly hatch. Runs through June here on the White River. The hatching of the May fly has been known to cause a fly fisherman to miss his own wedding. Might mean he'll miss the birth of his first child. (Fly fishermen don't mind sleeping on the couch. They got a hankering for miserable conditions.) Yes sir, a fly fisherman likes to make a narrow place pinch. The idea being that the harder it is to get a fish, the more growl you got in your gizzard. If it's unlikely as finding lips on a chicken, fly fisherman will be setting up camp.
    To understand fly fishing, you got to understand the "hatch" of the May fly. The May fly starts out under a rock in the river. He's called a nymph. When things get just right the nymph swims top side and hatches. Now it's called a dunn. The dunn flies off to find a bush for molting. Changes into a spinner, shimmyin' and sashaying' around in the sunlight, wings sparkling, tail twitching. Cause it's only got one day to mate—mid-air.
    Then it falls toward the river and when it does, it looks like it's "spinning" (a holy sight to a fly fisherman.) It drops its eggs into the river, and it's done for. Hits the water and lays there dying. Happy but dying.
    Trout and bass (the fish of interest to the May fly boys), can catch a May fly most any time along its journey. They can eat dunns in the morning or spinners in the evening. Or just wait till the flies fall and die, and sip 'em easy like. Cause them fish are just swimming around in a giant May fly soup.
    The whole river gets in on the May fly cycle, cause it just keeps coming round. The river itself is home to the fish that eats the May flies that fertilize the river plants, that feed the snails and stonerollers, that are grub for the sculpins and crawdads, that fatten up the bass and trout. And I haven't mentioned half the critters in the chain. Point is, it's a real smooth-running, pull-together without any help from the fly fisherman. Fact is, the May fly hatch wouldn't rightly miss them fly fisherman if it never laid eyes on 'em altogether.

So the fly fisherman's got his up-hill laid out for him. Course the fly-fishermen likes up-hill. What the fly-fisherman's trying to do is sneak into the May-fly shindig without being spotted as a phony. Now the primary critter he wants to fool is the trout or the bass. And the best way to fool them and specially to hook them is to look like a May fly.

So fly fishermen spend hours tying up little critters that look like nymphs or spinners. They tie them out of moose hair, calf tails, turkey wings, floss, copper wire, brass beads and a hundred other fixings to look as much like the hatch as possible. Why a fly fisherman begins to look at the world in terms of prospects: the lint on his sock, the fringe on the lamp shade, a lock of his wife's hair when she's sleeping. I promise you if a fly-tie boy thought he could improve a spinner, he'd steal a thread right out of his momma's own casket.

To make it more miserable and unlikely, nobody exactly knows when the hatch will happen. The exact moment is harder to predict than the winning lottery ticket. They've got them forecasts and charts, but ever thing depends on the weather. If it's too cold or too hot, rains too much or not at all, or if the wind comes up everything changes. If it gets downright ornery and hails, all the spinners get knocked right out of the only reason they were ever born in the first place.

It's a mighty bothersome and cussed affair. Which is why it's so appealing to a fly fisherman. (I think they put pea gravel in their wading boots.) Fly fishermen do a lot of standing around and waiting and suffering. But ever great once in a while, a fly fisherman happens on to the very stretch of river at the exact drop of the hatch! The sweet spot! If it's not too dark to see, they tie on a fly and crash the party. If they cast just right and don't hang up in a bush, or let the belly of the line swing onto a rock, or guess wrong on the leader, or overset the hook or the wind don't knot the line, they just might get a fish.

But if they miss the May fly hatch, there's always the caddis fly. Course, there are 134 kinds of caddis in the Ozarks. That's a lot of them flies to tie up. You'll see a fly fisherman, squatted down inspecting the road-kill on the grill of his pick-up truck. He's just trying to see what kind of bug is in the wind. He's ready to tie up anything that's on the menu.

Fly fishing! Tricky as straddling a barbed-wire fence with two sore feet. But if fly fishing ever got easy the fly-tie boys would be mighty disappointed. They'd have to give it up all together.

Anna's Third Notebook

It's been five years since I brought Momma to live with me. In the beginning my sister, Zoe, took a stand against it. "I think Momma would do best if I found her a private home," Zoe said. "One with two or three other ladies."

"I want to get to know her," I said.

"It's a little late."

"Sometimes she's her old self," I said. That's when Zoe reminded me that I never got along with Momma's old self.

"That's the point," I said. "I want to get it right while there's still a little of Momma left."

"This is about Momma's welfare. This is about her wandering around at night. You have those awful stairs!"

I told her how the nurse gave me a vest that Momma could sleep in. I was trying to explain how it tied to the bed, and Momma would be safe at night. But I never finished my argument because the phone rang. Momma had had a stroke. She'd lost consciousness and couldn't speak. Even the little scraps of the Alzheimers words were gone. After a week in the hospital, they put Momma in a rehabilitation hospital in Springville. Six weeks later she was ready to go home. She could talk again her Alzheimers talk, but she couldn't walk without help. Mostly she got around in a wheelchair.

In the meantime I had convinced Zoe I was up to the job of caring for Momma, and I drove to Springville to get her. But the hospital folks had their own doubts: "Did I realize that the majority of the nursing care would be mine? Did I know that I could never leave Momma alone? Did I understand that Momma would need continued therapy for the stroke?"

I just kept saying "yes," and finally Momma and I were in the hospital lobby getting ready to drive back to Cotton Rock. Momma sat in her new wheelchair with a scarf tied around her white hair and her coat buttoned right up to her chin. I think she thought I would push her wheelchair all the way to Cotton Rock. She clutched her big black purse against her chest like it held the winning lottery ticket.

"It's a warm day, Momma. I'll just unbutton your coat. You'll be hot in the car."

The word car set Momma talking, "Dade can't drive us home."

Poor Momma. "You've forgotten," I said. I knelt down beside her. "Momma, remember? Dade's dead."

"I know," Momma answered. "That's why he can't drive us home."

Well, I burst right out laughing.

Momma looked embarrassed. "I said stupid…numbers," she said. "No, not numbers…" She looked lost.

So I said, "Never mind Momma, you're coming home to live at my house. We're going to have good times together."

"Yes," Momma answered. "The doctor said, 'I just hope you and yours… have a…a…niceful'…course we never really had niceful."

Funny thing is Momma never tried to talk about the trouble spots till she got Alzheimers. It seemed like the more words she lost, the more she made the leftovers count.

I left Momma buckled in the wheelchair and went to get the old Ford. I parked it in front of the hospital lobby, then went in to get Momma. I pushed her wheelchair toward the door, and Momma pressed her house shoes hard against the foot rests. If there had been brakes in those foot rests, Momma would have left a line of rubber on all the way to the door. I just kept pushing the chair and saying, "It's all right, Momma. It's all right."

I kept repeating the nurses' rules to myself: "Keep the wheelchair at a forty-five degree angle to the location of transfer. Be certain to set the brake on the chair when you stop. A rolling wheelchair scoots out from under the patient. If there's a problem, don't panic. Don't lift with your back; lift with your legs."

"Shouldn't we call Zoe?" Momma asked.

"Zoe's teaching. I'm taking care of you, Momma. I went to classes. I learned how."

I was glad Momma couldn't see my hands shaking. I knew she felt uneasy about going to my house. I figured Momma would rather be going to Zoe's. That's where I'd want to go if I had Alzheimers. But the only baby Zoe ever birthed was still-born. So teaching school was Zoe's baby, and she was nearly ready for retirement money. I wasn't going to see her give that up.

We were nearly home when I rolled down the windows and let the sound of the woods fill the car. The cicadas were singing along the river. "Remember when I was in the third grade, and I told Mrs. Bedford I could play the steel guitar?"

Momma nodded her head and said. "Dade could…"

"Yeah," I said. "I used to sit beside him on the front porch listening to him play. Sliding that old lipstick case up and down the frets. I thought cause he could play I could."

Momma looked pleased and nodded her head again.

We rode along in silence, Momma tapping her fingers on the seat belt keeping time with the cicadas and me remembering Mrs. Bedford asking, "Anna McKerry, can you truly play the steel guitar?" And me, saying, "Yes Ma'am." Remembering the hospital nurse saying, "Mrs. McKerry, do you realize the extent of the commitment you're making—the extent of full-time care your mother will require?" And me saying, "Yes, Ma'am." Lucky for me Clyde Short, whose desk sat dead-center of the classroom, caught the measles that year. Half the third grade got them. Concert got canceled. I didn't have to play the steel guitar, and I didn't have to eat a helping of brag biscuits.

I could see the house now. Momma was flesh and blood beside me. I really was in charge of her care.

"Curtain's going up," I said, "and Clyde Short can't save me this time."

Momma smiled and nodded her head, like she understood exactly what I was saying.

Thoughts from the Back Porch   June 1996

    I sat with my cup of early morning coffee, its aroma spreading across the porch. The sun was still pink against the hills, and the early morning fog had just begun to dissipate. I heard a fish jump on the river and thought of Granddad. "Fish are jumping, Johnnie boy! Grab your tackle box. We'll fill the stringer before the sun can shine a rainbow on a trout's belly. Here! Take that big hand of yours and carry the lantern."

    He used to say with hands as big as mine the least I could do was learn to hold a hammer as well as I held a book. But Granddad's prospect of me taking over his construction business up in Kansas City didn't last long. By the time I'd finished college it was evident I'd be folding my long legs under a desk for the rest of my life.

    I took a sip of coffee and watched a hawk circle the outcropping of rock on the far side of the river. The town of Cotton Rock rests on a bedrock of dolomite—sediments carried grain by grain, by an ancient, retreating sea. For measureless millennia run-off water from surrounding hills chiseled its way across this stretch of bedrock to groove a bed and gather itself into a river.

    The rock and the river have engaged in ceaseless conflict and reciprocity ever since, like the French trappers, English farmers, and Scots-Irish Appalachian transplants who settled along its life-giving flow and yielded to the necessity of brotherhood. The dolomite along this section of river is unique—white and porous in appearance, and for which it received its name, cotton rock. Despite its soft appearance the rock proved exceedingly durable. The stone buildings along Main Street were cut from its quarries; it furnished the foundations for all the old clapboard houses lining the streets of Cotton Rock.

    Remnants of old rock walls that once declared lines of ownership on the surrounding farmlands were still visible, long after their owners were laid to rest beneath tombstones cut from the same shelf of bedrock. Whole walls of it shouldered the river through narrow gorges. Blocks of it were quarried to construct the courthouse on the town square—blocks as immutable as the laws it housed. And high up on the hill overlooking Cotton Rock the historical old prison looming over the town like a pale, ghostly museum from the past was constructed from blocks of cotton rock, some seven-feet long and two-feet thick.

I finished my coffee. On the table beside me lay the encyclopedia I'd been reading, its pages opened to another ghostly museum—a picture of Pearl Harbor the place where Anna's father had been killed. Just beneath the surface of the water the picture displays the pale shadow of a ship. The base of a single gun-mount thrusts above the water like a stark headstone marking the watery grave.

The words beneath the picture stated, "Below the silent, empty deck, the entire crew lies entombed in a steel sepulcher." The encyclopedia reported that on December, 7, 1941, without warning the Japanese began bombing the harbor. At approximately 8:10 A.M. an armor-piercing 1,760 pound bomb tore through the deck of the *Arizona*. In less than nine minutes the ship sank, carrying the entire crew to the bottom of the shallow harbor. For over fifty years, they have remained trapped there, a silent ship holding the skeleton of the man who fathered Anna. With the dropping of that bomb Anna's life was forever altered, and that alteration would in turn, influence the life of her daughter Leah, with the long dark hair dancing on the wind—Leah who had lost her courage.

I knew about losing courage, at least the courage to face the manuscript. I had to admit I was avoiding it. I spent my days running unnecessary errands to town. I'd chopped enough firewood to last through the winter that I didn't plan to spend here and fished enough hours to compete with the most avid fisherman on the river—anything but pull open the bottom desk drawer and begin serious work on the novel.

I'd hoped coming to the cabin would bring inspiration, but memories were all that the cabin seemed to offer. The little table that holds my coffee only brings me Grandma Rowden sitting here with her bowl of green beans, fishing them out one-by-one, pinching off the ends, snapping them into uniform lengths and dropping them into the cooking pot beside her.

"Hello darlin'," she would say to me each summer morning, aware of me without having to look up from her work.

"I've written a story," I said. I held out the fishing log book with its new red leather binding—a present from Grandma for my tenth birthday. I'd written straight through the boxes labeled "bait" and "weather conditions," kept writing till I told every word of the "Masked Man of Blackhorse Canyon."

Grandma didn't say a word about my misuse of the log book. She just set the bowl of beans aside, wiped her hands on her apron and took up my little story. She had retired from teaching, but she never really left the classroom. Learning to her was mandatory—like brushing your teeth and eating your vegetables—and books were sacred. She had read a number of great classics to me, and she read my little story as if it had come from the same canon of great literature.

She read it aloud enunciating the words as though each of them were worth a hundred dollars. My hero seemed to stand up on the page when Grandma read, "I never back down from a fight, you cattle-thieving varmint."

She finished the story, closed the little book and said, "Why John, you're a writer." She looked up at me, her face filled with frank approval. A grown man hates to admit how much he wants to see that same look of adoration on a woman's face. I had wanted it from Susan and seemed to have it in the beginning.

The story was a child's fledgling work, but it birthed a belief in my writing. I might have taken my Swiss Army knife and cut a benchmark in the little oak table beside the bowl of beans. I could have carved the surveyor's broad-arrow incisures with the horizontal bar through its apex, the bar on which all subsequent readings could be placed, resting with absolute certainty on the designated base so that I could now return as a man to verify my position.

"I christen thee The Benchmark," I said aloud to the little table. Perhaps I should chisel a piece of wood from its side and wear it around my neck, like Anna's buckeye for luck—embrace all the Ozark superstitions, let them seep into my mind like the early morning fog that lays along the hills.

It was after all, perfectly reasonable that the Ozarks, this isolated pocket of civilization cut off for years from all outside influence would conjure up its own rituals to appease the unseen forces of nature. It is also perfectly reasonable that writers who live in their own isolated wild—the undiscovered plot, the uncrafted story, the threatening blank computer screen—should have their own need for superstition. Writing is a singular act of self-reliance balanced with a good measure of neurosis. It forces the most fearlessly Spartan into endless rituals: pencils sharpened to the count of ten or seven or no pencils at all; pens a certain length or color; lucky socks; or computers facing East or North—endless little talismans that enable us to get words onto paper.

Each week I gave my students the same warning, "Remember a story must be told all the way to the end. A thousand demons wait to assault the unfolding of your story. Never quit until you type the last word!" Yet I could not follow my own advice. Each time I thought about working on my novel I got what Granddad called a "case of the slumps," a malady that he said, "drained the starch right out of the will."

Today, I have a severe case of the slumps. Today it's Granddad who fills the room. The swing of Granddad's arm is set in every nail. He stands there by the screen door dressed for work—like he dressed every day, even after he'd been retired for years—clean white shirt and striped carpenter's overalls with the bib holding a flat yellow carpenter's pencil. A tape measure hangs from a loop near his pocket, and the loop below that holds a hammer. His work boots are laced to the top with rawhide strings. "They don't come untied when you're half-way up a ladder," he's saying.

"You'd better not be going up any ladder," Grandma calls from the kitchen.

"I'm taking Johnnie boy into town to buy a watermelon," he calls back. "Unless old man Lushbaugh's started putting melons up on the rafters, I won't be climbing any ladders." He shakes his head and lowers his voice to a near whisper, "The children grow up, leave home, and the woman throws all that child-raising energy into making a quilt or altering a dress. When she runs out of projects, her child-raising energy takes up tailoring your manhood!"

"She's taught you to whisper real well," I say.

He pulls the bill of my cap down over my face and orders me out to the pickup.

Granddad and his tape measure. Every project, however insignificant, began with that tape. He wouldn't move a stick of furniture without first measuring rooms and doorways. He knew the dimensions of nearly everything in his daily life: the car trunk, the glove compartment, his tackle box.

"A tape measure is one of our most basic tools, Johnnie boy! It's the first thing they do to you when you're born, you know. Measure you. And when you're building you measure things twice. Measure twice, cut once. You either have the pain of preparation or the pain of regret."

But Granddad's preoccupation with being thorough sometimes made him magisterial. Grandma had learned how to curtail Granddad's meddling when needed. When she found him measuring her life too closely, she could be heard to shout, "Mr. Rowden! I'm not a block of wood!" On particularly intense days she'd devise a more protracted solution and announce that we were "out of fish for dinner." Granddad would set about organizing the boat, and we'd be gone for the afternoon. If it poured rain Grandma would select a project from the mental list she kept for inclement weather. "The little window above the bath tub is wedged shut. I don't think it's on the level." The thought of something being out of plumb in his own house was guaranteed to send Granddad to his tool box for the day.

Of course, we could always be sent to Lushbaugh's for a watermelon. Granddad would be found in a grocery aisle, unhooking his tape and measuring the diameters of melons.

"Ten inches," he'd say, putting a melon in the basket. "That'll just fit in the ice chest. We'll take it fishing this afternoon."

He looks quite remarkable in my mind's eye, strolling down the aisle, pushing the watermelon along in the grocery cart—full head of white hair, his back straight as a plumb line and his figure trim as the day he went to Kansas City. "Left here when I was a young man," he told me more than once. "Went to Kansas City with a hammer in my hand and a dollar-fifty in my pocket. Married your Grandma and built a construction business out of hard work and a good name. Always left the job site clean. A woman will hire you back if you sweep up and leave the place clean."

The cashier sees Granddad sizing her up with his keen blue eyes. "Good morning Mr. Rowden," she says and smiles up at him. She lifts the melon from the basket. "This is a fine melon," she says and slides a manicured hand across the melon's smooth skin. I know she thinks Granddad is telling me how pretty she is when he whispers in my ear. But Granddad is simply saying, "She's five-foot-six. I can estimate height within an eighth of an inch. She'd need her kitchen cabinets to be exactly thirty-six inches tall—she could roll out a pie crust without bending her back."

It wasn't that Granddad hadn't been known to succumb to temptation. It happened sometime after he severed his thumb. I learned the truth about his thumb over time. I learned about his affair in a moment. The loss of his thumb proved an imperfection he never fully accepted.

The loss of symmetry presented itself every time he used his hand. He had to relearn his trade. "The great opposable thumb," he'd say. "Try picking up a board without it. Separates us from the animals you know."

As a boy I'd often ask him how he lost his thumb, the way children ask for a story more than once. He'd just say, "Got to keep a close watch on a power saw. Truth is it was a sorry piece of equipment. I'd never ask a man to use such a blade. Made the board jump. Took my thumb with it."

When I got older, he told me a little more. "Lost my thumb during the depression. Always keep a savings, John. Never leave yourself penniless. Forces a man to take risks no man should take."

I heard the full story when I turned sixteen. I had just gotten my driver's license, had taken my first solo run to town. Grandma didn't hear me when I returned. I opened the cabin door to hear a full-blown argument. I often heard fighting between my parents when Dad was home. He was usually gone on business, and I've come to think he planned it that way. The constant fighting of my parents and the absence of my dad made me long for summers with Granddad.

So I wasn't ready for Grandma's shrill voice filled with hurt. I entered the cabin to hear, "I don't care if it was years ago. You slept with her! Left me alone with three little girls. I call it betrayal!"

"You want to talk betrayal? Let's talk about your crazy sister!" That was Granddad. I heard the screen door slam behind him.

But Grandma wasn't letting go of the fight, and she called out after him, "I knew you'd get around to Myrna. Sooner or later."

That brought Granddad back to the porch where he yelled, "Sooner or later! Try fifty years with no thumb! I'd never have used that sorry-assed saw if you hadn't stolen our savings! Myrna couldn't find her way out of a paper sack! Everybody knew she needed to be in the crazy house. Everybody but you! Took her to every doctor in Kansas City!"

"I planned to put it back," Grandma said. "I had a good teaching job. Who could know a depression was coming?"

"That's why you keep a savings, Rosalee! 'Cause you never know what's coming. I was the one who had to take to the streets with a shovel. Digging ditches with walls deep enough to fall on me. Knew that much without my measuring tape. I was the one sliding down an auger to free a jammed blade with my foot. And old man Tuttle did lose his foot—on that very blade. I did things no man should ever agree to. Cause you felt sorry for Myrna!"

"She was my sister!"

"Don't talk to me about a forgotten fling. I wasn't far behind Myrna in those days. I nearly went crazy myself."

I announced my arrival from the door: "Home with the dry cleaning," I called out.

The cabin fell silent. Neither of them ever spoke to me of the fight, but on rare occasions over the years when a similar kind of silence returned and things seemed out of sorts and strained, I wondered if old memories were passing between them. I never got around to asking Granddad how a man and woman learn to live together, learn to survive the betrayals, the resentments. We just grow up and never ask a single, important question, never even know the questions we should ask, resting free and young on someone else's hammered-out experience. When it finally occurs to us what it is we want to know, people have already died and taken the answers with them.

Memories. The cabins full of them. I'm looking at the patch there on the screen door. It's a large patch covering the hole where lightning sent a tree limb hurtling into the porch—a missile the size of a man's arm that shot into the chair where I had been sitting only a moment before.

What had Grandma thought as she stitched a piece of screen over the hole? How her grandson could have been killed? Had she pondered how randomly indifferent nature is, how it does not give mercy in place of its laws? No two things can occupy the same space. A foot or an inch can mean a life. A car—Susan's car—cannot occupy the same space with a loaded gravel truck. One of them, the less forceful, and that being the car, will be evicted, violently, coming to rest in its final place of capitulation, a piece of savage twisted metal against a blue-sky day.

Memories. I never saw Granddad without his carpenter's uniform till the day my father drove him to Springville and the nurses put a hospital gown on him.

"Doesn't cover the essentials," Granddad growled. "Might as well be a handkerchief!" When the nurses left, he announced, "I'm not going to die dressed like a derelict." In the middle of the night he got up and put on his clothes. The next morning they found him dead on top of the bedspread—carpenter's overalls, clean white shirt, pencil and measuring tape in place.

His leather work boots were laced to the top with their raw-hide string. He took care to fold the Springville Daily News beneath his boots to protect the bedspread. Always leave things clean when you go…

Time for a boat ride. I got up from The Benchmark and headed down the path toward the river. As a boy, I used to lie on my back in a johnboat, drifting along a quiet little branch thinking of Rat gliding along some stream in the *Wind in the Willows* telling Mole that there's nothing finer than "messing about in boats." I turned thirty-seven this month, and I still agree with Rat.

I returned from the boat ride with a couple of fine trout. I fired up the grill and thought about inviting my neighbor, Tom Ferguson, to eat with me. Tom bought the house next to my cabin a year ago and lived there alone. From my back porch I could see only a corner of his cabin roof through the thick woods. I hadn't met him yet, but I wanted to.

I went back inside, sliced a couple fresh zucchini to grill with the fish then phoned Tom, who accepted my invitation. Great. He'd be good company without too many demands on my writing time. He was a busy attorney, considered one of the best in the county. He was nearing retirement age, but from what I'd heard of him, it wasn't likely he'd ever quit working.

I carried the fish and zucchini out to the grill and looked up to see Tom sauntering out of the trees, carrying a six pack of beer. Gray-haired tall and lanky, he walked with his shoulders and head slightly forward as though he were used to ducking through doorways. He looked a bit like Jed Clampett of the old T.V. series, *Beverly Hillbillies.*

He offered me a beer, took one for himself and sat down on a tree stump, watching me with full attention. You couldn't look at Tom without considering his nose, a very large and determined part of his face. The second feature to appreciate was his enormous feet, which he planted firmly, one on either side of the tree stump. It proved judicious because he was given to volleys of laughter, and his feet kept him solidly anchored. Tom was an Ozark native. I asked him about his people and his life in Cotton Rock.

"I'm Scotch-Irish—an American word we put together as immigrants. Refers to us Scots who lived in the North of Ireland—Ulster." He took a drink of his beer. "Name might have become more a warning than a distinction." He grinned. "It was said we were 'the most God-provoking democrats this side of hell.'" He laughed a deep, hardy laugh. "When we arrived in this country, the aristocrats found us downright irritating. They used us as a barricade between their fancy houses and the Indians. But even the Indians found us a gripe in the bahooky. Many of them just packed up their ponies and went west. I guess we're even uneasy about one another. We say if you can see the smoke from your neighbor's chimney, it's time to move."

"I better hold off building a fire in my fireplace," I said. "I'd like to keep my neighbors."

The fish were nearly done. I added the zucchini to the grill. "My folks were British," I said over my shoulder. I turned toward him and confessed, "I think my ancestors fought on the side of the Loyalists."

"I've got some damn fine Scotch whiskey. I'll bring you a bottle to sweeten your British tea. Offset the taste of defeat."

"To the Scots and their whiskey," I said, holding up my beer.

Tom drank to my toast and said, "Actually Scots were on the forefront of most every battle in the revolution. They'd rather be ground to flint powder than coward to fear or subservience. Ozarks is full of Scotch-Irish. That fighting blood still runs strong in the natives."

"Makes you a good lawyer," I said.

"I hope so. Went through the university up in Kansas City. They nearly relieved me of all my common sense. But I was too simple to get a full purging. On the other hand I needed some modifications. I come from long line of outraged, fist-fighting, whiskey-drinking, story-loving passionate men. My granddaddy's advice about women: 'When it comes to making love, if you don't have six hours and a foot against the wall don't bother starting!' He threw back his head with a great gust of laughter.

The fish were crisp and the zucchini toasted. I took the food from the grill, and we headed to the back porch. We sat at the Bench Mark and ate, looking out over the river.

"You know before the dams came," he said, "river was wild and unpredictable. Travel was gut-wrenching labor. If you were going up stream with a load you had to push against the rapids. Men sometimes shoved poles against the river bottom a whole day. At the end of the day they might look down stream and still see the place they camped the night before.

"River's like a ribbon of time. Changing with each generation. Day came when steamboats made good their boast. Machines replaced men. Wagon loads of cotton lined up a hundred deep to wait for the ferry. Trains came down from the north. Ran along the river's flood plain. Hill men worked under blazing sun hacking railroad ties with a broad ax. For little pay. Men stood all night in the pouring rain. Making certain rails would hold the approaching train. Boys loaded ties that weighed as much as they did. Later died of creosote poisoning."

I had a sudden vision of Granddad sitting with me at the little table, talking river. It was a good feeling. Comfortable. "Do you know our neighbors down river—Anna McKerry?" I asked.

He nodded. "That poor woman. Probably married out of poverty. Alone with her little boy and no help. Like they say, 'Don't marry for money, you can borrow it cheaper.' Married Willis Sprule and had two more children. Two of the three drowned in the river. Just one girl left. A woman herself now. I don't know much about Willis except that after the divorce, he blamed his wife and daughter. It's half a man that whines on his family's hanky."

"I heard about the drowning," I said. "Tragedy. Didn't they blow the warning siren back in those days? Warn fishermen the generators were running?"

"Sure did. Corps of engineers up at the dam never missed. But Rayley Larkin was on duty down here at Cotton Rock. Got drunk they say. Never sounded the horn. Wasn't a drinking man either."

We had finished eating. Outside, storm clouds gathered along the river. An owl murmured its low-throated *t'whoo*.

"I was married thirty-five years when my wife died," Tom was saying. "Sure miss her. Moved down here to the cabin. Not so much housekeeping."

"Do you have children?"

"A son." He hesitated, as though he considered telling me something, but changed his mind. A gust of wind brought the fresh smell of rain and a flash of lightning lit up the river. "Looks like a storm's whipping up," he said, getting up from the table and thanking me for dinner.

"I'm in for a run home." He opened the screen door, ducked his head through and thumped his big feet down the steps, the rain already pelting around him.

"Careful," I called out.

"Yeah," he yelled over his shoulder. "Don't let your feet run faster than your shoes."

"Probably another old Scotch-Irish saying," I thought, watching him run across the backyard and disappear into the woods.

Anna's Fourth Notebook

It bothers me that Momma talks to the coffee grinder. It gives her something to do, but the thing is I can't seem to let her enjoy it. It's an old ceramic grinder the color of buttermilk with corn flowers painted on the front, and it hangs on the wall above the table. No matter how I study those flowers, they don't look a thing like a face to me. But to Momma it's a face, and she never forgets to believe it, even with her Alzheimers. The minute she sits down at the table she takes right up with a conversation.

I take it as a signal to get firm. "It's a coffee grinder Momma!" I turn the handle. "See?"

She nods her head. But I know she doesn't believe me. She's only agreeing to bring peace. This morning when I caught her in the very act, Momma gave the corn flowers a confidential look and whispered, "I'll talk to you later."

I wish I could have laughed. But I hung a dish towel over the grinder. The look on Momma's face made me feel pretty shabby. But I fought it off by telling myself that the coffee grinder wasn't the only problem. Momma thinks the floor lamp is Dade, and I'm not going to have Dade come back from the dead and boss Momma from under a lamp shade. Forty years of Dade bossing Momma was enough.

Momma talks to other things that somehow look like people to the scraps of her scattered mind. But most of these must be only passing acquaintances, because she just nods and says "hello" like she does to the rubber plant she passes on her way to the bathroom.

Anyway I hate seeing Momma talk to leaves and lamp shades 'cause it reminds me I'm losing her. Ever since I brought Momma to live with me, I've been trying to pull her back to herself, and she's been moving straight toward a gaping dark hole. Sometimes we pass each other and meet face to face. These are the times I step right into Momma's soul. These are the times when I think I make a difference in her suffering. Like that night when Momma first came to live with me. She had one of her worst nightmares.

Her cry sliced through the dark and cut into the deep place where I was dreaming. I climbed the stairs and switched on the lamp beside her bed.

She blinked in the pool of yellow light.

"Careful!" She pointed a finger at the corner. "There!"

"You're okay Momma," I said, but I couldn't help looking behind me.

"Shhh," she whispered. "They're watching!"

"You've had another nightmare Momma. That's all." I dropped down on my knees beside the bed and patted her face. The sag of that old cheek. The flesh moved under my hand like it had frayed from the bone. I smoothed the hair back from her face. I knew it wouldn't smooth away her fear, but women are smoothers. Always trying to smooth back the pain smooth away the disappointment, trying to smooth out the difference between what is and what should be. My daughter Leah thinks smoothing will make up for an excuse-me-I-gotta-go daddy.

She smooths little Harlo so much you'd think the child would have her skin rubbed off. No matter how much I smoothed, I wasn't going to smooth away Alzheimers. I knew that it was unraveling the strings of Momma's mind, leaving threads of memories, scraps of words, chips of old dreams.

Momma's eyes were wild. She lifted her head from the pillow and talked to the corner. "Don't hurt me! Zoe? Zoe?"

"No, Momma. It's me. Anna."

But it didn't do any good. She just kept calling, "Zoe!"

So I said, "Yes it's Zoe. I'm here."

"Oh, Zoe! See that big one? All frazlous?" Then she got hysterical.

You're never old enough, and I'm on the downward slope toward sixty, to see your momma hysterical. "God," I said to myself, "what am I supposed to do?" Momma continued to scream. I wanted to cry. Instead, I said, "Damn it!"

"My momma never swan," Momma said.

"Swore. Your momma never swore."

"Never swore," she repeated. She heard something and turned toward the wall. "It's melting! It's monsful..."

I snapped the bed rail down and climbed in beside her. I rocked her in my arms like I would have rocked a child and sang her favorite: "Amazing grace, how sweet the sound." But my voice wobbled right off its hold, and I had to try again. "Amazing grace, how sweet the sound." Lord, how the words of that old song hang lonesome in the middle of the night, the dark just pressing up against the window panes in silence. "Was blind but now I see." I can still hear its haunting harmonies floating out across Ozark porches, down church pews, beside coffins. Dreams and losses of whole generations seem to rise and fall with those words, rising and falling, hoping and grieving. Sometimes hope's on top, sometimes grief. Sometimes the momma rocks the child, and sometimes the child rocks the momma.

Leah still nursed baby Harlo back then. I heard her downstairs taking Harlo from her bed. I knew she held her to the breast. I heard pieces of her song in the spaces of my own: "Amazing grace, how sweet the sound… Hush little baby don't you cry…That saved a wretch like me… Momma's gonna buy you a diamond ring…"

Leah and little Harlo, Momma and me. Singing, rocking, smoothing and being smoothed. Each in a different place. All tied together by love and blood. And I knew that I was awake in the night to something bigger than words, something timeless and powerful like the White River running alongside my house. And I knew that rocking my momma was perhaps the finest thing I had ever done, and that little place inside the bed rails was a most holy place.

Lucy's Angel Gossip

They's all kinds a gossip. Lord knows! They's mean gossip, gossip that's stretched and gossip that's as satisfying as a good scratch on a chigger bite. But I reckon the sweetest gossip is stories swapped between angels.

The way I figure it, since every child has a guardian angel, there must be quite a passel of angels over at the Cotton Rock School House. Why there's several hundred youngens over there now, counting the sixth grade. That's a lot of angel gossip.

So I reckon I'll take up writing about their stories. I'm not saying angels talk to me direct, or that I eavesdropped on their gossip. People that claims that kind of thing are locked up down at Mount Boyle, and I know that. But I been teaching Sunday school at the Cotton Rock Baptist Church for most of my life, and my sister Opal taught school all her life. So between the two of us, we've got a double stock of stories about youngens. I figure the angels been collecting the same stories Opal and me been saving up. So I'm writin' them down for the angels and Opal. My husband Eb says that I should do my own snake killin' and not put you to the bother of correcting things. But I figure you'll tell me if I'm taking too big a dive into shallow water.

I'll start with a story at the school house. Maybe you don't know it but our school house was a one roomer for a hundred years or more, before the brick one come along in 1950. Why my grandma sat in the same room where I went to school.

My great uncles' names were still whittled in the desk tops when I come along. My momma's pen filled with ink from real ink balls grown on the sides of oak trees. In those days teachers knew how to boil 'em up with a little copperas. I got stories scratched outta old, old dirt.

Anyway this story is Opal's story. She's the one that did the teaching in the one-roomer, 'fore they tore it down.

Little Charlie Mills was her student. Them Mills never been to church a day, and when little Charlie first showed up at the school house, he just opened his lunch box without so much as a nod at God. Opal just followed her habit like always, rang her little bell, and all the youngens bowed heads and said their prayers. When Charlie's momma asked him 'bout the first day at school, Charlie said, "It was fine, but they's some strange parts. Before they eat, teacher rings a bell, and all them kids talk to their lunch boxes!"

Yes sir! I figure Charlie's angel couldn't wait to tell that one. Them angel wings did a little shakin' on that laugh.

Thoughts from the Back Porch   June 1996

"You must love being down here," Alex said, pouring himself another glass of wine. Alex taught with me at the college and had come down to spend the week-end at the cabin.

"To quote my Granddad, I drink 'lonesome water' when I'm away too long," I said.

"Well who wouldn't be lonesome for this place?" Alex asked, sweeping his hand across the view. He stood beside me as I cooked our steaks on the grill. A few minutes later he caught sight of a wild turkey eating shagbark from Grandma's hickory tree. He turned to look at me with wide, brown eyes, exaggerated through the thick lenses of his glasses. "You mean it just lives in your woods—wild? It's a damn zoo right out there in the trees."

"Can't say much for the mosquitoes though," I said, "and the steaks are done. Let's head inside." We sat at The Benchmark. Alex poured more wine, and I found steak knives. We ate and drank and talked about the cabin and tomorrow's fishing trip. We watched the sun set, sending long, wrinkled lines of pink and gold across the river. The frogs and cicadas began their drone along the bank, the woods faded into shadows, and the soft dusk deepened into night.

We opened another bottle of wine, and Alex leaned his chair against the back wall of the porch, his hands clasped behind his head of brown curly hair. I sat on the floor where I could see Alex and still take in the patch of stars through the screen.

"What's happening at the college?" I asked.

"Okay I've got a story for you," Alex said. But the thought of it started him laughing. It took a few seconds before he could say, "They asked Henry to give the opening address at the Summer Forum. He didn't notice his trousers were unzipped."

"Oh, god."

"Had on a bright pink oxford—tucked in so that the shirt tail stuck out through the zipper. You know how he lifts his head in that arrogant way. If he could ever bother to look down, he'd have seen the problem.'"

We were both laughing now.

"Strolled back and forth across the stage. Bright pink plume bobbing up and down with every step. It gets worse…" Alex laughed so hard, his tilted chair threatened to kick out from under him. "He mistook the laughter," Alex continued. "Thought it must be his great wit. Stuck his hands in his pockets, strolled around, made the shirt stick out even further. The faculty lost it. Even Henry finally figured something must be up. Shot a look to the president who tapped his watch and motioned Henry to sit down."

"Henry is such an asshole!"

"English Department's full of assholes," Alex said.

"Take Roland," I said. "He's actually developed a British accent."

"He's from Montana for god's sake." Alex held up his glass, "To the asshole dispensers of the classics."

"After you've explicated a Shakespeare sonnet for years isn't that the same as writing it," I said, trying to mimic Roland's British accent.

Alex nodded his head. "Absolutely. The great masters would be in trouble without us!"

"They really don't hold up their end—being dead and all," I said.

"But my Ozark runaway we, too, are assholes. I mean we are in the English department."

"But we, unlike the others, feel miserable about it."

"Yes. We are miserable assholes."

"You know why I really hate Henry?" I asked.

"Because he's an asshole who's had a book published?"

"Exactly! And I'm just an asshole. But, I've started writing again."

"That's great! You're writing?"

"No. I'm a little drunk."

"But you're writing?"

"Nothing on the novel."

"But you're writing."

"To quote Fielding," I said, rising up from the floor and holding my wine glass aloft, 'if one of the muses hath entrusted me with any inspiration, I am by no means guilty of discovering it.'" I drained my glass and set it down.

"So when did your novel get in trouble? I mean how long has the dry spell been?" Alex asked.

"I haven't written on the novel since Susan died." I heard the crack in my voice and fought to get control. I seized the wine bottle from the floor and drank straight from its mouth—a long, deliberate drink.

Alex brought the front legs of his chair slowly back to the floor. "Grief takes time. Maybe you need more time."

"I don't know," I said. "What if that's just a cowardly excuse? What if I haven't got a novel in me?"

"Well, what if you haven't?" he asked.

"Jennings retires next year from creative writing. If I finished the novel while I'm down here, I'd have the semester to market it. Even an offer would put me in the running. Otherwise the position goes to Henry."

Alex moaned. "Now I'm desperate! Let's lock you up in a hotel room like they did Faulkner. Reward you with whiskey. A pint for each new chapter."

I needed to stop indulging self-pity, but I'd had too much wine. I was determined to unravel. "Writing's the only thing I've got. It's my benchmark—there." I stood and pointed the empty wine bottle toward the table.

Alex pulled back the cloth and looked.

"No," I said. "The table's my touchstone."

"You lost me. . ."

"Doesn't matter—it's my own construct—more real to me than the light bill." I had trouble standing now. The wine had reached my knees. I sank back to the floor. "We have to get up early," I said. "I need to get my sleep if I'm to go on whining all day tomorrow."

But Alex didn't respond to my attempt at humor. A friend seems to know when silence should be allowed to speak. We sat for awhile longer, listening to the cicadas sing along the river and the June bugs hit against the screen, in search of the light.

We woke early Sunday morning. It promised to be a great day. I packed a box with canned sardines, crackers, rye bread and hot mustard, then filled the cooler with ice, beer, cheese and ham. I could hear Alex in the shower.

He arrived in the kitchen, and I handed him a cup of coffee, then drained the pot into the thermos. Alex sipped his coffee, and I closed a few windows in case of an afternoon shower. We carried things down to the dock—the food box and cooler, our rods and reels, bait and wire basket for holding fish. The sun broke through the trees, and the early morning dew on the dock caught the glint of its rays. A red-tailed hawk watched from his limb as we loaded the food and gear into the boat. Alex went back to the house for his sunglasses.

"Nice glasses," I said when he returned.

"Prescription. Cost me plenty. You know how I hate spending money. Don't want to lose them."

There were four seats in *Rosalee*. I took the back; Alex took the bow. We wedged the picnic supplies between the middle seats.

"The motor's loud; I'll row for a while." I gave a pull on the oars. "Catch the true serenity of the river."

Patches of fog lifted from the water. The hoarse cry of a blue heron carried down the channel.

Just below my cabin, we entered a series of hills shouldering the river on either side, their thick woods running down to the water's edge. Occasionally the woods gave way to meadows filled with willows. I spied a doe and her fawn feeding. They lifted their heads and gazed our direction, but being accustomed to boats sliding by, they resumed their feed.

"White-tail," I said, pointing. The meadow continued, ending at Anna's cabin. A light lit one of the windows. We rounded the bend and passed a fisherman in a bright yellow wind breaker and wading boots, standing knee-deep near the river's edge. He side-armed his rod, and the line skipped along the surface of the water.

"Catching anything?" I called.

"Nothing yet. Whites are schooling on top. Feeding on shads," he called back.

The next bend brought a string of cabins and the curl of smoke from a campfire. Laughter and the call of a name echoed across the water. We floated past, and the voices faded. The stillness intersected with the occasional hammer of a woodpecker.

We neared a stretch of sand, and a blue heron disturbed by our approach lifted off. For one brief moment it seemed to hang mid-air, wings bent, long legs dangling, as though suspended by an unseen thread. Then, reaching up with slow, strong wings, it pulled upward into the sky. To the right of us woods and willows gave way to a wall of cotton rock. Bunches of red columbine hung from crevices in the pale rock.

I headed for the confluence of a nearby spring. The water slowed there, as it entered the river and created a feeding lane, a place where the trout were likely to be waiting. We arrived at the spot, and I secured the boat.

Early mornings before the generators start running the water's down. For low water we would be fishing for trout, using red worms and rooster tails. I handed Alex a rod with the slower reel so it wouldn't get ahead of him. He hadn't done that much fishing. I wanted him to catch some nice ones. Granddad always did what he could to give his guests a good fishing experience and a love for the river.

"I'm hoping you snag a nice rainbow," I said. "They've got spirit—give you a good fight."

Alex inspected his rod though the lenses of his fancy sun glasses. "You know I'm a novice—any tips?"

"Cast carefully," I said. "Don't want to get a size eight rooster tail stuck in my ear lobe. Or snag those fancy sunglasses and break your cheap heart."

"So that's why you wear that ridiculous hat," Alex said, "Don't want to pierce your ear lobes."

"This is a wonderful hat! This hat brings good luck," I said. "I rent it out on week-ends."

Alex cast out, dropping his bait close to the feeding spot.

"Good cast," I said. "Let that rooster tail drop deep into the pool, then give short, slow pulls. The take will be soft. If you feel anything at all set the hook."

After a while, Alex said, "I think I may have missed the take." He cast from the other side of the boat. "Nothing."

"Once the fish has tasted the rooster tail and spit it out, he won't be fooled again," I said.

After a while Alex offered to trade me places. I took up my rod and cast off the front of the boat, dropping the bait into the seam between the river and the spring. The take was nearly a caress. I reeled in some line. Sure enough, I had a fish on the hook. I cranked earnestly tightening the line. The rod bent to an arc. A trout danced in the air sleek and shiny then plunged back beneath the water.

"Whoa! That was beautiful!" Alex shouted.

"That's what it's all about," I said. The trout took the line and ran with it. The ratcheting sound of the reel filled the boat. I wound against the pull, keeping the line taut. The hook set. I could feel the trout's body pumping the water. In a few minutes I had it in the boat—the first catch of the day.

"Okay," Alex said, "How much to rent the hat?"

I grinned. "Your turn to cast," I said.

Alex cast again and this time, he recognized the nibble. He jumped to his feet reeling in some line. The boat rocked as he lunged forward, letting the line feed out. If Granddad had been along he would have reminded me, "A bear could stand up in a johnboat without turning it over."

The battle waged. Alex straddled the middle seat. The reel jerked hard to the right. The trout headed upstream.

"Hear that *zing*?" I said. "There's no sweeter sound than a fish stripping the line."

"It's a fighter."

"You're wearing him out."

The trout put up a serious scuffle before Alex brought him up and over the side of the boat. I shoved the net underneath, and Alex had a fish. He went wild hopping from one seat to the other, whooping and hollering. On his final hop he put a foot down on an empty coffee can, skated wildly for a moment nearly lurching overboard. He collapsed in a heap laughing. "Ever fall out of a boat?" he gasped.

"More than once."

"I suppose there's an Ozark name for that, too?"

"Depends how deep the water is. Get a good soaking, they call you a forty-gallon Baptist."

We sat looking at the trout. The freckled rainbow, running the length of its side glistened in the sun. "Beautiful!" Alex said.

"It's bigger than mine. It's well over two pounds."

Now Alex grinned. "Do you want to rent my sun glasses?"

We put the fish in the bucket along with the other trout. "Hand me your roller skate," I said to Alex.

He passed the coffee can back and I dropped a couple of flies into it. We took turns tying on bait and casting. After awhile, I started the motor and headed down river. We were the only boat on the river, the exclusive guests of the rugged cliffs and thick forests. The water grew very clear. We could see small trout skittering at quick angles, and near the bottom the big trout, dark silhouettes against the pale gravel, holding their place, fins pushing against the current. I spoke of Schoolcraft, the great American geographer and his explorations of the White River, how the river—at times twenty feet deep—still revealed every rock and mussel shell with perfect distinction, how he wrote that his canoe seemed "from the remarkable transparency of the water, to be suspended in air."

We floated on in silence and after a time Alex said, "Keats believed that beauty obliterated all other considerations."

It was true. For these few moments, Susan's death, my unfinished novel, my dread of losing the creative writing position at the college, were suspended along with the boat. All that existed was the clear, flowing water beneath us, the wide, blue sky above.

The horn sounded its warning, and a few seconds later, sounded a second. Within minutes, the water swelled, and the current tugged at our boat.

"They're running the engines," I said. "Water can rise as much as nine feet."

"You'd want to be aware of that," Alex said.

"Right." I told him about Anna's children—how Mary and Sam had drowned.

We were getting hungry. I cranked on the motor and turned back toward the West. "There's a little stream not too far from my cabin. Has a nice beach."

We reached the stream a few minutes later and located the stretch of sand. I cut the motor, and Alex climbed into the shallow water, pulling the bow onto the beach. I tossed him the blanket, and I climbed out with the picnic basket. A kingfisher darted toward us scolding. "Very territorial," I warned.

The kingfisher circled back, head down, top knot blowing wild in the wind.

Alex waved the blanket, and the kingfisher retreated, gliding away downstream. "The place teems with life," Alex said. "I needed this. Reminds me I'm alive—not just an extension of books and florescent lights."

We spread the blanket, set out the food and snapped the caps off a couple of beers, taking long, cold gulps between bites of ham and cheese.

"How's Sylvia?" I asked.

"Busy. Nursing's a plethora of record keeping. Comes home exhausted. Finds me buried under my own paper." Alex mimicked Roland's accent, "Weekly assignments for Freshmen would provide helpful feedback."

I groaned.

"Making love to my wife would provide some helpful feedback," Alex said.

"God!" I said, remembering the conflict of work and marriage. "I never figured out how to balance things. I acquired a system just as Susan wanted a baby. Wanted to quit her job. All those years of supposed enlightenment—all those damned books we waded through. Nothing prepares you for marital conflict. You never imagine yourself a raving lunatic. Running down the hall in your shorts, shaving cream dripping on your knee caps. Waving your razor, screaming something right off the third-grade playground."

But I was spouting bullshit-lines that belonged in some superficial novel. I was far from telling Alex the real truth. That belongs in a book much darker and far more sinister. A setting where the water is not clear, like the water Schoolcraft described, where the husband finally scares himself with his own rage and retreats into the deep safety of silence. He's relieved that she, too, has retreated, and it's easy to let her adopt the habit of sleeping in the spare room, because he can get some writing done. But the husband never meant for her to go away for good. He just meant to grab a little time, while things worked themselves out. Then a gravel truck fails to stop at the sign, and a little time becomes eternity. In this book, the water is murky, and the big trout are not holding their place, fins pushing against the current, they have lost their balance, they are pumping blindly against the black heave of water. It's a Conrad novel full of ironies, and now the husband has all his evenings and week-ends free, and he can't write a single word. Maybe he never could. It's Conrad's "mysterious arrangement of merciless logic…some knowledge of yourself—that comes too late—a crop of unextinguishable regrets."

Alex interrupted my thoughts, "Let's take a walk." He pointed to a path leading into the trees. We passed a little spring, bubbling up from the ground. A wooden box, handmade and nearly collapsed, lay at its mouth.

"This was someone's refrigerator," I said. "Kept butter and milk in this box. Lowered it into the cold spring. There'll be other signs of a homestead nearby." The path ended abruptly at a dark hole in the hillside. "A fraidy hole," I said, pointing. We walked to the entrance. "That's what the hill people call it. It's a storm cellar. Nearly every path in these woods leads to a piece of the past."

We examined the sagging, cedar logs that braced the entrance—hand-hewn, smooth from weathering. Wild mint grew around the door. I picked several leaves. "I'll take some to the cabin," I said. "Makes great iced tea."

We took turns peering into the dark, cool interior of the cellar, the size of a large walk-in closet, the floor a carpet of velvet moss. "Dug out by hand," I said

"Must have been a welcome place in a tornado." Alex poked his head once more into the doorway.

We followed the path back to the boat. I stored the mint leaves in the picnic basket, and we loaded things into the boat, setting off once again for the cabin. After several minutes up river, I called up to Alex, "We're close to home. About a mile further."

We rounded another bend. A woman and child sat on the bank up river. As we drew closer, I recognized Anna and little Harlo. I slowed the boat and pulled up alongside them.

"Enjoying the day?" I called out.

"Mr. Sinclair," she nodded. "We're just resting."

I turned to Alex. "I'm her teacher," I said, explaining the "Mr. Sinclair" part. "They live just up the river. Not far from me."

"We've been picking blackberries," Harlo shouted, trying to pick up the bucket beside Anna as evidence.

"Want to give them a ride up the river?" Alex asked.

"Sure." I called out an invitation.

Harlo squealed with delight. Anna hesitated for a moment, and then seeing Harlo wading the shallow water beside the boat, she stood and picked up the bucket. I'd never seen her in jeans, but her hair, as usual, caught up in a knot at the back of her head.

Alex climbed out and lifted Harlo into the boat. She clamored over the picnic basket and squeezed herself in beside me. The child obviously felt comfortable with me. Alex noticed. I felt a certain pride about it.

Alex gave Anna a hand, then swung her bucket into the boat. Anna took the middle seat, near Alex, her dark eyes keen with interest. She loved the river. That was apparent from her journals.

I heard Alex introducing himself.

Harlo took up her own conversation, her little brows wrinkled in concern, "Captain, where exactly are we?"

I showed her the compass and explained, "The N is for north and the W is for west. We're headed northwest. And this is called the temperature dial, because it tells the temperature. And this is called a johnboat," I added.

"Yes," she said, "because your name is John, and it's your boat."

I laughed. "Well, most of the boats on the river are called johnboats." I explained about the Cajuns and the history of the boats, and I sounded like Granddad—like a dad, I decided. She looked up at me, her little face filled with pleasure.

"I could lean against you," she said resting her small head on my arm. Alex talked with Anna about the writing class.

The sun neared the horizon, and the sky filled with pink and lavender. I rowed out into the current. The water lapped against the wood, just the way Granddad loved. It was good—a good thing to have stopped and helped.

I started the motor, and headed up river. Anna's house came into view, a small, but attractive two-story, built into the hillside. The lower story was native limestone, the second story pine with bright blue shutters. A patio ran the length of the house, facing the river. Lawn furniture scattered at one end. An elderly woman sat at a table, beneath an umbrella, and a young woman with long, dark hair stood by her, painting at an easel. I recognized the woman I'd seen standing on the dock—Leah. I pulled in along the dock. Alex jumped out and held the boat steady for Anna and Harlo.

I suddenly wanted very much to meet Leah.

"I'll carry that bucket," I called from the boat.

Alex shot me a quizzical look. He was already on shore with the bucket, and I could hardly leave the boat with the motor running.

"Hey," I said, trying to poke fun at my mistake, "Why don't you carry the bucket—I'll manage the boat."

Alex nodded and started for the house with Anna walking beside him. Harlo ran ahead to meet her mother at the easel. She pointed toward the boat, and her mother turned to look. Alex and Anna joined them on the patio. I actually felt a small stab of self-pity—getting stuck with the boat, while Alex shook Leah's hand and stood talking with her.

Alex returned. "Nice people," he said.

I nodded.

Later, when we were cleaning fish at the river's edge, Alex said, "Leah is a good looking woman."

"I haven't met her yet. I'd like to."

"Yeah." Alex grinned. "Almost abandoned your boat, trying to get to her."

"I was just afraid you might collapse under that bucket of blackberries," I said. "You guys lift grade books down at the gym, right?"

But Alex wasn't going to be put off. The next day, as he headed back to Springville, he rolled the window down and said, "Wouldn't hurt you any to take Leah out. Have some drinks, see a movie. Maybe take a moonlight ride in that boat of yours. Or maybe you'd rather pack up and go live in that fraidy hole."

"Alex, go back to campus and get on with being an asshole."

"Yeah, yeah, nature boy. Just keep writing, or I'll send Henry down to give you lessons!"

Anna's Fifth Notebook

Zoe was as Scotch-Irish as the rest of us, but somehow she sidestepped the need to fail. Maybe she just got a bigger dose of English blood. Cause the English just rose up in her and planted a flag. Zoe turned eight, and I had just turned six when Dade Groves married my momma, and we left the things that make life good—the sweetness and the easy, gentle ways of Grandma and Grandpa Poinselot.

Dade moved us all into his log house. Momma stayed upright for the first few months. But she began having bad headaches and spent long hours on the couch. Grandma Poinselot said the best part of Momma just gave up and laid down on living.

Zoe was the kind of child every woman thinks she's going to have. Zoe was born agreeable and stayed that way her whole life. She always knew how to stay out of a fracas—especially with Dade. The truth is, Zoe didn't like Dade anymore than I did. But Zoe didn't see the need to say what passed through her mind. She just kept her mouth shut, and when her time came she left home, went to Springville got her teaching degree and married the right man.

In the hills when a woman gardened and couldn't keep an eye on her baby, she put its shirt tail under the bed post. That baby wasn't going anywhere. I used to say Dade Groves set the shirt tail of my life under his foot. Whenever Dade entered a room something I was dreaming to do turned ugly and broke.

Dade was born up in Kansas City, and that should have opened him out to a wider place. But Dade usually got mad sooner than he got the sense of a thing. The primary good that the city taught him was how to get money. Soon after Roosevelt declared war on Japan, Dade came down from Kansas City with a pocket full of bills. The funny thing was, he never bragged about those bills, and Dade never missed an opportunity to brag. He just took the hushed-up money and bought an old garage in Sugar Gum and filled it with things that the hill people couldn't do without.

Hill people hate to be beholden to anybody, so they do without a lot. But they can't seem to do without old trucks. So Dade filled the garage with rubber tires and fan belts and a hundred other things that old trucks need, and he made himself a living.

Dade was always mad. You could count on it. His face had a permanent flush, like his blood was always simmering, just beneath his skin. The smallest irritation could bring him to a boil, and things could steam off in any direction.

Zoe had taken up mothering me, so the first day Zoe went off to school, I felt pretty lost. Momma lay sick in bed. I got lonely enough to go and see what Dade was doing.

I rounded the corner of the garage and found him at the angry end of a crowbar. He was trying to pry up an old gasoline tank. The bolts holding it to the concrete island were rusted. Dade snugged the crow bar up around a bolt. It hung on by its last, tough groove. He pulled backward on the bolt till the lines in his arms stood tight like wire on a fence. His thick, stout legs spread wide, one foot braced against the concrete island. The bolt gave up without warning, and Dade shot backwards on the cement, came down heavy as a sack of sand. I burst right out laughing. Dade turned his steam on me: "I don't want no god-damned kid around here laughing!"

I took off for the house. But Momma was still behind her bedroom door sleeping, the house quiet and lonely. I stood looking out the window. Dade had the gas pump loaded on the wheel barrow. He headed down the path behind the house. The gate at the back of the lot was closed. I figured it'd need opening. I was out the back door in a flash and running alongside Dade. The wheelbarrow creaked under the weight of rubbish from the back of the shop, old rags, a broken fan belt, empty oil cans. A rusty gas pump rocked back and forth on top of the load. Dade struggled to keep the rubber tire of the wheelbarrow from running with the ruts. The sun beat down, and Dade's red face dripped wet with sweat. Now and then he shoved down extra hard on the wooden handles, cursing the path. I got to the gate first and called back, "I could open the gate!"

Dade needed to keep the wheelbarrow moving, so he snapped, "Well what you waitin' for?" He said it out of one side of his mouth, cause the other side pinched down on a cigarette.

I pushed the gate open and stood against it. "Where are you taking the trash?"

"Over yonder by the river," Dade said. The smoke from the red ash of his cigarette, clouded around his face. Dade squinted in the smoke. The rubber tire of the wheelbarrow hit a large rock, and the wheel came to a dead halt. The load swayed to one side. Dade's eyes flamed like hot coals, and his arms were red from the rage of his pulling against the sway, but the gas pump slid off the edge and most of the trash followed.

Don't laugh! I told myself. I squeezed everything down: my hands into fists, my eyes tight shut, and my chest till the air emptied out safe.

"Damned kid!" Dade yelled. He grabbed the gas pump up and slammed it into the wheelbarrow. The sides of the wheelbarrow shuddered. "I can't be workin' and talkin' to no damned kid!"

I didn't say a word, just jumped down and began picking up trash. When the things were reloaded, Dade shoved at the rock with the side of his boot, shoved till he had it propped against the opened gate.

He turned back to me, "Move!"

I stepped aside.

Then he brought his face down close, till his nose almost touched mine. "You should 'a told me there was a rock on the path."

This surprised me so, I didn't know what to say.

"I know about kids," he said. "I's a kid wunst. You's hoping I'd turn over the wheelbarrow wasn't you? You thought it'd be funny, didn't you?"

"No sir."

"You wanna be my helper? You gonna have to tell me the truth. You's hopin' I'd tip over the wheelbarrow, wasn't you?"

I looked back at the house, hoping to catch sight of Momma, but all I could see were dark windows.

"You want to be my helper?" Dade asked.

"I sure want to see the river," I said.

"You wanna work with me, you'd better tell the truth. You's hopin' I'd tip over the wheelbarrow, wasn't you?" His face streaked with sweat. He was breathing anger, and somehow it seemed like he needed me to say "yes" worse than I needed to say "no."

"Yes," I said. "Can I help you now?"

"I know kids," he said, clutching down hard on the wheelbarrow handles. "Don't never think I'm not smart about kids."

Once we were through the gate, the path narrowed with thick buckeye and dogwood. Virginia creeper hung from elm trees, and buck brush choked things down till we could barely find a foot hold. Dade wrestled the wheelbarrow with a heated will.

I followed along behind him. I knew the river ran somewhere behind the house, but I'd never seen it. I'd seen rivers from the car window, but never up close. Grandpa Poinselot told me, "They've got strong currents and undertows. You never know what a river's gonna do." I didn't know much about an undertow, but it sounded like if you got close to the bank, one would reach right out and pull you in.

I heard the river long before I saw it. It sounded like the buckets of bath water Grandma Poinselot poured into the galvanized tub, only it sounded as if all the women in Sugar Gum were emptying their buckets at the same time.

Dade stopped so sharp, I nearly bumped into him. I picked my way round him and looked down. The sound of water buckets joined itself to the picture spread out before me. It looked like the concrete highway on the way to Springville. Only it seemed like it had melted into gray-blue and moved all in a piece, like a width of shiny material from a bolt at the Five-and-Dime. One place ran smooth like a mirror, another stood up in little peaks like the meringue on a pie. One place turned spinning into a circle like the one that gurgled in the kitchen sink after the stopper had been pulled, and another place suds itself against a rock, then parting and joining like a smooth mirror on the far side, always moving, always talking. And that's when I fell in love with rivers.

Both sides of the banks were thick with the greenest ferns I'd ever seen. Willows hung their branches down to stroke the water. Here and there wild flowers bloomed. I knew violets, wild roses, and the tiny yellow flowers Grandma Poinselot called jack-in-the-pulpit, because they looked like a little preacher standing in a velvet pulpit.

Dade lit another cigarette, cupping his hands against the breeze. He straightened, looking out over the river and took a long drag on the cigarette, its red flame eating away at the white paper. He blew a cloud of smoke and looked down at me, "You never seen the river up close, have you, kid?"

It was good to give Dade an answer I could put my heart into, "No Sir!"

"Good place for dumpin'," he said, and forced the wheelbarrow up on its end. The gas pump went first, bumping and rolling its way down the hill. The cardboard and cans followed, scattering down over the bank.

Dade turned to me and said, "Your daddy's dead. I'm your Daddy now. And I don't give a god-damn about the Navy or Humphrey Bogart."

I decided two things that day. When I got old enough, I was going to live by a river, and I'd see every Humphrey Bogart movie I could take in.

In the meantime, I had to do what Dade said, and I had to learn to live with his temper. There were years of what I called "Dade's judgment seat." Maybe he'd lost a sale out in the shop, or lost a shipment of tires, something that caused him to swell up like the Sugar Gum River in flood stage, threatening against the limits of its banks. He'd set me on a chair while he circled around me.

"You always think you know more than me, don'tcha?" The speculation of his own question made his face red with anger.

I'd keep my gaze toward the floor, sit quiet. I didn't want him to think I wasn't listening, make him boil up and spill over. I'd sit so still my legs would grow numb. Sometimes my foot went to sleep, and I'd long to give it a shake.

"I was a kid wunst, and I know kids," he'd be saying. "Don't never think I don't know things." This thought would always make him feel better, make his face a little less red. Encourage him just enough that I might be able to wiggle ever so slight and give a little life to a cramped foot.

After a while, Dade would have enough of my hang-down-head, enough proof that I was sorry, and we'd move to the next stage.

"You didn't think you'd get caught, did ya? You look at me when I'm talking to you!"

Now I had to meet his eyes. It's not an easy thing to stare into eyes that are full of scorn. If you look often enough, you begin to feel deserving of it. Dade would draw his face down close to mine. His breath smelled like ash trays, and his eyebrow would be twitching. "I know you like a book," he'd be saying. He'd stand back then, jabbing his finger toward me, "You thought you'd get by without getting caught. Didn't you?" He'd keep his hand raised in the air, ready to strike any sign of disagreement.

I knew my part. "Yes sir. You're right, Dade."

It was the only way off the judgment seat, the only way to calm the rage flooding round my chair.

And finally, there would be the shift in his voice, a little less circling of my chair, and I'd know I was getting close to freedom. He would be spent—the flood waters would recede, but he'd ask for final proof: "You know I'm right, don't you?"

I would make sure now that the boil over had passed, "Yes, Dade, we're lucky to have you taking care of us."

His need for a cigarette, or his need to be back at the cash register would overtake him, and he'd be turning away from me, shaking his head at the bother of raising kids.

Sometimes I'd be sitting on the judgment seat for my beliefs. Like the time I said the Indians were the first Americans. That ended with me getting slapped, cause I refused to agree that "it don't matter what's written in some goddamned school book."

I knew Dade lived off-center. Didn't matter. Dade began to creep into my head. Pretty soon, I came to think of myself as off-center, too, came to think that Dade was my fault 'cause he married my Momma.

The thing is, Dade could get stuck on a subject like a June bug on a screen door. There was no letting go with Dade. He meant to get at the bottom of Momma's lay-down soul. So Momma took her pretty French eyes and dark hair to bed for the next five years.

It was Grandma Poinselot that finally got Momma out of bed, though she had to die to do it. She made Momma promise to play piano at her funeral, her favorite: "When They Ring Those Golden Bells." When Momma was a little girl she had piano lessons—only a few months each year. That's how long Grandma Poinselot's strawberry money held out.

Momma took those parceled lessons and a whole lot of hill country sounds and came up with a style that could soften a convict's heart. She could put a song together like the hill women put together a fine quilt from the left-over cloth of living.

Dade had never heard Momma play the piano. When she sat down at the keys and played for Grandma Poinselot's funeral, when she filled her hands with those deep sweet chords that swelled up the keyboard and spilled back down like dancing bells, Dade stood listening, still as a rock. Next thing we knew, Dade took Momma up to Springville. When they came back, there was a piano riding in the back of Dade's Ford truck. Momma never went to bed again.

Dade taught me to be two people. He taught me to feel one thing and say another. And just like that loaded wheelbarrow, I'd spend years swaying first to one side and then the other, first siding to agree, in order to be allowed to see the river, then siding to say what I really thought because it needed saying. But even when I said what I meant, it made me so uneasy, that I usually overshot, like picking up an empty milk jug that you thought was full.

A bird in a storm gets used to flying on a slant, to off-set the squall. I got used to pushing against Dade. When the storm clears, I reckon it takes a while to get the feel of level. Truth is, even after I figured out how to look level on the outside, to the folks at school and later at the tomato cannery, I never was able to feel level on the inside.

I let Momma know that I didn't plan to forgive her for marrying Dade, was never going to let her forget her mistake. And it makes me sad, now, cause I came to understand Momma was flying through a long, dark storm of her own. So that's why I'm taking care of Momma. I want to make things right while there's still some of Momma left.

Thoughts from the Back Porch   June 1996

Crooked Water lives up to its name. I maneuvered the *Rosalee* around the frequent, sharp bends with their accompanying eddies. A gust of wind riffled through the willows along the bank. Off to the right a bass leaped from the river, arching its silver-green body into the air, then smacked back into the water and disappeared into a deep pool beneath an overhanging rock.

I beached the boat on a stretch of sand and grabbed the coffee can from the boat floor. I flipped over a flat rock and grasped a startled crawdad just behind its little black, bead eyes. Its pincers opened and closed against the air as I dropped it into the can. I lifted another rock and several more crawdad scudded away from the unexpected light. Once the coffee can was full, I climbed back into the boat, heading toward the deep pool where I'd seen the bass and dropped anchor. I threaded the soft meat of the crawdad onto the hook and dropped my line into the water.

By four o'clock, I'd caught three nice bass. I dropped anchor, cleaned them at the water's edge, then laid them side-by-side on the middle seat, appreciating the dark green on black, the slightly forked broad tail, the characteristic vertical bands running over the sides. I stretched out on the seat, and closed my eyes. Sitting in the *Rosalee*, feeling her gentle rocking on the water, never failed to make me happy. "It's sitting in the sweet spot," Granddad would say.

The boat was Granddad's final achievement of construction. He undertook the project with his usual thorough and ritualistic manner, elevating it to a place of considerable importance. "I've been watching that yellow pine tree for the past fifteen years," he said. "It'll make a fine johnboat. The first of the year I'm having her cut. It'll take six months to get the water out and cure the wood. When you come down next summer, we'll build a johnboat worthy of her name."

Dad drove me down the following June, and as soon as I got out of the car, Granddad took me to inspect a stack of smooth, narrow boards. "They'll run crossways on the bottom," he said. "Been sanded so smooth they'll bond like bark on a tree. When they get wet, they'll swell. Seal tight, yet give flexibility. A metal boat bought up in Springville has no meaning, John. French trappers and Louisiana Cajuns never heard of a metal boat. They built out of native lumber."

In the evenings we'd sit on the old plaid sofa by the fire place, books piled between us, tracing the history of johnboats to the click of Grandma's knitting needles; the crickets outside along the river clicking their own kind of industry. Some evenings, Grandma would be sewing at her machine, making curtains, or a tablecloth. Granddad would stop reading, listen for a moment to the whir of Grandma's machine and say, "Listen. She sure can make that machine needle smoke."

Then he'd open his book and continue reading. "Now look here," he might say, marking the spot with his finger, "it says the Cajuns called it a jump boat. The Ozark folks changed the word to johnboat. Ozark folks can butcher a word quick as a picnic ham."

We worked on the boat early mornings and late afternoons when the sun wasn't so hot. Granddad explained, "The old timers measured a day from the time you kin see till you cain't see." He would wake me by saying, "We kin see, boy." All the while he sanded or glued, he'd feed me information. "John boats were common as buckeyes at one time. They're made to order for float fishing."

When we finished building the boat, we painted it forest green, and when it came time to name her, Granddad christened her Rosalee—Grandma's name—gold letters on a bed of pink roses, near the prow. When we put her into the water and took our first trip down the river, it was Granddad's finest hour. He sat in the stern, shaking his white head in affirmation, his hands—one absent its thumb—resting on the smooth silver oar locks. "Listen to the sweet, quiet sound of wood against the water," he said. "None of that cranky, rattling aluminum."

A fishing trip with Granddad meant a day on the river. We'd shove off early mornings with just enough light to find the river bank on the opposite shore. There'd be a thermos of coffee, heavy with cream and sugar, a basket of Grandma's baking, filling the boat with cinnamon, fog rising off the water and the cry of a blue heron somewhere in the thick woods flanking the shores.

Granddad would take up his river talk. "The Indians named the river, *Unicda*—White. French called it *La Riviere au Blanc*. Schoolcraft wrote in his journals that the river ran so clear that during the winter, when the ice formed, it was 'transparent as a window.' Ozark folks named the rock—saw how a splash of river water seemed to disappear into the dolomite's porous texture, like cotton—cotton rock."

On one of our trips down river, I made the mistake of telling Granddad that most johnboats had motors. He looked so disappointed in me, I wished I hadn't said it. He rode along in silence before saying, "I sort of think the old trappers keep us company now and then, John. If we turned on some whining motor to scold us all the way home, I think they'd climb right out of our boat."

But paddling back up river wasn't easy, and often in the late afternoons, Grandma would drive down river with the boat trailer and picnic lunch.

"You bring those pictures along?" Granddad would ask.

"You know I did," she'd answer.

"That woman won't leave the cabin without those pictures," he'd tell me. But I already knew all about the pictures, taken of her girls when they were young (my mother and her two sisters.) On Sunday afternoon when I was a boy, Grandma came to visit with those three pictures wrapped in quilts in the trunk of the car. "Well," she'd say defensively, "the house could always catch on fire." Granddad used to tease her about having to build her a casket wide enough to hold the picture frames. The pictures still hang in the front bedroom of the cabin, along with a gallery of relatives, though I can't remember ever seeing a picture of Aunt Myrna.

When it came time to load the johnboat on the trailer, Granddad would wink at me and say, "Good thing we've got this trailer, John. Paddling a johnboat upriver is like arguing with a woman. You find out your limitations in a hurry!"

"You never came close to finding out your limitations, Mr. Rowden," Grandma would say. "I didn't want to embarrass you altogether."

I wondered again how they had arrived at their gentle truce. Was it a matter of time—the slow friction of years spent together that scraped off the differences and left two people fitted, agreeable, like the small, pine boards on the *Rosalee*?

Susan and I had been married three short years when she died. Our discoveries were primarily of our differences—including the cabin. Susan didn't like coming here. She hated fishing and could tolerate a boat ride only if it were short-lived, only if I used the motor.

Granddad did have to add a motor when Grandma wasn't there anymore to meet us with the boat trailer and the picnic, when that great heart of hers just stopped beating. Sometimes I still turn the motor off, take up the oars and pay my dues to the trappers and to Granddad.

Today proved one of those times. I rowed quietly upstream and had just reached the bend, not far from home when I heard a child crying. I looked along the bank and recognized Harlo. She sat on the ground, clasping her legs. I rowed into shore and called out, "Are you hurt?"

"My legs are all scratched!"

I dropped anchor and climbed onto the beach. Harlo wore a yellow sundress, and as I neared she unclasped her arms from her legs and straightened them against the sand for my inspection. They were covered with red scratches. "I was picking blackberries," she said when I asked her why she was there.

"Would you like me to take you home?" I asked.

The prospect brought her crying to a halt. "Can I ride in the boat?" she asked, pointing.

"Certainly."

Once in the boat, she sat down at the place she'd come to think of as her own—beside me, near the compass and temperature gauges. But her attention divided between her injuries and the gauges. "We're going north," she said, whimpering, "and my legs are still bleeding, and it's eighty-nine degrees." She brightened with a new thought, "I can tell Momma I rode in the boat again." Just as quickly she wailed, "My Momma's gonna be mad."

"Oh, I don't think she'll be mad."

"I didn't tell her I was going."

"Oh." I nodded. "I'll get you home."

I started the motor and took the boat into the current. "Which direction are we going now, skipper?" I asked.

Harlo wiped at her eyes and turned to inspect the dial. "We're going west," she said and settled herself beside me. We were in front of her house within a couple of minutes. I tied up the boat, took her hand and helped her onto shore.

We were halfway down the walk when Leah came around the corner of the house. She saw us and came running, scooped Harlo into her arms and hugged her tightly. A second later she put Harlo down and grabbed her by the shoulders. I saw that Leah's hands trembled, and her voice was shrill when she asked, "Where were you! Do you know how frightened I was? Do you?"

"I wanted to bring you blackberries…the stickers scratched my legs." Remembering her wounds, Harlo burst into tears.

"There, there." Leah's voice softened, and she bent to examine the scratches. "Some band-aids will make it feel better." She hugged Harlo once again. Leah was—as I had remembered her that day on the dock—a younger Anna, taller, with richer darker hair. After a moment, she stood, and turned toward me. Her eyes were a remarkable blue.

"I'm Leah Gatewood, Harlo's mother," she said. She reached out her hand, then noticed it was smudged with paint. "Oh," she said, pointing toward the easel on the patio, "I'm covered in paint, I'm afraid." She brushed at her jeans.

"This is Captain Sinclair," Harlo told her.

"Harlo's convinced that my little boat's a yacht," I said. "I'm your mother's writing teacher. Please call me John." I explained how I'd found Harlo crying.

Leah thanked me again, and excused herself to attend to Harlo. We said good bye. I turned to walk to the boat when Harlo shrieked, "Captain, I forgot Bill! He's in the stickers."

"We can look later," Leah said.

I assured her that I didn't mind going back. I felt certain I could find the doll.

My hunch proved right. It didn't take long to spot Bill's red hair among the blackberry vines. No wonder Harlo had gotten her legs scratched. The tangled brush was thick with thorns. I returned, tied up the boat and knocked on the door. It opened at once, and Harlo reached out for Bill.

Leah arrived beside her, "Please come in," she said. "You must need a cold drink after all this."

Harlo took me by the hand and led me inside. Her face had been washed, and her legs were covered with a number of band aids, heading off in different directions.

The room, large and sunny, was a sort of family room. An elderly woman with white hair sat on a couch by the window. "This is Mayta," Leah said. "This is Harlo's great-grandmother."

Mayta reached for my hands and cradled them in her own. "I saw your ship," she said, pointing a thin finger toward the window.

The news of my mythical boat had permeated the family.

"I'm John," I said.

"John," she repeated. She looked once again at my boat, tied at the dock. "My husband…my husband…" She shook her head, and looked at Leah, hoping for her help.

"Grandma Mayta's had a stroke," Leah said.

"I'm…stroked." Mayta said, nodding her head in agreement.

"I live up the river," I offered, hoping this might answer her question. But she smiled a sad smile, and I decided she had not found the words she had wanted to say.

"Would you like something to drink—a glass of iced tea?" Leah asked from behind us.

"Iced tea would be great," I said, turning to face her. Leah nodded and left the room. Harlo had snuggled down on the couch beside Mayta, who put her arm around the child and patted her with a thin, veined hand. Bill lay on Harlo's lap, his steadfast look of glass-eyed worry cast upward at the two of them. Harlo would be asleep soon. Her blackberry adventure had worn her out. The grandmother, too, had begun to nod.

I walked to one of the many canvases that hung on the walls. They must be Leah's work, of course. They were all portraits of young girls painted in stark chiaroscuro—their pale faces surrounded by dark shadows—all with the same haunting eyes. The work was compelling, yet disturbing.

Leah returned and handed me a glass of iced tea. She held a glass of her own, but I felt quite certain it was something stronger than tea. She took a long drink from her glass. She seemed to forget my presence for a moment. I was to learn that she often seemed distracted.

"Are these your paintings?" I asked.

She glanced up, as though my question had come to her from a far distance. "Yes," she said.

"Your work is powerful."

She shrugged. "I don't feel very powerful." She located a cigarette on the table beside her and lit it. "I was so afraid she'd gone down to the river." She looked at Harlo who had fallen asleep, along with Mayta. "I lost people to the river. You've probably heard—small town. I…" She didn't finish. She took a long drag on her cigarette.

I looked at Harlo and Mayta, sleeping soundly. "Harlo's certainly peaceful now. Both of them are quite peaceful."

"Grandma Mayta did have a little stroke," Leah said. "But she also has Alzheimers."

"That must be terrible for her—for all of you."

Leah nodded.

A silence followed, and I said, "I've enjoyed having your mother in class. She's achieved an amazing amount of writing in a few weeks," I said.

"She loves your class. I think it's a kind of therapy for her, though she doesn't let me read any of her writing."

I finished my tea. "I should let you get back to your painting."

"Actually, I…" She stopped mid-sentence, then looked away.

The silence returned.

"Well, thank you for the tea," I said, setting the glass on the table beside her. "I'll be on my way."

She walked with me to the door.

I stepped outside.

"Oh—John?"

I turned back to look at her. The sun shone down on her there in the doorway, framing her in light, as though she had stepped from one of her own dark canvases. She smiled, a playful and unexpected smile. "Thanks for getting 'Br'er Bill out of the briar patch," she said.

"Born and raised in a briar patch," I said. I wished that I could tell her how very beautiful her eyes were. Instead, I said, "I'm not acquainted with many people in Cotton Rock. Maybe you'd join me for a movie sometime—or a boat ride. Maybe go to River Walk for a drink." (Alex would have been proud of me, I thought. I quoted him almost word for word.)

"That would be nice."

"I'll give you a call. . ."

She nodded.

I turned toward the river. The door shut softly behind me.

Emmett's Fishing Report

    The weather today is eighty-four degrees. It's blue sky all the way to the Mississippi. There's ever kind a fish you could hope to find in the White River. In the pothole below Cedar Shoals there's pickerel, bass, rainbow trout, walleye, channel cat, flatheads and crappie. All you got to do is wet your line and keep your hook from squirrel hunting in the trees. Night's been falling around sixty-three.

    Early morning fishing's about sixty-five. If you're going to wade and fish, you got to do it before the generators send down the water. Thing is, everybody's fishing the pothole below the dam. You can't find a place that you're not rubbing shoulders with somebody. Them fish just bumping up against your rubber boots, and so many fishing rods hanging above them, the fish think a grove of trees sprouted over night. That pot hole early mornings is like licking honey off a thorn. Like they say, "Just sweet enough to put up with the pain."

    In the afternoon, I come back down the White to ride along in Irvin's boat. Irvin's one of the best outfitters on the river. Had a couple of city fellas with him today. Didn't know which end of the hook to bait, but thought they were smarter than Irvin. They weren't catching anything, and they was sure it was Irvin's fault. Either the bait was bad, and that's why the fish weren't hitting, or the spot was bad, and Irvin didn't know the river. Imagine that! Irvin was wading in the river fore he was weaned. The final kick came when they said maybe the White wasn't all it was advertised.

    Irvin didn't say a word. Just reached over and took the pole outta City's hand and cast it out and got himself a hit. The reel took to singing, and Irvin doing the dance, keeping the line tight, then pulling her in. In a few minutes, Irvin had a fish in the boat. A beautiful big rainbow. Then he took the hook outta its mouth and throwed it back into the river. Watched it swim off free. "Why'd you do that!" City wanted to know.

    "I knew that fish," says Irvin. "Fact is, I know all these fish. They don't take kindly to strangers. So I reckon you just as well pack up and go on back to your car."

    "Whadda ya mean," says City. "I done paid for your time."

"Then we had a misunderstanding, I reckon," says Irvin, and he just opens his wallet and hands City his money back.

City will never know his mistake. But I know. When there's meanness in the boat, it gets so cramped there's not enough room to cuss a cat without getting hair in your mouth. But when the right fellers are in the boat, things just open out. A sweet spirit fills up from bow to stern, and Irvin starts sharing secrets about the river. Secrets he's been storing away since he's a boy. Irvin sells you a boat trip. But he gives you the river. Those are two different things to Irvin, and it pays to know the difference if you're riding in his boat.

Thoughts from the Back Porch   June 1996

It was Saturday. I anchored in a quiet cove, sipping coffee from the thermos cup while the fog lifted from the water. "There's history peeking out from the fog." Granddad would have said, "River's a great liquid legend, carrying history on its back."

The steam from my coffee dissipated into the swirls of fog curling around the boat, the damp air heavy with the pungent odor of the spice bushes along the bank. Old conversations with Granddad replayed to the rhythm of the water lapping gently against the wooden bow. "This river yielded its banks to the hooves of horses ridden by Cherokee warriors, to the carbon ashes of Osage fires, to the mocassined feet of women who fastened the heads of their babies to flattening boards worn patina smooth, to the wheels of wagons that camped for the night while white women eased the pain of childbirth by pulling against bed sheets tied to wagon staves, and their men brought buckets of water from the river, fired red from pine knot torches."

The fog cleared. The sun sparkled on the open patches of water. I finished my coffee, screwed the cup to the thermos, tucked it beneath my seat and pulled up anchor. The boat hitched itself to the current and floated silently along. The river does not discriminate, I thought. Whatever is overtaken by its current, gets carries away. Dee Lushbaugh said that within hours of the drowning a thunderstorm moved in. Spring rains continued for days, and the swollen river flooded thousands of acres of woodlands.

Anna had never written why they had failed to locate Sam's body. I could understand. Spring rains inundated the backwoods with flood water, sometimes to depths over ten feet. It proved sufficient run-off to contribute yearly to the Mississippi's delta region. The woods were a habitat for all kinds of wildlife: black bear, fox, raccoons, bald eagles and waterfowl—wildlife that didn't hesitate to eat what it found.

I'd seen the White River flood its banks only once—the summer I was fifteen. I arrived in the rain, which had been falling for days. The river swelled, like a glass over-filled, rounded, threatening to spill. By morning, it overflowed its banks. Our cabin proved high enough to insure safety, and the back porch provided a front-row seat to destruction.

Granddad and I sat for hours, watching uprooted tree limbs and bushes ride by on the surge of raging current. "The river is destroying years of its own work," Granddad said. "Like love tearing down its own house." Those words meant very little to me at fifteen. I had since experienced love, furious at its own betrayal.

Granddad and I had watched whole beaches—patiently sorted, carried and deposited grain by grain—tear off and churn back into the angry water, like love reversed. Passion that once invited entrance into the other, became the passion that slammed shut the door of intimacy. Emotions which once searched for words to caress and cherish, later hurled words to stab and blame.

I took up my rod and cast flies across the surface of the river—casting out and reeling in the line, casting out marital scenes and reeling in their implications. Susan worked in the college library when I met her. I had only been teaching a few months. I waited some time before telling Alex about her. We were eating in our favorite Thai restaurant. Alex held a spoon of Tom kah mid-air and asked, "Susan Sommerfeld?"

"A great name for a novel," I said.

"Careful, pal," he said, swallowing the spoon of coconut soup. "She's intriguing, I'll give you that. But…"

"Now, Alex. You are the one person who doesn't preach…"

"I taught her British Lit—or tried," Alex said. "She never handed in assignments. Took an incomplete in most of her classes. Dropped out of college. Went off to Europe or something. Came back. Hung around—doing nothing."

"You've turned stodgy-old fart on me!" I said. "And she is doing something. She's working in the college library."

"Stodgy old fart, maybe. But it's your first year of teaching. Scary as hell. Some of your students know as much as you do. They'll eat you for lunch. You feel alone—because you are. You meet a compelling girl. She makes you feel like King Kong. It's an opiate."

I thought of Susan, shelving books from a cart in the library aisle, her blond curls tied with some lacy fuchsia ribbon, her brown eyes wide with admiration, "You teach literature?" And later, "You write! How won-der-ful!" So excessive and so addictive. Alex was right—an opiate. But I could relax with Susan. She made me feel confident, certain that I could write something worth reading.

I was certain she had ambition. She'd spent a few years working before going to Europe. She'd studied fashion design—at least taken a few classes In Italy. She planned to pursue her interest at the Art Institute in Springville.

Alex interrupted my thoughts, "You must have some doubts, yourself," he said.

"I have the gravest doubts," I said, holding up my Singha beer and quoting Oscar Wilde, "but I intend to crush them." As usual, my humor didn't divert Alex.

"Exactly! How serious is it?" He continued, "Have you told your parents about her?" He didn't wait for my answer. "Never mind. Doesn't prove anything. We withhold the annoying little specifics we don't want family to know. Don't even want ourselves to know. I know this self-deception. On my second marriage, I practiced brutal honesty."

He was right. I disregarded his counsel. I dismissed my internal warnings. We disregard counsel when we're determined. I saw the little pop-ups that appeared on my mind's eye, and I chose to click the mental option that read, "Don't show me this again." But the disregarded data base continues to store all the entries, only to retrieve them later, usually in a marital fight, where we can fling them at our partner as though we were deceived, swindled.

A few months after the wedding, the data started its unmistakable crawl-line across our lives. Susan didn't seem to follow through with her objectives. She could manipulate the language of fashion, chat easily about her plans on the phone or at a party, but she hadn't done her transcript work or actually gotten herself enrolled at the Art Institute. It was difficult for her to quiet herself, to organize her world.

She excused herself by saying she had decided to teach Yoga. She would attend school in the spring. But in the spring, she had a new interest. Some afternoons, I came home to find that she was just getting out of bed, or sitting in her pajamas watching television. She no longer talked about her plans for fashion design. She seemed lost, and I didn't know how to help her.

By our second anniversary, she turned thirty and became obsessed with having a baby. Meanwhile, I had arrived at my self-described "golden year"—the year I had time to write. I had finally accumulated enough lecture notes to coast a little.

"This is my year to write," I reminded her.

"It's always your time to write!"

Round and round the circle—different versions of the same fight. In the end, I agreed to carry a full teaching load till after the baby was born. Susan was ecstatic with the news that she was pregnant, and then, she had a miscarriage. We became two sides of an unbearable equation. I hadn't wanted the baby. She'd lost the baby. She couldn't forgive me, nor could she accept my comfort.

She couldn't bear for me to talk about the baby, and she had no interest in talking about anything else. I was the lumbering husband in Frost's poem who cried, "A man can't speak of his own child that's dead."

Then, as a flooded river ultimately spends its rage and sags into a narrow, tired lake, Susan and I arrived at a period of despair and silence. She took a position at a marketing agency. I'd hear her come in from work. We would exchange brief news, and she would proceed to the kitchen.

"Do you need some help?" I'd ask, but I knew she'd say no. We were getting good at not occupying the same room.

Silence is the bunker of defeat. Silence is a game that pretends. I will pretend not to hear you come into the room. You will pretend that I am not sitting here. I will pretend not to notice that you pretend not to notice.

"A river will heal itself, in time," Granddad had said the summer of the flood. "Nothing is lost. Everything the river has torn loose is suspended there in the brown water. Now that the rage has passed, the river will restore itself, largest debris first, then smaller and smaller rocks, down to the smallest grains of sand. It'll put everything back. Naturally, it'll be in a new place, and the river will alter its course. But when it's finished, the water will be clear again, and the river will have a richer flood plain than it had before."

But I knew the statistics. Most marriages don't survive the loss of a child. Yet sometimes I believed that our marriage might heal. There were moments of sweetness. Then something would snag an old wound, and the bitterness would surface without warning—like one of our last dinners together.

Susan tied the fuchsia ribbon in her hair, the one she wore when I met her. Her brown eyes were bright and hopeful, again. She'd lit candles, and I'd been careful to tell her how lovely she looked. Yet things were awkward.

There were painful silences. I simply tried to fill a silence when I said, "I've finished the fourth chapter today. I have some good ideas for the fifth."

Her response edged in sarcasm, "By all means—go write!"

"No—I didn't mean. I'm glad to be with you."

"Your novel's the important thing," she said. The anger in her voice was unmistakable. She gathered up the plates, letting them clatter together sharply, maybe letting them break.

"You're important," I said.

She turned away with the stack of dishes.

"Susan—there's got to be a way through this. People lose babies. Somehow they make it through."

She turned toward me, her face filled with contempt. "Which baby are we talking about, John? My baby that I lost, or your baby?"

"What?"

"Cause your baby didn't die—it's right in there on your desk—all four chapters of it!"

She began going out with friends. "Quiet house—you can write," she'd say.

"Fine with me," I'd tell myself. But it wasn't true, because she was hooked to my gut. I couldn't write. I could only stare at the computer screen and brood.

Granddad was right about the river. In time it did rebuild itself. Today, it flows by the cabin with no apparent sign of its former destruction. But the destruction that had surged through my marriage had no time to rebuild. Susan died. Time stopped, and whatever debris suspended in the sagging, retreating water, dropped abruptly.

It was early afternoon when I headed back up the river. I drove the boat slowly past Anna's dock, hoping I might catch sight of Leah painting on the patio or playing on the lawn with Harlo. I saw no one and felt disappointed. I wanted to see her, yet I couldn't seem to phone her or follow through with my invitation for a drink or a movie.

I was nearly home when the warning whistle—shrill and unmistakable—pierced the air. A few minutes later the second whistle sounded. The generators had turned on, and the river would swell quickly. It was still early. I decided to continue on up river, dock at the River Walk and pick up a cup of good coffee.

As I came in sight of Tom Ferguson's dock, I saw a commotion—two men wrestling on Tom's dock! Within seconds, I was close enough to see it was Tom—wrapping his long arms around the other man and pulling him down, then spreading himself out and pinning him to the dock. It was bizarre, nearly surreal, and something just as strange was the fact that Tom had taken the man down with deliberate care, almost kindly.

I cut the motor and hesitated. Tom's head shot up from the deck, where he still lay spread eagle on top his victim. He recognized me. "John! I need your help!"

"My god, Tom! What did you get yourself into?"

"It's my son! Dock that damned boat and help me!"

I wasn't at all certain I wanted to get involved, but I stopped, threw a rope around the piling and climbed onto the dock. Tom looked terrible, red-faced, sweat running in little furrows along his cheeks, his white hair stuck wet to his head. He continued his struggle, holding on to the man beneath him who looked half Tom's age. The man, moaning, grappled and fought to be released.

Tom panted out orders: "Get to my cabin. Back bedroom. Get the doll—in the bed. Bring it here."

"Doll?"

"You'll see. Run. Can't hold him much longer!"

I sprinted to the cabin, thinking how there was something wrong in the way the man moaned—almost rhythmically, almost chant-like. I located the back bedroom. Sure enough there was the doll, lying on a pillow. It could have been a relative to Harlo's Bill—same sagging cotton body. I raced back to the dock. "Got it."

"Put it in his hand!"

As soon as the soft cotton body touched the convulsing hand, the man's body ceased to struggle. Tom rolled off him and sat up, resting his head on his knees and breathing hard. The man, vacant eyed and expressionless, sat up and hunched over the doll cradling it and rocking back and forth.

Tom got his breath, lifted his head and said, "Autistic—severely autistic. Can't swim a stroke. Don't know how he got past me. Whistle blew just as I saw him out here on the dock. Loud noise makes him wild. He went crazy. Throwing himself around. Don't know what kept him from going off the dock. That doll's like morphine. Guess I shouldn't have brought him home. Just wanted to get him out of the institution for a day or so."

"God, Tom. I'm so sorry!"

"Had to put him there when my wife died. Just hope she understands."

I nodded.

"I better take him inside." Tom stood and bent down to give the man a hand. "Come on lad. Let's go get us a cold drink of water." He pulled the man to his feet, and the two of them walked down the dock toward the cabin. The man stumbled a bit, and Tom wrapped an arm round him. A few steps later, I heard Tom singing softly—his head close to the man's ear. I could tell by the lilt of the tune, it was something old and Scottish.

Much later, nearly too late to be calling, Tom knocked on my cabin door. He held a bottle of scotch. "The best they make," he said. "No, can't stay. Just wanted to say my thanks."

"You know, Tom, no thanks are needed."

"Well that's the Scots for you. Can't be beholden. Damnable arrogant pride, you know." He turned to go, hesitated and turned back. "Took my son back to Springville. He calls that doll, 'Angel.' Can't say five words, but named that doll Angel. Makes you wonder, what he might be seeing, doesn't it?"

Anna's Sixth Notebook

I gave birth to Sam at the Sugar Gum Hospital, just one year before it got buried under Marble Head Lake. I sat holding him, studying his little face to see if he was handsome like his daddy, Jake. No doubt about it. But when his baby eyes opened and he looked up to inspect me, it hit me what I'd done. I'd brought a fine little fella into a hard place that he had nothing to do with.

Like my own birth, there was no Daddy's shirt for good luck. So I wrapped Sam in my petticoat, which some folks say brings the same good luck, but not in Sam's case. I know God's stronger than any petticoat or shirt tail, but I know a daddy would have changed both our lives, and I don't reckon God, himself, would argue that. So I just rocked little Sam, whispering, "I'll get up early, and I'll work late. I'll make things right." And I believed it. But I was young.

Like my momma, I went to work at a tomato cannery, and little Sam stayed with a friend from school who waited on her own baby to be born. By the time Sam celebrated his first birthday, Marble Head Dam was ready to hold water. Like I said, Sugar Gum got buried somewhere under the 50,000 acres of Marble Head Lake. Everybody in the town had to move to higher ground. Most folks moved up to Willow Grove or Crawford's Landing.

Dade and Momma moved to Springville to be near my sister, Zoe, and her husband, took the last of the family blood with them. Grandma and Grandpa Poinselot had been dead for years. Grandma McKerry held out up in Walnut Hill, but she died just before I delivered Sam. I had to decide where I was going.

The Sugar Gum Cannery moved to the tomato fields outside Cotton Rock. They offered to make me a supervisor along with a little raise. So I moved to Mrs. Spencer's Boarding House. Celia Calhoun baby-sat Sam. She lived with her husband in the apartment above me at Mrs. Spencer's. I paid Celia five dollars a week. My rent came to ten, and my food was eight. That left me just enough change to ride the bus out to the cannery every day. On a short week, I couldn't put much food in the cupboard. I saw the empty cans I didn't recognize in my trash basket. I figured Celia sneaked a can of soup or sardines in her purse so she and Sam could have enough to eat.

I hadn't figured how many pairs of shoes a boy might need, and that wasn't the only thing I hadn't figured on. By the time Sam turned three, we were pretty well down to the clothes on our backs. The ground under me grew so thin you could see through it.

"You need to be going to church," Celia told me. "The church helps its own."

Next Sunday, I sat in a row at the Cotton Rock Tabernacle. That's how I came to marry the wrong man.

"Mind if I sit down by you?"

I looked up to see Willis Sprule staring down at me with eyes the color of a cold, gray sky. "Congregation's thick as dog hair," he said. He spoke with the same voice the bus driver used after he'd been saying "ticket please," saying it over and over to a bus load of tomato workers, saying it till it sounded like nothing but tired.

I saw several empty pews Willis could have sat in, but Sam and I slid over. Still, I left my Bible on the bench between Willis and me. The organist began to play "Shall We Gather At the River," and Willis sang like he talked, all on one pitch. After church ended, Willis introduced himself. His face was just like his voice. It didn't change with the using.

I had no more interest in Willis than a gray-sky day, till he said, "I teach math at the high school." Anybody that went to college would have to be worth knowing, I thought.

The next Sunday he sat down beside me without asking, and when the service ended he said, "You look like you need a good meal. The hotel serves a good Sunday dinner."

I said, "I've got my boy with me."

Willis never looked at Sam. He just said, "The boy can come along." We ate dinner with Willis every Sunday after that. I decided that I shouldn't care if he wasn't like Sam's daddy. Didn't have Jake's dimples or dancing blue eyes, or that he didn't make my heart flutter like a hummingbird's wing. That's what I thought one Sunday when I was cutting my pork chop, and Willis sat across from me saying, "I'm a very methodical man."

"Well," I said, "a teacher would have to be orderly."

But that's not what Willis meant, 'cause he said, "You've upset my routine." There was just enough rise on the word routine to tell me I should consider myself honored—routine must be important. Then he said, "I've decided I need to marry you."

I didn't answer. But it didn't matter, because Willis didn't notice. He was looking at his appointment book, turning it page by page, unhurried and orderly, deciding when he might have time to go to the court house for a marriage license.

I was thinking that marrying a man who'd been to college might be almost as good as going to college, myself. A man who'd been to school would appreciate the sweetness of books. Maybe he'd even speak about some of that sweetness. Most of all, I figured Willis wouldn't be running off like Jake. That was the only part I got right.

Willis didn't seem excited about getting married, but I didn't take it personal. Willis wasn't excited about much of anything. His voice was just one sound held flat, like a teeter-totter held level between two children. His gray eyes didn't see anything particularly exciting, either. They weren't happy or sad, just eyes looking out of his head. If a woman in love will lie to herself, a woman in poverty will hock her brains altogether.

After we were married, Willis moved Sam and me to his farm. He raised pigs, outside pens of feeder pigs headed for market, and a barn filled with sows and their litters. He taught school during the week. On Sundays we sat in the Tabernacle pew, looking for all the world like a family. I learned that a man's silence can be rage, forced level like his voice. I learned that it's possible for a man to read any number of books and still get up every morning, shave himself, and never see more than a face in the mirror.

I first saw Willis's temper poured out on the pigs, a sow that wouldn't load, or pen of pigs running off through a broken fence. I saw his temper first fall on Sam when he turning five, and Willis said he was old enough to help in the barn.

 I heard Willis yelling before I got the door open, saw Willis standing over Sam, small and squatted down above the baby pig. I heard Sam crying through the dust and the smell of manure.

"Grab it by the leg, Sam!" Willis screamed. "Knock its head against the cement! What's the matter, Sally? Got lace on your shorts? Kill the god-damned pig!"

A patch of sunlight had come through the barn door with me, and Willis turned toward the light. "It's a runt pig," he said when he saw me, his voice wild and unfamiliar. "Needs putting out of its misery. Gotta teach sissies to be men!"

I did some yelling of my own then: "He's just a little boy! He doesn't know anything about killing!" I took Sam by the hand, pulled him up from the cement floor, felt the gladness of his little body against me.

Willis's stepped in front of us, his washed-out eyes, now wild and accusing. "You want to keep him a momma's boy!"

I didn't answer, didn't turn back, just stepped out of Willis's way and kept walking out into the sunlight holding tight to Sam's hand.

"You think you're too good to hear me?" Willis called after me. "I didn't have to marry you!" He was at the barn door now, yelling across the rows of field oats, where Sam and I were walking fast, but not fast enough to shut out the words I knew might be coming, words that a woman might even believe she deserves, when she's hiding under a swamp of shame.

"I didn't need to take in a god-damned, pack-saddle woman with a pack-saddle kid!" Willis was yelling from the barn door.

I came to understand that whatever drained off the joy from Willis's life and left him bleached out and dried, had funneled his spirit into a dark place, shoved down, and resentful.

"You're choosing the boy over me," Willis said, later, when he came into the house. "I know kids best. I'm a school teacher. I know kids!" he repeated. Something in me remembered, and it came to me that I had married something familiar, something I must have felt comfortable with, something I hated. I had married myself a "Dade!" But Leah was a baby in the house, and how could I feed two children? And I had more excuses than the river has fish. So I stayed.

I reckon there are many ways to steal a young boy's confidence. Willis had his way. Castrating a hog requires a special kind of vice grip, a kind of trough that holds the pig on its back while a board slides across one end and locks down over its jaw. This leaves a man's hands free to hold the knife and do the cutting. The squeal is unforgettable and is partly responsible for the saying, "squeal like a pig."

If you wait to castrate a pig till it's half-grown, it can go into shock and die. And if you wait till it's full grown, it'll turn five-hundred pounds of insulted pork loose on you. So you castrate it while it's still a baby, under thirty pounds.

If you're going to castrate a young man's confidence, you have to do it when he's still a boy. A grown man would never allow the amount of outrage it takes to cut out his natural store of self-respect. By the time Sam was ten, Willis had cut away most of his spirit.

The third child, little Mary, was robbed of her confidence mostly by what Willis didn't do, ignoring her shy smile and her sweet ways, shoving aside her butterfly touch. She was always dancing, always twirling with some old dress of Leah's or a scarf of mine. She was graceful as a snowbird on a lake, till she came near Willis's chair.

My Leah had enough fight for the whole family till the drowning. She never backed down. She figured having her say was worth swats from Willis's paddle. I'm counting on Leah to find her grit once more. Somewhere between the wine bottles and the strange times, when she goes into those dark places, I'm praying she'll run right into herself.

In those early days, I looked around at church to see who I might ask for help. It's a fearful thing to let a church know that one of its own elders is mean to his children. A church doesn't like that kind of problem. Elders are leaders. They work hard for the church. They put money into the offering plate. They're not easy to come by. Troubled women are an embarrassment. A church wants its pews filled with upstanding folks, a kind of proof that the church is one of God's favorites.

It's amazing how ordinary good folks, once banded together, can kill their own wounded. I'd seen it often enough in the barnyard where a runt pig gets starved out or a hen is pecked to death. There was a pamphlet in the pew that told what the Tabernacle believed. But I found out it isn't what the elders write down that matters. It's the things they would never put on paper, things they're not likely to admit to themselves, their fears and prejudices that hush trouble and blame the ugly.

I reckon I forgot that Jesus was never angry with folks for telling the truth. I reckon I forgot that Jesus didn't have much truck with fear.

But I did what many a woman has done. I tried cashing in Bible verses to pay for my coward's heart. I strung the verses together and made hope for my life. But all I was stringing together were the passing days.

"Never mind," I sing,
"Momma and God can fix everything."
Standing on the promises of Christ my Savior,
Add another bead to the necklace of days.

Children born in hope or despair are still beautiful. And children can be a sweet solace for the mother. I promised myself I would do better than my Momma did. I would never go to bed and be a quitter.

Wrap a soul in a flannel blanket and take it home.
A child's body is a sacred skin, to keep its sacred spirit in.
I am the Momma, the keeper of the children.
When I fail them, it feels like I am failing God.

Children are raised by their daddy, too. A daddy can have his own obsessions. Willis thought children were born to help carry the load. Children were good for work and to use for taking out your anger.

Bake a cake. Bake a happy family
Add another bead to the string.

Willis says a child must obey. It will be over soon. The shutting of the bedroom door, the counting of the swats, calmly, orderly. Willis is a methodical man. Now he is praying with the child, kneeling there on the bedroom floor, praying in his level voice, bloodless and dead. He is telling the child that God wants children to obey. And little Mary, the little one who only whispers when she talks, must she be spanked?

Can this be true?
Must she bend over and grab her ankles, too?
Add another bead to the string

And in the field, when he's mad, he leaves his bleached out voice behind. He shouts God's name in curses. In the field, he can slap without praying. He can kick without quoting verses. He's a teacher-preacher. He teaches math at school, Sunday school at church, and rage in the field. He has a temper only when he's home. He's careful about that.

Prayer can tame a temper.
Prayer can make a temper walk on the water.
Add another bead to the string.

Willis carries a pig-herding stick to crack across the pig's snout and across the back of a boy. My boy. I see Sam with his fragile boy-pride. I see him walk that desperate path that mocks and shames him into manhood. I see him with his young heart under his young cotton shirt, where hope sits sick, and courage bends crooked. And Willis calls Sam "Sally" because he cannot kick the big, red boar who's as long as the kitchen table and bites and whirls with five hundred pounds of fury and cowers Sam against the corner of the pen.

And one day Sam is thirteen and ready for his first hunting trip. It's early morning. The roosters are still crowing around the barn. I'm in the kitchen washing up the breakfast skillet. The smell of bacon fills the room. Sam's wearing his bright-orange hunting vest, taking aim down the barrel of the broom handle at the cat, warming herself by the wood stove. "You be careful," I say. "Don't shoot anything without antlers."

Sam grins and sets the broom back in its corner. But he can't sit down. He just paces around the kitchen. His gear is packed. He's been checking it for days: flashlight, hunting knife, sharpening stone, all stowed in his backpack. Today's the day. His bacon and toast are half eaten on his plate. I figured he hasn't slept much.

"Do you think a boy could get a deer on his first hunting trip?" Sam asks. He's by the sink now, leaning on his elbow, looking up at me.

"Why I suppose he could," I say. But I have no idea. I just liked seeing the happiness inside him.

"A whole day to try," he says. He stops leaning on his elbow and begins drumming his hands on the counter top.

I've already said, "Settle down, Sam." Said it more than twice. But he can't quit jumping around the room the way a boy will do when excitement is jumping around inside his rib bones.

Willis comes into the kitchen, "Did you get the cow milked?"

"Yes, sir," Sam answers. "And finished grinding the last auger of grain, too."

They shouldn't be back till late, long after supper. So I don't know what to think when I see the truck coming up the drive middle of the morning. Willis came to the house, carrying Sam's backpack. I watched Sam, walking slow to the barn, head hanging, shoulders slumped.

Willis' voice was level and cold, "No sooner got there till he was sick. Lost his breakfast. Excited as a fool." Willis dropped Sam's pack on the floor. "First sight of deer, he lets out a holler like a girl! A buck and a doe! They ran clear to Little Rock by now, I suppose. Don't need a greenhorn with buck fever in hunting camp. I'll be heading back now. I gave the boy work to do in the barn." He turned to the door, kicked Sam's pack aside with his boot and left.

But there were some good times, and good times can lie the most, times of singing in the car on the way to Grandma Mayta's house in Springville; riding the feed wagon to the river with a picnic lunch; Christmas morning, the turkey smelling sweet in the oven; Leah stirring peanut brittle in the cast-iron skillet, and Willis helping little Mary glue the roof on her doll house. Maybe Willis is beginning to understand, I tell myself. Maybe I can tell him the things he needs to know about the children. And desperate women will believe that words can make a river run backwards, against itself. Choose careful words. Speak the finest argument.

And words are only sounds that sit
a second in the ears, and maybe never in the heart.
Rock-a-bye baby, the sky is blue,
Rock-a-bye baby, I saw, I knew.

I must tell someone. I tell the elders at the church. They sit stiff-jawed around the table, with faces I cannot read. All that's missing are the poker cards. They've got a church to maintain and a mortgage to pay. Willis has a paycheck. I have none. When they do nothing, it comes to me that they are cowards, just like me. So they give me a verse:

Wives can change their husbands
without a word,
by their godly behavior.

And I swallowed this promise easy, cause if Willis was my fault, it meant I could make him change. But verses can be twisted in the hands of cowards. And faith doesn't hide at the bottom of a swamp. Faith doesn't marry cause it's scared, and it doesn't keep children in a mean house.

And one day Sam is eighteen, and Leah's fifteen. Little Mary's just turned ten. And Rayley Larkin, at the Osage Bend Look-Out Station, never had a drink in twenty-five years. Twenty-five years of steady watching the river and sounding the horn when the generators start running, until the day my Sam and little Mary were fishing in his care. And that day, whatever broke Rayley Larkin's heart came down the river to Sam and Mary, and God turned his back.

And the knock came on my door. The knock that all mothers work against. Check every danger. Is there something in the baby's mouth? Are the children near the road? And did you turn the stove off? Always working against that knock, and the sheriff was standing on my door step.

And I go to see little Mary. They are carrying her on a stretcher with a sheet over her face. I feel my heart tear out of my body and go away on the stretcher with her. I feel the animal inside me, and I want to claw my way up to God and bite him. I keep my hand over my mouth all through the funeral so I won't scream. If I let the screams come, I won't be able to stop. Women cry every day for a year after a child dies, and then without warning, for a lifetime. And they never, never, forget.

And now the string of beads
is held up to the light,
nothing more than empty stones of hope,
a thousand beads of useless stope.

And the teacher-pig-herder goes out to feed the pigs. And he goes about his chores. At night, he sits silent and cold in his chair. And one day he says, "Sam always had a streak of sissy in him."

Now my sixteen-years-of-waiting leap at him, like a too-tight coil. I scream my say. Sixteen years worth of say. A word for every broken hope. I word him to his knees. He does not answer back. He does not even moan. He sits in silent bitterness. God has let him down!

And I am choking and cannot find any air in the rooms where he sits. I sweep the floor. The broom rakes against the boards. I stack the dishes on the shelf, plate on plate, the pottery scrapes. And I know I cannot stay where he is.

And God came walking in the cool of the day,
and called, "Adam, where are you?"
"I was afraid, Lord. So I hid myself."

"And I am hiding, too Lord. Here at the bottom of a swamp." I haven't climbed out yet. But I did put my things into boxes and moved to town, and I took Leah with me. Willis sold the farm, and the divorce court ordered him to give me half the money. That was fifteen years ago. Leah's a grown woman now, with a child of her own. I've had fifteen years of sitting beside graves and thinking. So I'm writing my way to the place that leads up and out of the swamp.

Lucy's Angel Gossip

    Little Nettie Box asked if she could be forgiven if she warn't "advertised." I knowed she meant "baptized," 'cause Nettie's older brother's gonna be baptized in two weeks. Little Nettie's been asking her momma if she could be baptized, too. But her momma says Nettie's too young.

    It's no real blow to God's kingdom. Cause Nettie's true interest in being baptized is to cure her biting habit. Little Nettie's in trouble most every Sunday. She's tough as a pine knot. She has five brothers and never had on a dress. She comes to church in left-over boys' clothes. I reckon she's had to fight for ever helping on her plate. Like most girls that have to fight boys, she's learned to scratch and bite, and mostly bite. You always know when she's close to chompin' down on someone, 'cause her lip gets to twitching. Worse than a rabbit's nose.

    "Biting habits take more than baptism," I says. "Next time you want to chew on somebody, you pray and ask Jesus to stop you. He'll be standing there at your right hand, ready to help.

    But before class was over Nettle was in another fight. It ended with her a biting Dixie Jones on the finger. "Nettie," I said. "Did you remember to pray?"

    "Yes. And Jesus was standing there on my right side. But the devil was on my left. And you know, Miz. Lucy, I'm left handed!"

    Well, I was plumb outta ideas for Nettie, till a scarlet tanager came tapping on the window last Sunday morning. If you don't already know it, Mr. Sinclair, Ozark folks are a mighty believing people. I know outsiders call us superstitious.

    But when folks and animals are all sharing a river and a woods for a long, long time, they get a language that ain't got words. Like when folks get together for music. They don't have to talk, neither. One starts out a playin' maybe the banjo, and the fiddle player hears what the banjo's saying, without speakin' a word. He knows how to make the fiddle answer back. Ozark music folks play notes that ain't written nowhere. The guitar, dulcimer and all the rest. Just sharing the magic.

    That's the way it is in the woods. We been a listening and a seeing for a long time. I reckon the reason they's not much magic up in the city is cause they chopped down all the trees and run off all the animals. Filled all the hearing and seeing places with concrete.

Anyway, everybody in the Ozarks knows that a scarlet tanager brings a warning. Nettie knowed it, right well. So I just says, "They's a scarlet tanager at the window. He's bringing a warning to somebody in this room."

Nettie stepped right up to the judgment. "I reckon he's a warning me about biting," she says. And that was that. Nettie was cured of the bites. I knowed her angel was ready for a rest. I figure that scarlet tanager might well have kept Nettie's angel from puttin' in for a transfer.

Thoughts from the Back Porch   July 1996

I spent the weekend in Springville checking on my house. I gave Alex a call before heading back to Cotton Rock. He met me for a beer at Blicks, a bistro just down from the college. In the winter, Blicks is crowded with students. On this summer day, it was nearly empty. Only a scattered handful of students, hunched over their books. Out on the sidewalk, a young man sat playing his guitar.

Alex examined me through the thick lenses of his horn-rimmed glasses. "Look at you," he said, "Tanned — relaxed."

"The benefits of fishing."

We talked about Cotton Rock and the construction of the new library at the college. Two girls stopped by the table and discussed an assignment with Alex. They left, and Alex finished his beer.

"So how's Anna McKerry?" he asked, setting down his empty bottle.

"Still circling her sacred stick," I said.

"Is this another Ozark expression?"

"This one's from Australia—an aboriginal legend."

"Wait," Alex said, "This will take another beer." He signaled the waiter. When the beer arrived, he gave a mock toast and said, "to the Aborigines."

I began again. "The Aborigines believed God led them on their daily journeys with a sacred stick. The appointed leader carried it. As long as the tribe walked behind the stick, they found game, water, protection."

The label on Alex's bottle had come loose on the corner, and he began slowly peeling it from the bottle as he listened.

"Every night they planted the stick in the ground. Every morning, they took it up, and a new day's journey began." I took a drink of my beer and continued. "One morning, as the leader started to pull the sacred stick from the ground, it broke in half."

Alex stopped tearing at the label and looked up.

"The tribe was devastated. No one knew what to do. They couldn't leave the broken stick, nor could they replace it. So they just sat there—immobile—until they died."

"And this is Anna?" Alex asked.

"Possibly. She's not leaving the scene of the drowning. She's desperately seeking an answer from the god she fears has betrayed her. It's the great dominant theme of her life. It's as though every cell of her existence is committed to its resolution."

"So, what about Leah?" Alex asked. "Had that date yet?"

"No, but I did meet her."

"And?"

"I said I'd give her a call."

"Did you?"

"Not yet."

"I'm talking about a simple date."

"She's a little strange—preoccupied, I suppose. Her brother and sister drowned. I think she's trapped in some kind of guilt."

"Didn't that happen years ago?"

"True—I guess Leah's circling the stick too."

Alex stared past me, at the young musician on the sidewalk. He was silent for a moment, then asked, "Think you might be circling that stick yourself? All of you circling your losses. Some indefinite hiatus."

"I don't see myself like Anna and Leah. I mean, my hiatus—as you call it—doesn't feel deliberate."

"They would probably argue the same thing."

I shrugged and looked at my watch. "Should be heading back," I said.

Alex looked annoyed, but followed me to the door. "Leave some fish in the river for me," he said.

"When I catch the last one, I'll throw it back."

I thought on Alex's words all the way back to Cotton Rock. Dusk darkened the road in front of me. I switched on the lights. "E. L. Doctorow!" I said aloud to the windshield in front of me. I thought how Doctorow said that writing a novel was like driving a car at night, how you could see only as far as your headlights, but you could make the whole trip that way. Well, that proved my point—I had no light for my novel—no vision. So if I'm circling, I told myself, it's because I'm just waiting for the lights to come back on.

I arrived home far too late to catch the sunset, missing the chance to drift by Leah's house. I got up early next morning, climbed into the *Rosalee*, cranked on the motor and shoved out into the river. I slowed the boat, as usual, when I passed Leah's house. I had no excuse for not calling her. Alex was right. I was stalled—an indefinite hiatus, Alex called it. Whatever it was, it made me restless. I kept moving down river.

I passed a new construction site that promised to be a very expensive, elaborate vacation home, and further on the shell of an old log cabin with its remnant of split-rail fence. Rounding the next bend, I encountered still another sophisticated vacation home, with its deck of colorful umbrellas and backyard pool.

The same incongruity proved true of the town, itself. The old water mill at the side of the river with its multi-storied, weathered walls, where hill people once took their wheat and corn to be ground, rose up between McDonalds and Pizza Hut. Some of the stores on Main Street had been here since Justice Taney handed down the Dred Scott Decision, while many of the little boutiques and shops along the waterfront were built in the past ten years.

The river connected the past and the present. Like Ferguson said: "The river's like a ribbon of time." For this summer in 1996, it connected all the people who lived along its banks, caused us to live on the same long street—the wealthy, the common, the transplants, the natives, each of us living on the recycled land of the past. The evolution of the river was Granddad's favorite topic: "The Civil War reached these very river banks," he'd say. "Troops from both sides took livestock as they grazed, tore entire crops from the fields. Between the lead mines and the logging companies, the land was nearly destroyed. Starving miners took up mining tiff—leftover barite from old lead mines. Left the land so scarred with scabs and stripped of life, they used to say that a vulture would have to pack a lunch if he tried to fly over it.

"World War II was the last of the simple life. Hard times rationed gasoline, and Americans drove on worn tires. Life along this river slowed and was given back to the hill people. Those were the last of the best days."

The closer Granddad got to modern times, the more his opinions accelerated, along with the heat of his temper: "The whole country raced toward the future," he said, "like dogs in heat. Like progress was a new name for greed. The Ozarks might have escaped the insanity, but they started building those confounded dams and making those confounded lakes, and now those confounded tourists are everywhere!"

I spent most of the day nosing up little creeks that emptied into the river, ate my lunch by a stand of cattails and toward late afternoon, headed home. A bank of dark clouds rolled in from the east. The sunset would be lost to blue-black haze. Just down from Leah's house, I turned off the motor and reached for the oars.

The river banks filled with the drone of cicadas and frogs. Something fluttered near-by, and I thought it must be a bat, feeding on the evening moths. It turned out to be a scarlet tanager which had flown into the boat and landed on the bow. It tucked its little black wings against its sides and stood very still, looking at me with its round eyes. I stopped rowing. "Lucy would say you've brought a warning," I said softly. The little bird cocked its head as if listening, but did not move. The boat began to slide backward with the current. I reached for the oars, and the little bird flew away. I'm not superstitious, but I had to admit, later, that the little bird did seem to be telling me to be aware of something upriver.

A chill arrived with the approaching storm. I pulled on the windbreaker, from the seat beside me. I had just passed the outcropping that marked the threshold to Anna's property when I caught sight of him. I almost missed him—the gray form sitting lifeless in the anchored boat, as though he were carved from the stone cliff of dolomite. He gazed through a pair of binoculars, so intently he didn't move or hear the sound of my oars lifting from the water.

A light went on in Anna's house, and he drew forward, intent on his spying. I felt a rush of anger. "What are you doing at Anna's place!" I yelled, surprised at the sound of ownership in my voice.

He wrenched to look at me, the binoculars falling from his hand. He didn't answer, but started his motor. Turning the boat round, he headed down river, opposite my direction. For a wild moment I considered following him. I had never met him, but I was willing to bet it was Willis Sprule.

Anna's Seventh Notebook

Maybe it was the way Dr. Anderson said it, so offhand: "And of course, your mother's having hallucinations," as though he was saying, "your mother's having indigestion." He'd already said Alzheimers and degenerative disease. But those words sort of hold back like company that's introduced themselves but haven't taken off their coats yet. Hallucinations, people seeing things that aren't there, that just sits right down at your kitchen table.

I said, "I don't think my momma's having hallucinations."

Dr. Anderson opened the file, read over his notes and said, "Your mother saw water rolling in through the windows on the fifth floor of her retirement home. According to the resident manager she was hysterical."

There was nothing I could say to that. But I've got Momma with me now, and if she wants to see water rolling in through the windows, it's a possibility. Cause we've got the White River a few hundred feet below our house.

After the divorce, I took my part of the money and bought a house. It was a fine thing to own a piece of ground. It was a fine thing to walk through the rooms and know I had a place for Leah and me.

"Will you feel comfortable living by the river?" The real estate lady asked. She was trying to say a hard thing in a kind way. I knew what she meant: "Will you be reminded of your children each time you see that river?"

"I'd think of Sam and Mary every day if I was living in the middle of the desert," I told her. A river brings death and life, sort of like God, and until God gives me an answer, I don't want to live very far from the question.

Anyway, it wasn't a natural river that took Sam and Mary. When a man puts a dam on a river, he walls up a powerful resentment. He has to keep an eye on that resentment, day and night. The White River has five dams on it, and that takes a lot of looking after.

It was the Cedar Shoals Dam that sent a wall of water down on my Mary and Sam. Rayley Larkin worked at the Osage Look Out for twenty-five years, warning all the fishermen who loved to fish those little quiet pockets of fish when the river's low.

They found Rayley Larkin sitting on the office floor at the bottom of a whiskey bottle the day Sam and little Mary decided to fish below the dam, the day that God shot a hole in my heart.

There's time enough to wade out of the river after the generators start up and the warning horn is blowing. Some folks felt Sam should have noticed the swelling of the water, even if the warning bell didn't sound. Sam was a good swimmer, and Mary was small for her age, easier to rescue. I only know Sam would have saved Mary if there was any way to do it.

Anyway I want to live right here—on the bank of the river. Leah would live somewhere else if she could. But the river broke our hearts, so I think the river holds our healing.

Down at Terra Port the White River joins up with the Black River, before the two are conquered by the mighty Mississippi. The Mississippi's been collecting rivers since it left Minnesota. But the ocean's waiting to collect all of them, and even then they're not done for. The ocean just rises up into clouds that ride back out over the land, rain down and run back into a riverbed to begin things all over. And that's what I love about a river. It's just a piece of eternity sliding by. My house is pretty small, and the kitchen isn't much, but it has a great view of the White. There are six windows in the living room that look out over the river. Six views of eternity.

Leah used to love the river. You wouldn't know Leah by seeing her today. She had a heart big as Sunday dinner. By the time Leah was four years old, she'd nursed a number of little runt pigs from the barn. She'd sit on an egg crate by the wood stove with a baby pig wrapped up careful as baby Jesus, feeding it a bottle. She brought in more than one raggedy cat from the hayloft with pink eye, cleaning its eyes with a cloth and boric acid. Even after she caught pink eye herself, she never gave up her nursing career. When she started school, she branched out, started taking care of classmates.

By the time she was ten, she gave herself to serious charity. She took five swats from the principal's paddle. The swats should have gone to Buddy Burdett. I got a call from the school. When I got there, Leah was sitting on a bench outside the principal's office, her face was red from crying. The secretary was typing up a paper. She handed it to me and said, "Leah's suspended for the week."

It was a long walk through the school. Children in the halls stopped to look at us. Someone whispered, "principal's office" and "paddling."

I opened the school door, and Leah stepped outside. The wind was up, and Leah stopped for a minute, closed her eyes while the cool breeze blew across her hot cheeks. Those swats were real as a toothache.

When I got her in the car, I said, "You stole milk money?"

She sat twisting her handkerchief around her finger. "I don't know who stole it," she said. "But Mrs. Murphy was going to paddle Buddy. Just cause he's dirty, and never has any milk money."

"She wouldn't paddle him for a reason like that," I said.

"Yes, Momma!" She stopped twisting the hanky, "Mrs. Murphy thinks not having milk money is bad as not knowing multiplication. She says Buddy's milk tickets are paid by the government. She says she'd rather eat scraps off a buzzard's beak than take help from the government."

"Well, that's Ozark for you," I said.

"Buddy never has anything in his lunch. He's so skinny, and he wears his daddy's britches. They're all hitched around his belt. Looks like he's wearing a ruffle. Anyway, Buddy's already had five paddlings this year. Mrs. Murphy asked who stole the money and looked right at Buddy. I could tell by his face, he just wasn't up to another paddling."

That was Leah. She was only fifteen when the drowning happened, and life came collecting on her tender conscience. I should have realized she would need help paying the cost. I came across her in the middle of the night flung on a chair in the dark, like a rag doll, with an open-eyed stare that would sicken the heart of God himself. She came to herself when I said her name. She just kept saying, "I'm fine, Momma. I'm fine." But neither one of us was fine. That was the beginning of her going off into those strange, dark places. Leah and I moved to town after the drowning, rented a small apartment near Lushbaugh's Grocery. I found a job behind a counter at the Ozark Gift Emporium. Leah kept going to school every day, but I noticed how she stopped dropping into a kitchen chair to visit while I cooked supper. She stayed in her room. "Studying," she said. But Leah never had much homework. I knew she wasn't studying. She stopped seeing her friends, never returned phone calls. Pretty soon, the phone stopped ringing. She graduated and went straight off to the university and earned a degree in art. Eloped in her senior year. Graduated the following May, came home with her degree in art, a broken marriage and little Harlo on the way. I knew the minute I saw her that whatever had been pretending to hold together inside her, had let go with both hands. I figure God shot a hole in Leah's heart, too.

But Leah says, "First, you've presupposed that God exists. Secondly, you've supposed that God sends evil." She stands there at her easel, painting and lining up my suppositions and presuppositions. She says if my presuppositions are wrong, then every one of my box cars has been hitched up to the wrong engine.

I say, "Never mind box cars, how many engines are there?"

Leah stops painting for a moment. She looks over her easel and says, "Engines are tricky. Just when you think you've found an engine, someone comes along and shows you it's a box car."

So I try to start at the beginning. I go to the kitchen and sit on a cane chair and ask myself, "Does God exist?" But God is so much a part of me, I'd have to step outside my own skin to get a fair look at the question. So, I had to give up on looking at my presupposition, and that makes God the engine for me.

I start with the box cars. The first car seems plain enough: God shot me. Even if human hands pulled the trigger, God could have yelled, "duck," and he didn't. Box cars only go where the engine leads.

I go back to Leah's easel. I tell her my argument. Leah lays down her brush and lights a cigarette. She smokes a moment and then says, "People spend whole lifetimes deciding whether God has the power to yell duck. If he doesn't have the power, how can he be God? If he does have the power and turns away, what kind of God is he? It's not an easy reconciliation, Momma. The attempt to reconcile is called a theodicy. People have been writing theodicies for years."

Early the next morning I went right down to the Cotton Rock Library and checked out all the theodicies I could carry home. Most of them kept cooking up the same jar of jam: God doesn't send evil, but he allows it. I call these writers the "Grimsled Believers." Bonnie Grimsled lives up on the ridge, just where the White River makes a sharp bend below Bald Eagle. We all know that Tom Grimsled runs around on Bonnie. But Bonnie has six little children and no place to go. So Bonnie has more excuses for Tom than warts on a pickle. But I know all about making up excuses for a husband. I did my own staying in a bad marriage.

But there's tragedy that I didn't bring. There's tragedy that God alone could have stopped, and it's that tragedy I'm talking about. I'm not a Grimsled believer anymore, and I'm through making up alibis for God. I've come to think more of God than that.

In my theodicy reading, I came across Keats—the poet. He didn't think we could come into the world ready-made. He thought we had to experience the "Vale of Soul-making." I reckon I'm somewhere in the Vale.

When my Sam and Mary drowned, everything tilted off course, and nothing went back on track. All my religion ran off with its tail between its legs, but God stuck. When I stopped going to church at the Tabernacle, the church people said I quit on God. But I know that when a coyote pounces on a rabbit, the rabbit hangs limp and looks dead. But it's not dead; it's waiting to see if there's a way out.

I never had any proper church training, but between Grandpa Poinselot's Atwater Radio, and the visits to Grandma Effie McKerry's house, I got a powerful introduction to God. Grandma and Grandpa Poinselot were too old to drive the Hudson to Church by the time we took up living there. So they went to church in their living room, almost every day, listening to Brother Lester Roloff on their old Atwater Radio. After Brother Roloff's program ended, Granddad would run the dial back and forth, hunting down a barber shop quartet. He'd throw back his bald head, cocked sideways to the radio, so the ear piece of his hearing aid lined up with the speaker. He'd find his pitch, close his eyes and slide into the harmony, finding his note in each new chord, brown leisure shoes tapping out the beat, stroking the cat curled up in his lap, and he was no longer in Sugar Gum. He was somewhere in New York or Chicago, singing bass.

Grandma Effie McKerry, Daddy's momma, was the only live churchgoer in the family, but I never went with her much. Walnut Hill took two-hours in the old Hudson, and Momma only drove us there a couple Sundays a year. But those trips gave a lasting sway to my faith. Hymn singing was as much a part of Grandma Effie's house as her crocheted doilies and her endless pitchers of iced tea. Sunday afternoons at her house meant uncles and aunts, cousins and friends, singing harmony about uncloudy days and circles being unbroken. Sometime during the singing, Grandma Effie would always lean close and remind me, "God respects you if you work, honey. But he loves you if you sing."

Besides the singing, there were platters of sugar-cured ham and tables polka-dotted with every color of vegetable. God got stored away with the taste of fried chicken, hot apple pie, and the strum of guitar strings. It isn't easy to give up on that kind of God. So Grandma Effie's unflinching faith got passed on to me, along with my Momma's dark French eyes and hair, though my hair's mostly gray now, and my eyes faded till they look no different than an Englishman's.

Anyway, after God shot a hole in my heart, I stopped asking him for things. There's prayer that expects an answer, and there's prayer that just talks. I just talk. Once you've been spooked by God, you live with handcuffs on your hope.

Hope rides on a big ocean, looking for a place to plant its foot. Leah says they did an experiment on rats. They put them in a tub of water. After a few minutes, the rats began to drown. That's when they were lifted out of the tub. The next day, the same rats were put back in the tub. This time they swam fourteen hours before they drowned. That's called hope.

I have two pictures in my Bible: One's a picture of my sister Zoe's dead baby, pink and sweet, with eyes that never opened. The other's a picture of Leah's baby, Harlo, her eyes wide and shiny with life. I keep these two pictures in my Bible, God's "no" and God's "yes," to remind me of the kind of tub we're swimming in.

Emmett's Fishing Report

Things have been pretty dry lately. Last week's rain was just in time. River got so low I was afraid we'd have to start hauling water to her! But today's a no-complaint-sunshine day, and I took off north to the state line. The White River and its tail waters wander back and forth between Missouri and Arkansas borders. Course, the river don't give a buzzard beak about border lines and neither do the fish. Those fish swim from one state to the other without the slightest prick a conscience.

But the game warden cares more than his share about the law. So if you're planning to fish the border lakes above the dams, you got to look up from your pole now and then and get a fix on your horizon line.

Take trout, for example. The slot restriction for Missouri side is between twelve and twenty inches. That means you can keep anything less than twelve or over twenty. Fish twelve to twenty inches are the best egg producers. So they have God's protection or at least the Department of Conservation. On the Arkansas side, it's the Fish and Game that does the tending. Arkansas says you can't keep a Cutthroat or Brown under sixteen or a Brook under fourteen. Today, I come across a Missouri feller, standing up to the top of his hip boots in Arkansas water. He's just reeling in a cutthroat. The game warden showed up just as he's putting away his cleaning knife.

The cutthroat was laying on the rock, all cleaned and ready for the frying pan. He wasn't an inch over twelve, and that was plain to see—four inches too short to keep, according to Arkansas law. Course it's nothing for a fisherman to stretch the size of his catch, and that ole boy commenced to saying what a fight that cutthroat had given him, all sixteen inches of him.

But the warden wasn't taking the bait. He says he's got a tape measure in the truck, and he'll be back. When the warden came back, that cuttthroat was nowhere to be found. Missouri says how that nice big fish was a true fighter, all right. He says he just jumped off the rock and swum off.

But that game warden sees the guts laying in the grass, and he knows that cutthroat was dead as the rock he's cleaned on. So he just says, "Well then, I guess I'll just have to write up the ticket for the other citation."

"What citation is that?" asks Missouri.

"Well, for using live bait stead of flies or lures."

"But I didn't use no live bait!" Missouri says.

"Too bad that fish swum off," says the warden. "We might a looked in its belly and proved what bait was used. But like you said, 'he swum off.' Unfortunate, too. Cause fishing with live bait's a durn costly fine."

I couldn't wait to get home and tell Lottie this story. She said she may as well go up the ridge and visit her momma for the day, 'cause I wouldn't be home till I told that story to half a Cotton Rock. She said she reckoned I'd be busier than a goose with nine rectums.

Thoughts from the Back Porch   July 1996

    I was on the back porch with my morning coffee when the phone rang. "It's Henegar, over at the garage: "If you want to bring your jeep in, we'll take a look at the engine today."

    I showered, shaved and headed for town. The traffic would be substantial. An endless number of tourists passed through Cotton Rock on their way to Cedar Shoals Lake or one of the numerous resorts along the shores of the White River. The town had capitalized on the culture of a bygone era. Shops sold items ranging from handmade quilts to so-called "hill whiskey." Some establishments were run by valid historians who tried to capture the past in museums and galleries. Like Granddad, they had great respect for an isolated culture developed in an arrested frontier. Their shops offered handsome, hand-crafted dulcimers, split-oak baskets or hand-woven rugs. But most of the shops sold a commercial and badly crafted collection of junk, claiming to be souvenirs of the Ozarks.

    When the residents of Cotton Rock were in a hurry, it was easy to resent the crowded sidewalks and slow-moving cars filled with gawking tourists. There were usually were no serious accidents, though we were sorely tempted to give a tourist a bumper-nudge across the street when they stopped, camera in hand to take a picture.

    I reached town to find the expected crowd of tourists. The car in front of me had slowed to a near stop. Its driver leaned from the window to ask directions. It was Friday, and the town would remain invaded for the week-end. I couldn't find a way to cut through the congested traffic. By the time I reached Henegar's Garage, it was mid-morning.

    George Henegar, a large, friendly native of Cotton Rock met me at the garage door, wiping his hands on an oil rag and shaking his head. "Hydraulic went out. Just got her working. Got cars backed up to the street. Leave your jeep out front, and I'll get to her soon as I can. Might be afternoon."

    I ate lunch at a nearby restaurant and walked to the library. I would be teaching Hawthorne's *Scarlet Letter* when I returned to the college, and I had located a good edition at the library. Later, I walked to the book store to order a similar edition for myself.

It was afternoon when I returned to Henegar's Garage. George leaned over the counter, totaling my bill when George's son, Lingo, burst into the office. Lingo had a variety of jobs: helping his father in the garage, mowing lawns and working Saturdays at Mumford's Feed Store. Lingo's hair was as orange as Dee Lushbaugh's, though Lingo's came naturally, along with a helping of freckles.

"You'll never believe this one!" Lingo yelled. He glanced my way, gave me a quick nod of recognition, and turned back to his father. "Sam McKerry isn't dead after all! He never drowned below Cedar Shoals Dam neither! He's downtown right now — in the Cotton Rock jail house!"

No one spoke for a moment while we registered Lingo's words. Then, George whistled and shook his head. "Sam McKerry—alive. Don't that bring a rising in your brain? How long's he been missing? Must be about fifteen years." He whistled again and asked, "What's he been hiding from for fifteen years?"

"I don't know," Lingo said, "But Anna must be awful happy—Willis too."

"I don't know about Willis," George said. "That ole boy has a thick rind—don't know if anything gets through to him. Fifteen years," he said again.

It was as though Sam had returned from the dead—an unbelievable miracle for Anna. Yet George was right. Why had he allowed his own mother to believe he was dead?

It was late when I arrived home. I cooked dinner and ate on the back porch, leafing through the library's copy of *Scarlet Letter*. The sun had reached the horizon as I put the dishes into the sink. I should begin making an outline of the Hawthorne course, but I felt far too restless to concentrate.

I pulled on a wind breaker and headed for the dock—plenty of time to catch the sunset. It felt good to be out on the river. I knew that I would go down river toward Anna's house. I wouldn't stop, of course, just pass by. As I drew near, I switched the motor to low.

There was no sign of movement—only the silent house. I kicked the motor to high and drove several minutes on down river. The cicadas had begun their evening ostinato. An occasional lonely call from an owl punctuated the steady drone, and the water lapped relentlessly against the rocky shoreline.

By the time I reached Willows Branch, I admitted to myself that I didn't want to see the sunset. I turned the boat around and headed back up river.

My hope of seeing someone at Anna's place paid off. Leah sat on the dock. As I drew near, she stood and motioned to me.

I took the boat in alongside the dock and cut the engine.

"I saw you go past earlier," Leah said. "I waited here for you to come back up river."

"Are you okay?" I asked.

"Yes. I'm sure you've heard about Sam."

"Yes."

"Small town," she said, shrugging her shoulders. "It's the week-end. Sam can't see a judge till Monday. So there's no getting him out on bond. It's like he came back from the dead. Only…" She didn't finish. Instead, she lit a cigarette.

"You want to sit here in the boat—talk?"

She glanced at the boat and said, "Do you have time for a walk?" She waited while I tied up the boat. "There's an Osage tree we can sit on," she said.

I nodded, and she turned to lead the way.

"What's an Osage tree?" I asked, walking behind her.

"A sacred tree," she said without turning around. "One that the Osage Indians tied down when it was a sapling. Made the tree grow at an angle so that it points—like a finger—toward healing herbs. Served as a marker for the returning tribe."

"Oh, my Granddad called those Buffalo Trees. Squaws hung buffalo hides on the low limb. Used them to tan hides."

"Well theirs was a practical religion," she said, smiling over her shoulder.

We passed Harlo's blackberry patch. Once around the curve of the river, Leah left the path and walked a few yards to the Osage Tree. Its trunk ran parallel with the ground a good six feet before returning to its natural, upward growth.

"The holy place," Leah said, pointing to the tree.

I pulled off my windbreaker and spread it out on the low limb. "White man's denim hide," I said. "For maiden of the healing tree."

She smiled, again, and sat down on my jacket. I sat down beside her.

The sun painted the surrounding trees with the last of its gold. The crickets and cicadas pulsed along the river. Leah had been drinking. A breeze caught at her hair. She smoothed it back from her face and said, "I guess my dad—Willis Sprule—never believed Sam was dead. Although none of us knew it, he's been looking for Sam for years. He knew Sam was good at fishing. Figured he'd find him near fishing boats. He hired a detective who found Sam up in Sturgeon Bay—Wisconsin. He went to the state's attorney who got the judge to issue a warrant for Sam's arrest. Sheriff Milby made a trip up to Wisconsin and talked Sam into coming back peacefully. He said it wasn't hard. It was as though Sam had been waiting to be found."

I thought about the man I'd seen several days earlier, watching Anna's house from his boat. I decided not to alarm Leah until I knew for certain it was Willis. Instead I asked, "Did your mother get to talk with Sam?"

"No. Momma's not allowed to see him until tomorrow at visiting hours. She's beside herself. I finally got her to rest a little. One minute she's laughing, and the next she's crying and asking why. All these years and never letting us know. And, of course, she's upset about him being in jail. He's asked to see me, too. The thing is…I dread seeing him."

"Why?"

"I don't know—I just hate talking about the drowning. Actually, I can't remember much of it. I had some kind of black out." She dropped her cigarette on the ground and slid off the tree to press it into the dirt with her foot. She sat back on the tree limb and continued. "Mary was ten when she died. She loved two things. Dancing and fishing. She always dressed in a some kind of costume. That day, she had me tie a collection of ribbons around her waist. Streamers of red and yellow. She spent the whole morning dancing. Ribbons twirling.

It was my day to take care of her, but I wanted to be with my friends. When Mary found out Sam planned to go fishing, she begged to go with him. I insisted he take her. It's the only time Sam ever refused. I gave him a hard time. He finally agreed, but he was angry. I wasn't sure he would take good care of her. He hadn't been himself for awhile. I got worried. I left my friends and went to check on her. She and Sam liked to fish from Sleeping Rock." She turned to look at me, "Do you know Sleeping Rock?"

I nodded. Sleeping Rock lay near the center of the river, marked with buoys to alert boats. It got its name both because it "slept" out of sight and could sink an unsuspecting boat in seconds, and because it resembled a large mattress. When the water ran low, the rock stood above water line, in clear view. People often sat there fishing, or eating a picnic during the hours when the water level was low.

"When I got to the river," Leah continued, "Sam was standing in the middle of Sleeping Rock, throwing this duffel bag. I remember seeing it sail through the air. Remember seeing the water slide over the rock then and swirl around his ankles. That's all I remember till I woke up on the Dawson's front porch. They said I had fainted. But not before I screamed that Mary and Sam had drowned."

She stopped talking. We could hear the river, lapping along the shore and the faint song of a nightingale. A breeze rustled the limbs around us, carrying the scent of Leah's perfume—lavender, I decided. Her hair hung down around her shoulders. She wore jeans and a sweater that looked soft. Another man, another woman in different circumstances, would have used this sacred limb for a romantic tryst.

Leah had proven so unpredictable. I knew she would excuse herself, knew any moment she'd be gone. She turned to look at me, and she became the freed spirit I'd seen that day in the sunny doorway. "Indian maiden will give you gift," she said. She smiled. "I will listen to one of your sorrows. It must be a sorrow never told to anyone."

"Wait," I said, "I tell you a sorrow I've never told anyone, and that's a gift for me?"

"An untold sorrow makes the heart sick. This," she patted the limb, "healing tree." She was playful, yet earnest. She kept her eyes fixed on me, as though she could already see my thoughts, even in the fading light.

Maybe it was the ancient tree, or her remarkable blue eyes like some sacred shaman's. I heard myself saying, "My wife was killed in a car accident." I had to look away from her now. "After the funeral, I got a call from the wrecking yard. They wanted me to collect the personal items left in the car. I'd been there once before—seen the car from the outside. I dreaded going. It was sunset when I arrived. That unique light that paints everything gold—like now," I said, looking around.

She waited for me to continue. "I located the car. Getting the door open wasn't easy. It was sprung—made a terrible sound, like a cry. Metal scraping metal. There was the sad, musty smell of a place that has been unoccupied. The interior was torn apart. Glass, twisted metal. Things scattered. The front seat was nearly unhinged—gaping—one of Susan's running shoes in the back window. A book on the floorboard—tube of lipstick, a jacket. Pieces of her life. I decided I had to leave. Just wasn't up to it. I sat down on the edge of the floor board, and looked away, out at the sea of cars, like twisted coffins. I don't know how long I'd been sitting when noticed something shining—reflecting the sunlight. It was her locket, hanging by its broken chain from the door handle, just beside me, eye level, so close it was almost touching me. I gave it to Susan on our wedding day. It was heart shaped. I'd had our pictures put in it—hers in one side, mine in the other. Sitting there in the wrecked car, holding the broken locket, I could finally cry—for all the broken things. The broken love, the baby that died."

I could have stopped there, but I wanted to tell her the rest of it. "Susan measured every day by our baby that died—always sounding the depths of a child that wasn't there. The day of his birth, if he had lived. The day he would have been a month old, and then two. 'Baby days,' she called them. She started drinking too much, especially on the baby days. She never believed that I understood. I suppose she was right. Maybe a man can never know what it's like to carry life, and then to lose it. Anyway, I failed her—really failed her."

I looked up at Leah. Tears ran down her cheeks. *God! I thought—the death of a child, the feeling of guilt. How could I not have recognized it? Leah—with her drinking and her sadness—was Susan! I was recreating my failure. I felt resentment rising. I was barely out of my own quagmire. How could I have gotten myself into another one? I wanted to do what I came to do. Sit in some quiet cove and fish, till I could make the hands on the dead clock start ticking again.* "Some healing tree," I said, not hiding my anger. "We must have had an allergic reaction."

Leah fumbled around in her pocket and produced a cigarette and lighter. She smoked too much. Someone should tell her that. She lit the cigarette and exhaled slowly.

"Now I will tell you something no one knows," she said. "The day you found Harlo crying and brought her home…I'd had too much to drink. I intended to close my eyes for a second. I must have fallen asleep." She took a deep breath, "No, I passed out. I don't even know how long. When I woke up, I couldn't find Harlo. I was terrified."

I knew she would be leaving now. True to my prediction, she slid off the limb and handed me my jacket. "I better get back and check on Momma."

I watched as she walked to the path and faded into the gathering shadows. I pulled on my jacket and followed.

When we reached the boat she turned toward me. "Thanks for stopping."

I nodded.

She reached out and touched my arm lightly for a moment. She started to say something, but thought better of it and turned back into the shadows.

I climbed into the boat and yanked hard on the throttle. The engine coughed once and caught. I headed toward the middle of the river. How many times did I want to make myself the source of a woman's pain? I brought it on myself! Nobody had asked me to get into my boat and drive by her house every afternoon, like a sixteen-year-old school boy. Couldn't wait to encounter a hurting woman—see how fast I could summon up her pain—then retreat into some kind of emotional catatonia.

"Backing and forthing," Granddad would say. "You're backing and forthing. Sit down and fish or get out of the boat, boy."

Well I was through inviting trouble. I would avoid any further involvement. It was a promise!

I switched on the headlight. Its beam glared against the water. I headed home, listening to the lone motor grate against the night.

Anna's Eighth Notebook

I'm sitting in the Cotton Rock Jail house between two other women talking to their kin folks through the thick glass window. A mother's asking her son if he's read all the newspapers she brought him, and a young wife's saying she couldn't make the rent payment.

My people have been in the Ozarks for over five generations, and nobody was ever in jail before now. The far door behind the glass wall opened, and a guard brought Sam into the room. He was wearing one of those orange jump suits. I never knew about the slippers. Everything about jail says you can't be trusted, not even with a shoestring. Sam sat down on his side of a thick glass and said, "Hello, Momma," like he'd just come in from the field and sat down to visit.

There's no getting yourself ready to see a child you believed was dead. No getting ready to see a lost son and not be able to get hold of him and hang on. All you can do is cry and touch the glass where his hand is pressed and wrestle down the moans that want to howl their way up your throat.

Sam leaned forward and asked, "Can you hear me okay?"

"It's all right. I can hear," I said.

And I think how he's hearing the men talk on his side of the glass, hearing them and trying not to. The young wife on my right, is still talking rent, and the momma on the left, asking if she should bring some *Readers Digests*, and I'm sorry for all of us. Sorry that we have to be here like this.

"I sure appreciate you coming down," he said.

I nodded. I always thought he looked like his father, and now I'm sure of it. He has the same sandy-red hair and the same Irish eyes as Jake. He was burnt brown from working in the sun, and his shoulders and arms were strong from hauling heavy nets of fish. But more than hard work was written on him. He died an eighteen-year-old boy and came back to life a worn man looking ten years older than thirty-three.

"Look at you," I say, "you're a man. Look at your shoulders! And your arms!"

"Yeah, well, I've been working on a fishing boat. Wish you could see Sturgeon Bay," he said. "You'd love it, Momma. Fishing boats are amazing. You'd have to work on one to understand."

"I'm sure it's a grand adventure," I said.

"I had some pictures I wanted you to see. The police took all my stuff. I want you to meet Raymond. He's in my cell. He wants to go back to Sturgeon Bay with me. A real, good person. He was with this guy who robbed a convenience store. Raymond didn't even know what was going on."

I know it won't do any good to ask him to go easy on plans with Raymond. To ask him if it's likely Raymond's lying. The little boy inside Sam didn't seem to grow along with the outside. He just kept his boy's heart, even when he grew to be six-foot tall. Maybe it was just the Irish he got from Jake. Irish that likes to come to grief when it can. Sam's heart was always fighting with good judgment. Hill people would say he was "green for kindling." Willis saw it right away and took it personal. Willis was determined to change him.

Sam could draw, like Leah, soon as he got big enough to hold a pencil. It gave him an uncommon joy about everything, specially the outdoors. Maybe it was the pleasure I got watching Sam's joy that bothered Willis. Maybe whatever drained the joy out of Willis, caused him to resent seeing it in Sam. Or maybe Willis had been born without a need for joy in the first place, and seeing it in Sam offset his balance, made him crush the sight of it under his heel.

I did what I could to keep Sam out of Willis' way. That's not easy on a farm, where a boy needs to be in the field, and his momma's tied to the kitchen. Anyway, I tried to make up for Willis. Maybe I pushed past the truth and made my own kind of lie.

When Sam was little, he loved to play checkers. I let him win, gave away my moves. I guess I did that in real life, too. I didn't hold him to the game, you know. I let things slide so he'd come out feeling okay about himself. I reckon it's not honest, but I keep on playing the game, giving away my moves. I don't demand to know what happened at the drowning fifteen years ago, why he ran off and let me bury him in a funeral that never should have taken place.

I sit and wait for him to get to the truth. It won't be much, just the part he can manage, and he finally gets to it: "I couldn't face everyone." And he's choking up, and he says, "I couldn't get to her! I couldn't save her! How could I come home with that news? I didn't plan to run for so many years. It just sort of happened. A day at a time. Then fifteen years went by."

And I don't tell him the pain he's caused, or how I would never have done anybody that way, running away and leaving them to carry that kind of weight alone. Instead I say, "Everyone knows you would have saved Mary if you could. I see Tom Ferguson today. I'll do everything I can to get you out of here."

And he says, "I sure appreciate you helping me, Momma."

He asks me about Leah and little Harlo. He's never seen little Harlo, of course. He asks me about the town, and especially about his friend, Phil Hutchins. Phil was Sam's best friend in high school.

I tell him I believe Phil still lives in Cotton Rock. And he's hoping maybe Phil will come to visit him. I'm hoping he'll be set free before there's much need for visiting. He tells me about his life on the fishing boat, and I say, "That's just the way the story goes, all right!" It's as though he's four-years-old, and he's brought me a picture, saying, "See my rainbow?" And I can't say that it doesn't really look like a rainbow.

After I left the jail this morning, I came home and sat at my desk. I just sat looking out the window, watching the river and writing in my notebook. Mainly, I've been thinking about dreams. There's all kinds of dreams. There's day dreams for one. Take Orey Whitaker for example. What Orey dreams about when he sits fishing along the banks of the White River tells a lot about the level of his losses.

I happen to know something about Orey's dreams because Lingo Henegar, who cuts my grass every Tuesday, told me about Orey. Lingo unloads feed sacks every Saturday at Mumford's Feed Store where Orey works. Orey unloads feed sacks all week long. In between shipments, Orey parcels out the sacks into customers' cars. Orey's nearly sixty-years-old and too worn out for those sacks. Some of them weigh a hundred pounds. Orey's never going to retire. He's just going to die under one of those sacks.

Anyway, Lingo saved up his money for three summers. He and a friend took the money and drove up the Alaska Highway. They hiked the Talkeetnas, lived in a tent, ate ptarmigan and fresh-caught fish roasted on an open fire. Lingo says the only time he sees Orey smile is when he gets a minute to hear about Alaska. He leans his sore back up against the loading dock wall, lights up a cigarette and says, "Lingo, tell me about Alaska." Lingo says Orey goes into a kind of trance. I call it day-dreaming. And that's how I know what Orey dreams about. I figure he's catching Alaskan trout when he sits down there on the White River.

I'd like to think that Orey's wife treats him right. I'd like to think she has a warm meal and some gentle talk waiting for Orey when he comes home at night. I'd like to think that she thanks him once in a while for unloading forty years of sacks. But Resa is a hard woman. If Orey never smiles, Resa's never even tempted to smile. Orey knows he's never going to Alaska, except in his dreams.

But there's a second kind of dreams. They're the dreams that we believe will happen, dreams we work and scrape for, like the dreams a mother has for her children. Anyway, I figure God wrung the necks of my dreams. I used to watch Grandma Poinselot kill chickens for dinner. She'd take a chicken by the neck and whirl it till the body flung out in a great circle, like a rock sailing round in a sling-shot. A moment later, the head hung limp in her hand, while the body sailed through the air, hit the ground and ran crazy, zig-zagging across the grass, like it was looking for the rest of itself.

The thing about dreams is, they live on after their necks have been wrung, after their bodies have flung through the air, zig-zagging across strange ground, wrung from all their reason. They live on in dogged living, because doing and doing seems like living. They zig-zag in tears down cheeks from eyes filled without warning by the spill of old memories. They zig-zag along broken pieces of sleep, along old fissures of the heart. They come up in the night, erupt in the throat, in a cry, in the bed, where there are no more dishes to wash or clothes to fold, or floors to sweep and sweep again.

Lucy's Angel Gossip

Little Ben Northington's another child that's never been to church. His folks come down from Kansas City ever summer. I figure Ben's Momma was needing a baby sitter, and I figure she wouldn't get one none too easy. Ben got rotten long before he got ripe. We've been holding a vacation Bible school over at the Baptist Church. I figure Mrs. Northington needed a rest, cause little Ben come to Bible School ever day last week.

That youngen's got hair red as a sumac leaf, and he's freckled as a turkey's egg—just like me. Except on him it's cute, and it's a good thing, too, cause he'll be needing a heap of clemency.

On the first day we took the church bus and a picnic lunch down to Buckeye Knob. Eb, my husband, did the driving. We hadn't gone five miles 'til two little girls was wanting the bathroom. I's just trying to find out if the need was serious. So I says, "Do you have to go number one or number two?"

Ben figured the higher the number, the more serious was the case. He yells right out, "I have to go number five!" I liked to never got the screaming under control after that. Youngens was having to go number eighteen and thirty. I thought Eb was gonna have to pull off the road, he's laughing so hard. Course, turns out Ben didn't have to use the bathroom no way. He's just interested in ferreting out the Super Quick Stop.

Ben's momma is a strong-minded woman. Truth is, she's persnickety. And it's too bad, really. Cause being persnickety makes for a lot of extra work, and Ben already gives her enough of that. Ben says his momma believes in "a varied curriculum." He said his momma visited ten schools up in Kansas City hunting for a school with a varied curriculum.

Anyways, I figure Bible school weren't much of a variety. Cause on the third day Ben met his momma at the door, shaking that sumac hair and a rolling his eyes and a saying, "Momma! Jesus again today!"

On Wednesday, Mrs. Northington come in just as I's finishing out the story of Abraham sacrificing Isaac. I had the picture up on the flannel board. Course Abraham didn't really sacrifice his son. But Ben knew his momma was in need of coaching. So he yelled right out, "Don't worry, Momma, they take that kid off the barbecue grill!"

On Friday, Bible school was over, and Mrs. Northington hadn't come for Ben. She called the church to say she's sitting down at the Cotton Rock Beauty Shop. She says she's right in the middle of having her hair done, and could I please be a darling and drop Ben off on my way home.

Ben and I was driving along when Ben asked me where God lived. I was right pleased he's thinking such thoughts, and I says, "Why he's everywhere, Ben. We can't see Him, but God's right here in the car with us at this very minute.

"Well," says Ben, looking around, "He's not wearing his seat belt."

Yes, sir! I reckon Ben's angel always draws a crowd of angels when it's time for gossip.

Thoughts from the Back Porch   July 1996

It was Monday morning. I heard a soft knock on my cabin door and opened it to find Anna dressed in a gray suit.

"I'm on my way to the attorney," she said. "Just wanted to drop off my notebook. I won't be coming to class tonight." Her dark eyes, usually intense and anxious were tired, as though she hadn't slept, and she looked pale. "Leah said you knew about Sam."

"Yes. Come in, Anna."

"Only a minute," she said.

"I make great iced- tea. We could sit out on the porch."

"That sounds nice, but I won't stay long."

I took her notebook, led her to the back porch and found her a chair. I put the kettle on. It took a few minutes to brew the tea, ice it down, and locate glasses and a tray. I added some of the mint leaves I'd brought from the fraidy hole. "Be careful," I reminded myself. "Anna is Leah's mother. You made yourself a promise."

I carried the tray of tea, with its fragrance of mint onto the porch. Chunks of ice kept rhythm with my steps, tapping against the sides of the glasses. Anna stirred in her chair. She'd been dozing. The rest had been good for her; the color had returned to her face.

"Mint," she said, lifting her glass, and taking a long drink of her tea. She set the glass down and shook her head slowly. "I've lived in Cotton Rock over thirty years. Never been down to the jail house before. Sam's thirty-three. Looks forty-three. Sheriff Milby asked him to come back voluntarily to answer some questions. It was Willis's doing. It's amazing what hate can do—even find a son everyone believed was dead." She fell silent, took a drink of her tea and then continued. "I wasn't allowed to see him till Saturday. Wouldn't let him go home. Sheriff Milby said they had to hold him over till today for an appearance in court. At eight o'clock this morning, the judge advised Sam that though there was the suspicious matter of leaving the scene of a fatality and feigning his own death, he was actually being charged with grand larceny! Grand larceny! Seems that the day of the drowning, Sam hid in the woods till nightfall. Then sneaked into the barn and took Willis's Winchester. Some kind of valuable Model with a powerful scope. We'd had a round of coyotes helping themselves to the feeder pigs. Willis took to leaving the gun in the barn. I guess Sam knew it'd bring him enough money to get a bus ticket and a new beginning."

"So Willis suspected Sam was alive," I said.

"Yes. A secret Willis kept to himself. Must have visited every pawn shop in the county before he found the gun. Could of have been anybody that took it, of course. But vengeance is a powerful persuader."

"Grand larceny," I repeated. "But isn't there a statute of limitation? It's been fifteen years. Do you have an attorney?"

"Tom Ferguson."

"Well if anyone can fight for Sam, it's Tom Ferguson."

"I have a meeting with him in an hour. He says rumor has it that they're just detaining Sam while the Grand Jury looks into the drowning. They're saying Mary's death was neglect on Sam's part. Milby's been sheriff since Sam was a first grader. He knows as well as anybody that Sam would have saved Mary if he could have. Milby just says there's evidence to back the charge, but he isn't saying what. They wouldn't release Sam on bail. He's considered a risk—running off and hiding all these years. I'm sorry to be rattling on so. I ought to go." But she didn't move from her chair. She just sat looking out over the river. A gentle breeze blew across the porch.

"Smells like rain," I said. "It won't be much of a shower. Just enough time to finish your tea and sit awhile. Your meeting isn't for an hour, right?"

She smiled and nodded.

The rain started. We sat listening to its gentle drumming against the porch roof. A meadow lark sang in the hickory tree.

"The very first poem I ever wrote was about a meadow lark," Anna said. "Cora Eckert laughed right out loud. She was in my poetry class last winter at the library. Cora said my poem sounded like a greeting card. She said the class was a workshop for serious verse."

It wasn't hard to imagine Cora mocking Anna's poetry. Cora managed to criticize someone's work every week. She worked as a tour guide at the old mill, and never failed to tell us how she'd been on her feet all day. She always added, "And I have bunions—big as toadstools."

"Anyway," Anna continued, "The poetry teacher said there's all kinds of poetry. Gave me the names of some poets to study. I looked them up in Leah's college books. The next poem I wrote for the class was serious. About a little boy I'd seen sitting on a freeway ramp outside Springville. I wrote how he looked abandoned, like a puppy left beside the road. We had to exchange poems. Write each other a critique. Cora wrote that my simile—abandoned like a puppy— was condescending. She wrote, 'Animals are just as important as humans'."

I smiled, and Anna continued. "That was quite a surprise to me. I loved my dog, Sugar. Much as I think it's possible to love a dog. But no matter how I thought about it, I didn't think Sugar was as important as that little boy on the freeway ramp. Next month, Cora wrote a poem about her dog, Ishmael, and her son, Albert. Turns out, Albert was allergic to dogs. She wrote about having to say good-bye to Ishmael."

"Did you write a critique?" I asked

"Yes," Anna ginned. "I wrote, 'You were caught between a rock and a hard choice, Cora. What made you decide to keep your son?'"

We both laughed—fine, rich laughter—and I poured us another glass of tea. It felt like being with an old trusted friend.

For a wild moment I thought of telling her about my writing problem, but thought better of it.

"I have to sell my house," she was saying.

"You love your house!"

"I had no idea how expensive lawyers are. I had to take out a second mortgage. Ferguson tries to do right by his boy. He's autistic. He's in a fine institution. Folks say it costs Ferguson nearly every dollar before he makes it. I can't blame him for doing right by his boy. I do the same."

She finished her tea. The little shower had passed. "I've talked too much—stirring the wind as they say."

"You needed the rest," I said, "We both needed the laugh."

At the door, she said, "Writing is holding me together right now. I'm mighty grateful."

"I'm glad you're in the class," I said, hating the sound of formality in my voice. I should have told her how very important her writing was to me, told her how courageous I thought she was. I watched her walk down the path to her car, saw the defeat in the sag of her shoulders, and the slowness of her step.

I walked back to the porch and picked up the tea glasses. "Don't worry," I said to myself, "you're safe—safe as shallow water." I was angry at Alex for suggesting I get involved, angry at Leah, angry at myself. I needed to get out of the cabin.

I decided to go to town. Run some errands. I backed the jeep out of the garage, up the drive and pulled onto River Road. That was as far as I got. A snapping turtle, as big as a washtub, sat squarely in front of my car. The Ozarks has a high concentration of snappers. Folks in the hills call them alligator turtles because of the spikes on their tails and the bite of their deadly jaws. When they clamp down, they hang on.

I killed the engine and took a tire iron out of the back. I planned to slide him across the road into the grass. His head was as big as two of my fists, his neck as thick as my arm, and his shell nearly three feet across. I had barely touched him when he whirled and snapped his bony jaws down on the tire iron.

I whistled and let go. "Scared me, old boy," I said. But he held tightly to the tire iron, held it high, like a kind of flag. "Take it easy, fella. I'm just going to grab hold of the iron and drag you to the edge of the road. Otherwise, you're road kill." I kept talking quietly, dragging him slowly. When I got him to the edge of the road, I let go of the tire iron, but to my amazement, he just kept clutching it in his fierce jaw—carrying his perceived enemy across the grassy embankment.

"Hey! Hey, that's my tire-iron!" I yelled.

He disappeared from sight. All I could see was the tire iron, threading through the tall grass. The old guy kept right on going down the bank and slid off into the safety of the river. The tire iron, like a kind of periscope, was the last thing to disappear beneath the water.

"It's all confounded turtles and tire irons," I yelled at the river. The whole confounded language is confounded turtles and tire irons." I sounded like Granddad at one of his worst harangues, and it felt surprisingly good.

I jerked the jeep door open, climbed in, letting the fury parade through my mind: *Confounded turtles and tire irons! I said I didn't think it was time to have a baby. It didn't mean I wanted the baby to die! May as well talk to confounded turtles. A loaded gravel truck fails to stop, and Susan is dead.*

Professor of English for god's sake! Professor of that which ultimately walks off into the river. A complex code of tire irons and turtles—that's what we've generated.

Make little sounds with your mouth and call them words, think we can use little sounds to mean what we've lived, what we've suffered, or loved. Write the words in dictionaries and believe we've pinned down their meaning. Look up the word "pain," and it sends you looking for "injury." "Injury" sends you looking for "harm." Every new word just keeps walking into the river with your tire-iron. And Derrida with his French deconstruction is right—the language ultimately collapses. What little sounds can I utter to describe Susan's pain? I must go to the graveyard and point to the grave that holds a small white casket. There—there is pain. What word expresses the defeat in Anna's eyes or the slump of her shoulders, when language sits stick in the heart. What word means the way Leah drains a glass of wine or rubs out a cigarette only to light another and stare off at something no one else can see?

And what word is there for you, John Sinclair? What word is there for the self-absorbed husband who spouts a cheap excuse? I jammed the key into the ignition. "Chicanery! The human heart can hear without words. The human heart can read the human body. And what did my body say to Susan? That I was marking time? Pretending to listen to her, pretending to care? Did my body shout that the only time I was alive, fully committed, I was writing? And now I cannot commit to anything.

And what is my body saying to me with its stagnant will? That my creative flow stopped because it is blocked, or because I have too meager a talent to sustain it?

Anna's Ninth Notebook

When Momma came to live with me six years ago, I wanted her room to look like home. I covered the rented hospital bed with her favorite bedspread and brought her lamp and night stand from her apartment. I hung pictures on the wall beside her bed. There was one of Momma as a young woman, one of Zoe and me as little girls, and another of Momma's mother, Grandma Poinselot.

Momma spent many early mornings looking at those pictures, waiting for me to come and untie her from the sleeping jacket. She often started the morning by saying, "Have you seen my pictures?" She usually said Zoe had hung them.

I would say, "They're nice, Momma." But one morning, I said, "I hung them, Momma. Me—Anna."

"Yes, you're Anna," she said.

I unbuttoned the sleeping jacket and crawled under the bed to untie the jacket straps from the bed frame.

"I just hate this...I hate this... salamander."

"Sleeping jacket," I said.

"Sleeping jacket," she repeated.

"It keeps you from falling in the night," I reminded her. I undid the paper diaper and helped her to sit up. "You have to go to the bathroom, Momma. Pee." I planted my feet and pulled Momma upright, and turned her around. It was then that I remembered the portable commode was still against the far wall, but Momma was ready to sit down.

"Wait, Momma!"

"They usually fall slow," the therapist had said. "Don't panic. Just step behind her and catch." Sure enough, she sat down slow, bare-bottomed, right on my lap.

Before I could make sense of what had happened, Momma said "pee," and it was too late. She peed all over both of us. Right then and there, it mattered who I was. "Who did you pee on Momma? Did you pee on Zoe or Anna?"

"I peed on Anna," Momma said. Then she laughed.

"You got that right," I said. I laughed too, sitting there on the bedroom floor, my nightgown stuck wet on my legs, holding my momma, laughing.

There were other times when I could still laugh. Like the time Momma thought I was Dorothy, her care giver. When she thinks I'm Dorothy, she tells me secrets. She was sitting at the kitchen table, cutting coupons. I was stirring gravy on the stove. She laid her scissors down and whispered, "Don't tell Anna…"

She looked around, and whispered again, "Don't tell Anna."

I stopped stirring and leaned forward to hear.

She wrinkled her nose a little and whispered, "Anna's putting on weight."

Well, I cut back on the pie, right then and there.

But sometimes I can't laugh. The day I brought Momma home from the hospital, it was turning dark. When we entered the house, Momma was still belted into her wheelchair. She was trying to stand up, but the belt pulled her back. She'd put her hands on the chair arms and try to stand, pushing against the belt, and then fall back down, worn out. Her white hair was wet, against her hot face.

"What is it, Momma?"

She didn't answer. She just pointed to the dark windows around her, like they were the portals to hell itself. Her eyes were wild, like a cat's eyes when it's made to ride in a car.

I called the number the hospital had given me. "I've never seen Momma like this," I said. "She's looking at the windows like they're full of demons."

"Sundowners," the nurse said. "It's one of the many phenomena of Alzheimers. It's an anxiety that comes with the setting sun. Windows, any reflective surface—mirrors, T.V. screens—can be confusing. Sometimes these will frame a different reality for her."

It was true. Sometimes Momma nodded hello to her own face in the mirror. And sometimes Momma thought the people on T.V. were sitting in our living room. Yet there were times when we were watching an old movie on television that it felt like we were really together, like I'd always wished we could be. I'd make us a cup of tea and a plate of cookies. Momma likes chocolate with black walnuts, and if there's one thing we've got plenty of in the Ozarks, it's walnuts.

We'd sit in the two over-stuffed chairs, Momma, wearing her blue fur slippers and her velour robe. It seemed like she was really understanding the movie. She'd laugh when I laughed. Then a commercial would come on, and maybe a man selling Preparation H would ask, "Do you have hemorrhoids?" Momma would answer, "No. Never bothered by hemorrhoids." She believed for all the world that Mr. Preparation H was sitting in the room with us, as though she expected him to say, "Good for you, Mrs. Groves!"

And I felt the anger coming up inside, because I knew I was losing Momma. Though last week Mr. Preparation H was more help to Momma than I was. We were watching television when Momma said, "Well, I think I'll just go get a little…" Her voice trailed off. She stood and walked out into the hall. She hadn't gone two steps till she was back.

"I just need a little…" But the word was lost in her snowy old head, and she just dropped down into her chair.

"You need something," I said. I was trying to get clues, so I asked, "What do you do with it?"

She looked at Mr. Preparation H and said, "I don't know. But if I was him, I'd go get myself a cold drink of water!"

"Do you need a cold drink, Momma?"

"Yes!" she said, like she'd just won the lottery. "Water!" She was so glad to find the word.

Poor Momma. She'd probably learned to say, "I want a drink," when she was three years old. Almost eighty years of saying those words, and she couldn't find them anywhere in her troubled, old head.

I thought I knew why I wanted Momma to live with me. I thought it was to get to know her, make a little friendship before I lost her. That was only partly right. There was something else I wanted from Momma. I wanted her blessing. I wanted the birthright.

I've come to think a child is born twice. A child's body is born once at birth, but a child's place is not born till a parent gives it. Without a birthright, a child never feels at home anywhere —just goes through life feeling like a counterfeit. Like the children of old who waited for Abraham and Jacob to stretch out their hands and give them the blessing. Children can wait their whole lives for a birthright.

I glimpsed my birthright once, when I was very small. It's the only memory I can find of Momma before sadness took her to bed. It was early, and I had come to the kitchen. Momma was the only one there, and on her face was the blessing, shining out just for me. I tried to write a poem about it, but I couldn't remember anything in the room. Couldn't remember the press of the cane chair against my girl legs. Maybe the feed sack curtains were riding a little on the morning breeze, but I couldn't feel its touch on my memory. My nightgown and the tablecloth brought no pattern to my mind. I couldn't smell the biscuits, still hot on the oven door. The morning birds were singing in silence. Nothing was stored in my girl-memory, but this one clear knowing: I had my momma all to myself, and I was a child-cup, help up to her face shining down on me.

I wanted to see that blessing again. Growing up I tried to find to find it on Momma's face. Maybe there were times when she almost gave me the blessing. Maybe there were times when she looked at me, and she felt the blessing rise up in her, till it almost broke through to her face. But the weight of her sad heart was so great, that it held her face prisoner. The blessing just couldn't overcome its heavy mask. Just sank back down and faded out of sight.

After a while, I told myself I didn't need her blessing. I didn't know then that truth is often the backside of what we insist on. Safer to say I didn't need anything from Momma, because I needed so much. I came face to face with my lie when I was packing up Momma's things and found a little piece of paper tucked inside her Bible. The words written there were made by a lost hand: A-l-m.—she stopped, and began a new line: A-l-z, and finally a third try: A-l-z-h-e-i-m-e-r. Below this Momma had tried to write my name, but she couldn't remember it right off. First there was A-n-a. She had marked through it again and finally: Anna. My name. And I was crying.

Fifty-one years of waiting for my birthright held on to the little piece of paper where Momma had written my name—where she was trying to find me in her memory. There's a lot of fear wrapped in so great a need. So my fear clutched up an alibi. It turned itself around and said that Momma needed me. She had Alzheimers, and she wouldn't make it without me. Truth was, Momma had no way to say no. I took no risk in asking. So I brought Momma home to take care of her. Now I know I was bringing Momma home so I could see the blessing one more time. It came a few days ago. I was writing at my desk, and I looked up to find Momma looking at me. "Do you need something, Momma?"

"No." Then, came the six little words: "I just enjoy looking at you." For years, her grief kept her from thinking of such words. And now, in the midst of a dark night, she had found those six words, had strung them together on one thin thread, held them together long enough to say them out loud. "I just enjoy looking at you." The blessing!

All those years when I was trying to please Mrs. Bedford at school, or Mrs. Tilden at the tomato factory, I was looking for my Momma, and I didn't know it. And now, shining clear as the kitchen window, was the blessing, streaming out to me from Momma's eyes, like God, moving on the face of darkness, bringing light.

The blessing brought a new thought: I'm thinking that the great empty place I carried, grieving for its birthright, got itself mixed up with Sam. Maybe that's why it feels like I have to give Sam the blessing every time I think he's in need of it, every day, every moment, no matter what's happened. It's possible that a whole heap of my giving to Sam was really giving to that little four-year-old girl who got up from the cane chair early one morning and went looking for the another helping of the blessing—went looking for over fifty years.

Emmett's Fishing Report

She's a sunny day on the White River. Temperature is eighty-six this afternoon. If you're fishin' lakes today, dangling a spinnerbait and buzzbait means you'll have fish sittin' in your boat! If you're fishing the river, look for stumps and laydowns. Fish like hugging up against the shadow of a log. They also hanker for rocky shoals and drop-off points.

I won't be carrying no fish home to Lottie, today. Seems I'm gonna eat my catch from yesterday. I've had some surprises on the end of my line, but this one took the rag off the bush! I come home tired yesterday and leaned my pole against the screen door jam. Left a big night crawler still a wiggling on the hook. I was a coming right back to tend to it, but the U.P.S. truck (we call it the "ups truck") come down the road, and the ups man was asking directions for the Boxley place. I got to talking to him about fishing and one thing led to ten.

Lottie's pet goose come along down the walk and sees that worm a dancin'.

That goose hasn't noticed nothing since she stepped outta the egg, but she spied that worm and took for it straight away. She swallowed it down and then set up a racket worse than a kicking mule in a tin barn. She's all over that porch. Wings flapping, feathers flying, honking and spitting, and whipping that fish line around good as any bass. She had that pole pulled tight as a trot line.

It took me a spell to figure out what got hold of her. Then she took off backwards, like a crawdad with its tail tucked under. She run backwards the length of the porch, her wings spread and honking like a stuck horn. Didn't stop till she went right off the end of the porch, fishing pole jumping and clattering along behind. That goose run backwards clear down to the barn, 'fore I could get a step on that pole and bring the whole parade to a halt.

Nothing to do but kill the old goose and put her outta her misery. The goose wasn't real happy about it. But she was a good deal happier than Lottie. Anyway, we're a having roast goose for supper tonight. I suspect it'll be a pretty unfriendly meal, all in all. I give my word to Lottie, I'm through fishing on the front porch.

Thoughts from the Back Porch   July 1996

It was Wednesday. I sat beside The Benchmark, trimming the fingernail I'd torn on a fish hook. To Ozark natives, cutting fingernails on Wednesday means you will receive a surprise. A few minutes later, I acquired my second portent—a cricket hiding under my newspaper. Between the cricket and the fingernail, the Ozark folks would say I was to receive a surprise and little luck.

The day brought both, and caused me to eavesdrop, shamelessly, on two different conversations. The first began at the coffee shop on River Drive. I sat at one of the outdoor tables overlooking the river, drinking coffee and reading an article about the number of trout in Cedar Shoals Lake. Three people sat talking at the table next to mine, and the name of Anna's ex husband caught my attention.

"Didn't Willis Sprule teach you algebra?" asked the older man. (I decided this must be the father.)

"Yes. Did me as much good as tits on a boar," the young man said.

"That's vulgar!" (This was spoken by the woman I assumed to be his mother.)

"Is Sprule wanting to know about Sam McKerry?" the father asked.

"Must be. Asked me to meet him for lunch at Molly's Diner. I'd rather eat razor blades."

"Willis must have heard you wound up in jail with Sam," the mother said.

"I suppose."

"Well, did Sam say why he's been missing for fifteen years?"

"No. Just talked non-stop about fishing boats and Sturgeon Bay."

"I can't imagine being in jail," the mother said.

"You got that right. One rubber mat, one wool blanket apiece. Four of us in there. Three of us been drinking. Took turns pissing all night. There was only one toilet—not a foot from my head. You can bet I was quick to sit up anytime someone pissed."

The woman groaned.

"Next morning," the young man continued, "a guard knocked on the door. Asked us to state our names if we wanted breakfast. We each called out our name. We told the guard Sam was still sleeping. But he said, 'You snooze, you lose.' Few minutes later, he slid a tray through the slot. Three pieces of toast and three cups of coffee. Sam woke up. We tore up our toast and gave him some. But none of us was sharing our coffee. I made that cup last as long as I could. No more food till lunch time. One bologna sandwich apiece—no mustard, no mayo and one cup of cool-aid."

"That's terrible," said the mother. "Someone should do something about the food."

"It's not a bed and breakfast, Mildred. If you don't like the food, don't drink and drive," said the father.

"But it's barbaric!" the mother insisted. "I'm certain we never had those conditions in New Haven. Anyway, you need to settle down, Phil. You need to get married. You're thirty-two years old."

"Don't start—"

"What are they going to do with Sam?" the father interrupted.

"They're talking about manslaughter—saying it's his fault his sister died. Anyway, it looks bad for him since he ran off and hid."

"So why does Willis Sprule want to see you?" the father asked.

"He's got it in for Sam. Always did."

"But that's his son," the mother said.

"Step-son. Sam was always clear on that. But still—family."

"Why does Sprule want to talk with you?" the father repeated.

"Trying to get something on Sam, I'd guess. He thinks cause he taught me algebra in high school, I owe him. As if I ever used that dumb shit. I'll have lunch with him—nothing more. Be right back. I need a pack of cigarettes."

The young man passed my table and headed inside to the cigarette machine. His long hair was pulled into a ponytail, and the back of his tee shirt read, "Where's the Party?"

When Phil was out of ear shot, the father said, "Sprule must have something on Phil or Phil wouldn't bother meeting with him."

"Well, Sam and Phil were friends in high school."

"That's just it, Mildred—Sam and Phil were friends. Not Sprule. Something's fishy."

"Phil needs to get married," the mother said again.

"Please, Mildred. Who do you think had to pay the hundred dollars to bail Phil out? That's all we need—a wife and kids added to the basement."

The young man returned then, and the three of them left.

I remembered that Anna had mentioned Phil in one of her notebooks. I decided I would eat lunch at Molly's diner, myself. I wanted to see Willis Sprule. I felt certain he was the man I'd seen sitting in the boat, spying on Anna.

It was close to noon when I entered the parking lot at Molly's. A worn, green Chevy pickup pulled into the parking space just ahead of me. Its truck bed held a lawn mower, rakes and shovels and some lilac saplings several feet tall. A man in his late fifties, climbed from the cab of the truck. Sure enough—the same man I'd seen on the river. For a man of order, as Anna had described him, he was strangely inconsistent in his dress. He wore a pair of dress slacks, with a frayed, faded shirt and scuffed work boots, as though he had dressed in the dark.

However, Anna's description of his stiff, implacable manner was apparent. He strode across the gravel parking lot—a methodical, rigid stride, the gravel crunching beneath the gnawed heels of his boots Though his hair had been resolutely slicked down, sprigs of it stood out stiffly from his head, the way a board might thrust over the edge of a roof, as though bits of his stubbornness had sprouted.

Molly's Diner was one room, dominated by a central counter and stools, and behind the counter a pair of swinging doors led to the kitchen. A row of booths ran along the outside wall. Willis took a seat in one of the booths, and I sat at the counter.

A woman, spatula in hand, entered through the swinging doors, ushering in a momentary clatter of dishes and the smell of bacon from the kitchen. She saw Willis seated in the booth and called out, "Willis Sprule! I haven't seen you in years." Her round face broke into a smile. She wore an orange and brown uniform that said Molly's on the pocket. "Yes sir." She nodded her head of frizzy, gray curls. "It's been years."

Willis did not answer.

"Hey!" the waitress said, jabbing the spatula toward Willis, "You taught my boy, Harold. Harold Malloy. Course that's been fifteen, sixteen years ago."

If Willis remembered Harold, he didn't say so. He studied the clock on the wall by the kitchen door. "Is that clock correct?" His voice—neither friendly nor unfriendly—remained monotone, just as Anna had described it.

"Right on the money," Harold's mother said, pointing her spatula at the clock. "Mr. Collins wouldn't have us open one minute late or close one minute early."

"Good for Mr. Collins," Willis said in his monotone.

A young girl, dressed in the same orange and brown uniform entered from the kitchen. She wore her hair in a pony tail, and her earrings had little gold hearts that swung when she walked. She carried a stack of menus on her arm.

"That's Patty," Harold's mother said, as the girl stopped at Willis's table. "She's our new waitress. First day on the job. Today's her birthday — sweet sixteen."

The girl blushed, and she held out one of the menus toward Willis. But Willis didn't notice. He was confirming the time on his watch. The girl laid the menu carefully on the corner of the table, then came to hand me a menu.

The front door opened. It was Phil, from the coffee shop, his tee-shirt still asking, "Where's the Party?" He walked to Willis's booth and held out his hand, "Mr. Sprule."

Willis shook his hand. "You're late, Phil," he said in his flat voice.

Phil glanced at the wall clock. "Only five minutes," he said.

"If you're not five minutes early, you're already five minutes late," Willis answered. "That makes you ten minutes late."

"Sounds just like sophomore math class," Phil said and laughed.

Willis did not laugh.

Phil slid into his side of the green plastic booth.

The young girl brought a menu to Phil.

"You're new here, aren't you?" Phil asked.

The girl nodded, the little gold hearts swinging at her ears.

"What's your name?" Phil asked.

"Patty." The girl blushed a second time.

"Where you from?"

"My folks just moved here from—"

"I'll have a hamburger. Well done," Willis interrupted.

"The girl, uncertain, stopped and looked at Willis. When it came to her that Willis must have placed an order, she said, "Oh," and took a pencil and tablet from her apron pocket. "What would you like, sir?"

"You weren't listening," Willis said, looking at her for the first time, his voice never betraying its drone.

Patty stared down at the tablet, her cheeks now scarlet. "I'm sorry," she said. "I—could you repeat that?"

"I said you weren't listening," Willis repeated.

"No…I…meant…"

Patty turned to back to Phil, clearly bewildered.

"I believe he said he wanted the hamburger well done," Phil said. "I'll have the same."

Patty wrote on her tablet.

As soon as she was out of earshot, Phil spoke. "I really don't think I can help you. Sam's been gone fifteen years."

Willis held up a warning hand.

"Sorry," Phil said and leaned closer and lowered his voice.

From time to time, I heard him say Sam's name. More than once, Phil held his arms out and shook his head, as if saying, "Believe me—I don't know anything."

Willis sat stone-like throughout the conversation, altering his posture only three times: first, when his food arrived, and he leaned slightly forward to pray—out loud—a second time, when he examined his burger to see if Patty had, indeed, brought it well-done, and a third time to check the bill after she placed it on the corner of the table. He found a seventeen-cent error, which he pointed out in his calm, flat voice.

"I'm sorry," Patty said. "I's adding too fast I guess."

Willis ignored her apology.

She began clearing the table, balancing the plates in one hand. And then, as though performing an overused ploy from a very predictable scene, she reached for Willis's water glass and everything collapsed. The plates struck the floor, and the glass of water rolled into Willis's lap.

Willis jumped to his feet. For one, brief moment his lifeless eyes filled with rage. Then as quickly as if he had flipped an unseen switch, he resumed his indifferent gaze.

Harold's mother, who had heard the crash of dishes, came with a dry towel. "She wouldn't of had that happen for the world, Mr. Sprule. She's a sweetheart. Her first day, you know."

Willis didn't answer. He took the towel from Harold's mother, folded it in half and began wiping methodically at his dress slacks.

"I'll just go get a dust pan, honey," Harold's mother said to the girl.

Patty dropped to the floor, picking up pieces of broken glass. She kept repeating, "I'm so sorry. I'm so sorry."

Willis stood looking down at her. The girl, kneeling on the floor, her hands holding the jagged glass, looked up at him through her tears.

A small, unmistakable smile formed on Willis's lips.

And though she was only sixteen years old—as of that very day according to Harold's mother—Patty seemed to understand that Willis enjoyed her misery there on the floor beneath him. She whimpered like a small animal, got to her feet and ran for the swinging doors, bumping into Harold's mother, who had emerged carrying a dust pan and a broom. "Slow down, honey. It's sure enough all right!"

The girl vanished into the kitchen. Willis sat back down in the booth, and Harold's mother swept up the broken plates.

"Say, I've got another appointment," Phil said to Willis. "Better be five minutes early, right Mr. Sprule?" He gave another nervous laugh and reached for the ticket. "Listen, lunch is on me, okay?" He walked to the register and paid Harold's mother. He returned to the table with a five dollar bill for Patty, placed it carefully under the remaining water glass, gave a final nod to Willis and headed for the door.

Patty eventually returned from the kitchen carrying a dishcloth. She stopped abruptly when she saw Willis, still seated in the booth. She looked around for Harold's mother, and found her busy clearing another table.

Willis pointed to the remaining water glass. "You can take this," he said to Patty.

She walked to the table and picked up the water glass. The five dollars lay between them, exposed, on the empty table. Willis reached out, slowly, deliberately, and took the five dollars. He folded it carefully in half and put it into his shirt pocket. He did not look up as he spoke, "I believe that will just cover the dry-cleaning of my slacks," he said and stood up. He walked to the door, his boots striking methodically across the wooden floor.

Patty stared after him, the dishrag hanging from her hand, watched until he was through the door and it had unequivocally shut, before she slumped down into the booth.

I finished my lunch and left a double tip for Patty beside my plate. I paid Harold's mother at the register, stepped out into the sunshine and took a deep breath of fresh air, glad to be free of Willis Sprule. However on a side street, two blocks from the restaurant, I received my next surprise of the day.

Willis's worn Chevy sat in front of a steep terrace, leading up to an old, pink Victorian house with an even brighter pink door.

On the sidewalk Willis crouched under a lilac bush, resting its burlap-covered root-ball on his knee. The pink door opened, and an elderly woman, broom in hand, headed down the front steps. "There's three holes dug back there," the woman called down to Willis, pointing her broom handle toward the backyard. "Lingo Henegar dug them for me."

By the time I reached the pick-up Willis had carried the lilac bush up the hill, and the old woman had arrived at the sidewalk. "I'll just sweep up this dirt and mud," she said to me. "No need to get it on your shoes."

"Looks like you'll have some lilacs to put in a vase," I said.

"Yes! I will. Thanks to Willis Sprule. Comes every Wednesday. Rain or shine. Gives me a hand with things. He's our Sunday school teacher. Over at the Tabernacle."

Willis returned, striding down the steep terrace.

"I was just singing your praises," the woman said to Willis.

But Willis was having no part of her praise. He gave a nod in my direction, grabbed a shovel from his pick-up and headed back up the hill.

The woman shook her head, "That Willis is all duty!" she said, sweeping the last of the dirt from the walk.

Yes, Willis was apparently all about duty, I thought, because his dress slacks were covered with dirt and mud. "Enjoy those lilacs," I said and resumed my walk.

Apparently the urgency of duty was Willis's only consideration, because he'd known when he put on those slacks that he'd be planting lilac bushes. I decided Willis probably always wore whatever was handy at the moment. And I was quite certain those slacks would never find their way to the dry cleaners.

Based on Anna's writings and my encounters today, I would say that Willis was a man who was relentlessly committed to his definition of responsibility. Surely he had never missed a day of teaching school, or a Sunday morning service. No doubt his tithe envelope was never cheated— no matter the personal cost. Undoubtedly, he took care of his animals, even if he missed a meal or a night's sleep. It must have been this quality that Anna, as a young, abandoned mother, had found so reassuring. And she would not be wrong. Willis would never have left her, even though the marriage was empty and bitter. He would have done his duty.

He probably had never allowed himself to measure the rage and resentment that his addiction to duty had accumulated over the years. Nor would he would acknowledge the pleasure he derived from releasing that rage on someone caught at his mercy—someone like Anna's boy, Sam, or the young waitress at Molly's diner.

I walked several blocks, reaching the cool green shade of Cotton Rock Park, and there under a wonderful old oak tree, I met my last surprise of the day: Leah and Harlo, sitting on a picnic blanket.

Harlo was the first to see me and call, "Captain John!" She jumped up and waved excitedly, then twirled around the blanket in her pink sun dress. She wore a crown woven of clover and skipping about the grass, she might have been one of Shakespeare's elfin fairies. Leah, wearing a yellow sun dress, also wore a crown of clover, and Harlo's doll, Bill, who leaned his sagging body against a stack of books, sported a dandelion in his lapel.

"Sit," Leah said. She brushed aside the scattered clovers and patted a place on the blanket. Taking a sandwich from the picnic basket, she held it up and asked, "Have you eaten?"

"Thank you. I have," I said.

"Then you'll read to us." She motioned to the pile of books on the blanket. She was in one of her playful moods, I decided.

Harlo chose *A Child's Garden of Verses* and brought it to me. "This one, please."

I opened the book and began, "How do you like to go up in a swing, up in the air so blue?" When I finished reading the poem, I asked, "Is this a celebration?"

"It's library day!" Harlo cried, handing me a cup of lemonade.

"To good books," I said, lifting my cup for a toast.

Harlo danced through the grass, her arms held out as though she tiptoed along a high wire. Her dance ended with a run to the nearby swing. She soon sailed high into the air, singing, "Up in the air so blue, up in the air so blue."

Leah and I watched her from the blanket.

"Your celebration's made her very happy," I said.

"I have my moments," Leah said. She turned to me and asked, "What do you do all day? Down there in your cabin?"

"Fish, read, watch the river," I answered, but I was thinking, once again, how remarkably blue her eyes were—almost turquoise.

"And you're a writer," she said. "So you must be writing."

"That's what I came down here to do."

"And are you doing it?"

"I have a novel I should be working on. I haven't written for over a year."

"Oh…is that when—"

I didn't want to talk about Susan. I interrupted her and asked, "And what do you do all day in your house by the river, besides paint and raise an angel?"

"I do illustrations for a textbook company. They allow me to work at home."

"Your degree is in art, isn't it?" I asked.

She looked startled.

"Anna mentioned it, I think."

"I hope she's not writing about me in those notebooks! She thinks I need to work outside the house—meet people."

"And what do you think?"

She shrugged and began putting things back into the picnic basket and stacking the books into piles. "Help me fold the blanket," she said. We stood and folded it between us.

"Death does something to the people who are left," she said. "People like you and me. We stay in a kind of holding pattern. We don't die, but we're unwilling to let go and live."

She reached for her purse, rummaging through it. A cigarette, I thought. Time for her cigarette and her departure. I should tell her she had a habit of abrupt departures. Instead I said, "You have remarkably blue eyes."

She looked surprised. "Sometimes I think your eyes are brown. Other times they're almost amber—they're uncertain—like you."

"Uncertain?"

"Perhaps, I should say vacillating."

"I think of you as vacillating," I said.

"Let's see," she said, "you mentioned taking me out. Promised to call me. Never did."

"I'm an idiot," I said.

She smiled. "Well, that might be an understatement."

"Tonight at seven!" I said. "How's that for decisive?"

"I have a child, remember? I'll need to make some arrangements. What about this weekend?"

We agreed on Saturday night, and I helped her carry the picnic things to her car.

I walked the final blocks to the garage to pick up my jeep, thinking again of Willis and wondering if Leah knew he was in town. I tried to imagine him at the little picnic with Leah and Harlo, or sitting with Anna and me, drinking the mint tea and enjoying the rain. I could not imagine the oppression he must have inflicted on his family.

Ultimately, when the drowning happened, and their pain was unbearable, his cold self-righteous pursuit of the trite would have destroyed their remaining toleration. She had written of it in her notebook: "I am choking and cannot find any air in the rooms where he sits." So she had chosen to leave.

It had been a long day, but I wanted to talk to Tom Ferguson before I went home.

I phoned his office from town. "Can I drop by for a minute? Unofficial visit."

"Come at your own risk. Got a devil cold." He sounded miserable and sat with his head in his hands as I entered his office a few minutes later. His office occupied a couple of small rooms in an old stone building off Main Street. The rooms were in general disarray. Stacks of files covered the floor. His desk lay buried under a load of papers.

"I know. I need a secretary," he admitted, watching me as I looked around the room.

"Well, you've got an impressive wall of books," I said, trying to affirm the positive. "That's a lot of laws to learn."

"There's a pile of them alright. Aristotle warned us—the more laws we make the less justice we get. But we seem to avoid common sense whenever we can."

I grinned. "Aristotle must have been a Scotsman."

"Scotsmen don't mind having laws. They just believe they should ignore the ones that are stupid." Tom blew his nose, long and loud. Poor Tom—his nose, not easy to overlook on a good day—now glowed red.

"Sit down," he said, clearing files from a nearby chair.

"I wanted to talk about Anna McKerry," I said.

"You know she's hired me to defend her son."

I nodded.

"I can't discuss the case, John. Only in general terms."

I nodded again. "She's my student. Comes to my writing class. A good writer incidentally. She stopped by several days ago to tell me Sam had been indicted for grand larceny."

"Well they can't make that stick. They'd sooner bail the river with a creel. Statute of limitations ran out years back. Just an excuse to hold him over cause he's a flight risk. They're working on a manslaughter charge. Grand Jury's investigating evidence. Trying to see if they've got grounds. Police are holding their cards close to the vest. They've got something they're not telling. Manslaughter's a serious charge." Tom blew his nose again and looked at me questioningly, "Why are you here John?"

"I guess I care more about the family than I knew. I don't want to see Anna lose her house. I don't have a lot of money, but I'd like to put something toward the bill."

"I tried to get her to let the public defender take the case. She wouldn't hear of it. I tried to take the case *pro bono*. She wouldn't hear of that either. It's that stubborn Ozark pride. She'll lose her house first. And she may lose it for nothing. I'm not sure I can get Sam off. But I can tell you right now, she'll never take your money."

"If anybody can win the case, you can."

Tom shook his head. "If I could use my fists to whip Willis Sprule's ass, I'd have more confidence about winning."

"Anyway, thanks for talking." I walked to the door. "I need to let you get back to what you're doing."

"Yeah, I'm behind on blowing my nose."

 "Come over and have a drink of your good Scotch whiskey. It's supposed to cure a cold."

"Well, it may not cure it, but it's top of the list of satisfying failures."

Anna's Tenth Notebook

When you make more out of something than you should, Ozark folks say you're filling it with wet corn, 'cause wet corn swells up bigger than it started. "Maybe I'm filling hope with wet corn," I said to Leah, "but I believe Momma's getting well!."

"Have you asked Dr. Anderson about this?" Leah wanted to know.

"No," I said. "I'll just wait till Momma gets well. Then it won't matter when Dr. Anderson tells me it can't happen."

"Momma," Leah said, "Grandma Mayta was diagnosed with Alzheimers."

"And I don't think we should say the word Alzheimers anymore," I said. "Not around Momma. Besides, Momma did have a little stroke. So when she can't remember things, we'll just remind her she's had a stroke. You can recover from a stroke."

Leah tells me she thinks I'm walking myself to the end of a thin limb.

I tell Leah we have to keep an open mind.

Leah says, "Don't be so open minded that your brains fall out."

But I've got a reason to believe Momma's getting well. It all started with the stomach medicine. It's nothing more than a fancy antacid. Last month, when I went to refill it, the druggist gave me a little slip of paper, listing the side effects. One was confusion. Why would anybody bottle up confusion for an Alzheimers patient!

I called Momma's care giver.

"Even a simple, over-the-counter medicine can have serious consequences for an Alzheimers patient," Dorothy said. "Ask Dr. Anderson."

Dr. Anderson said, "I suggest you stop giving her the medicine and see if it makes a difference."

For the first week, I didn't see any change. On the ninth day, Momma's confusion got worse. On day ten, Momma was so confused, that I called Dr. Anderson again.

"The medication must have been addressing the Alzheimers in a way we can't evaluate," he said. "Perhaps she needs to resume taking it."

But each time I picked up the bottle and thought about confusion, I set it back down. I figured I'd wait one more day. On day eleven, I was in the bathroom, helping Momma pull up her slacks.

"I'd rather be dead," Momma said.

I stopped fussing with the zipper. "What's wrong, Momma?" I asked. Momma glared at me. "I hate …"

I tried to zip her slacks again, but she pushed my hands away.

I didn't know what to make of her. One thing was clear, she didn't want me to help her. I went straight to the phone and called Dorothy. "Momma hates me," I said. "She's in the bathroom and won't come out."

Dorothy was at my door in ten minutes. Momma was still sitting in the bathroom. Dorothy got Momma's slacks zipped and helped her to her room. I could hear them talking. After a while, Dorothy came to the kitchen where I was washing dishes. Mostly, I was waiting.

"Taking your mother off the medication seems to have brought her into a new level of awareness. With it has come humiliation. She doesn't hate you, Anna. She just needs some independence. I think it's important for her to go to the bathroom alone," Dorothy said.

"She could fall. And she can't even get her pants zipped."

"It's important to let her try. Taking her off the medication might allow her to execute new levels of functioning."

And Momma did get better. A lot better. She went to the bathroom by herself. She didn't need a diaper in the daytime. The wheel chair was put away, and she could walk all the way across the kitchen, before reaching for the back of a chair. Zoe paid to have Momma's piano brought down from Springville, and Momma sat right down and played "Golden Bells."

That's when I decided that maybe Momma didn't have Alzheimers. Besides, Momma didn't eat well when she lived alone. Maybe her troubles were a combination of the stroke, the medicine and not eating good food. I went right out and bought Momma a bag full of vitamins from that health food store down on River Drive.

Maybe I was filling the story with more wet corn, but a black hole was swallowing my Momma. She was living in a place where doors closed that she couldn't open, where the lights went out on important moments, and words melted like snowflakes in the river. So it was easy to grab hold on a sliver of hope and hang tight.

Dorothy tried to warn me. "You need to consider that her improvements are limited. Your mother is simply recovering abilities the medication prevented. Do remember once she's reached her plateau, the Alzheimers will continue its work of degeneration." I didn't tell Dorothy that I no longer believed Momma had Alzheimers. I wanted to prove it first.

Part of proving it meant taking charge of Momma's life. Momma liked to choose her clothes each morning. She liked to stand in front of the closet doors, deciding what to put on, taking out first one thing, then another. But Momma had a way of picking the very thing I was hoping against. If I was taking her to the doctor, she'd put together a collection that said, "Hello Dr. Anderson. I'm a lunatic!" If Dorothy was coming over, Momma would put on something that said, "Anna neglects me." So I began deciding what Momma wore. I'd help her with her bath, and then I'd lay out her clothes on the bed. Momma would point toward the closet door, and I'd pretend I didn't see. I'd slide a blouse over her head and have her dressed and on her way to the breakfast table before she had time to sort out what happened. I'd see the look on her face, like there was some disappointment she just couldn't remember. I'd try to make up for it by giving her a nice breakfast and a good helping of vitamins.

But there were days when the word "Alzheimers" whispered that it hadn't gone anywhere. Like the day Momma got her signals crossed. She was sitting by the telephone when it rang. She took her hearing aid out of her ear, laid it on the table, slid her glasses on and said, "Hello."

I should have been able to laugh at that. But I stepped in front of Momma so Dorothy couldn't see what happened. I reckon I was stepping in front of Momma more than I was willing to admit.

On Tuesdays, Ruth came for speech therapy. Momma hated to see that stack of cards in Ruth's hand. It meant she'll have to hunt hard for answers she might not be able to find.

Momma tried to escape:

"I'm…tired," she told Ruth. "I…"

But Ruth took charge. "What is this?" Ruth asked, holding up a picture of a hairbrush.

"Oh…it's a…"

"A hairbrush," Ruth answered. "What do we do with a hairbrush?"

Momma rubbed her hair.

"Yes," Ruth answered, "We brush our hair."

The painful questions continued. Momma got more miserable. "I've have… tramples," Momma said.

"Troubles," I said. "You have troubles."

"Troubles," Momma repeated.

The stack of cards continued.

If Momma got the answer right, I cheered.

Today Momma said "square" instead of "rectangle." So I explained to Ruth, "Anything with four sides was always a square to Momma."

After she finished the cards, Ruth took me aside.

"Your mother does better, Anna, when you're not in the room."

"Really?"

"She wants to please you a little too much," Ruth said.

This sent me outside with my cheeks burning. I was making things harder for Momma? She wants to please you a little too much. Momma wanted my approval! That idea wouldn't fit into my head anywhere. Momma was sliding down into a black hole, and she was worried about not disappointing me! That put a squeeze on my heart, for sure. I had to save Momma!

But all my efforts came to a showdown. Momma was sitting at her little dressing table. She likes to sit there each morning, combing her hair and putting on her lipstick. She puts on strings of beads or sprays of perfume, usually too much of both. This morning she found the hair clips. She clipped a hand full of them in her hair. Some hung in the front, some on the sides. They swung in all directions, each time she turned her head.

Leah had been painting Momma's portrait in watercolors. "You need to come with me, Momma," I said. "Leah is ready to paint." I took the clips out of Momma's hair and led her to the living room. The early morning sun filled the room with light. Momma looked beautiful sitting in her chair by the window, the sun shining on her white hair. Leah stood at her easel, holding a palette in one hand and her brush in the other. I sat on the couch where I could see the portrait and still read to Harlo, soon as she finished sorting through her stack of books.

Leah was spreading pale lavender on the paper. "Her white hair allows maximum transparency," Leah was saying, mostly to herself. "The light reflects from the lavenders and blues."

"Your hair is beautiful in the picture, Momma."

"It's message," Momma said.

"Messy," I corrected.

"Messy," she repeated.

"But it's beautiful in the painting. Come look, Momma." I lead her to the easel.

"You made me good," Momma said, touching the picture.

That gave me an idea. "Guess what, Momma! I'm taking you to the beauty shop! We'll get you a permanent! Your hair will be pretty as the picture."

I called for an appointment. The girl on the phone said I could bring Momma right in. In twenty minutes, we were driving down River Road. The sun was shining yellow and the river running blue. We were going to town to get Momma some pretty hair, and Momma was getting better. I was sure of it.

We reached town and pulled into Sylvia's shop. I helped Momma out of the car and shut her door. I was nearly inside, before I saw Momma wasn't behind me. She was still standing by the car, talking to the window. She was saying, "Momma? Momma, are you coming with us?"

It took me a moment to understand. Momma was talking to her own white-haired reflection in the car window. Worse than that, she thought she was talking to Grandma Poinselot. Grandma Poinselot's been dead over forty years!

I took her by the arm. "Come on, Momma." But Momma kept looking back at the car. "There's nobody there," I said. I should have faced the truth about things, right there in the parking lot. Instead I said, "We have an appointment. We have to hurry."

Once we were inside the shop, she seemed to forget about Grandma Poinselot.

Sylvia Henegar, Lingo's sister, was leaning across the fancy counter, full of bright bottles.

Momma looked around at the glass shelves filled with shiny nail polish and bottles of shampoo. "I like it here," she said.

"Just what a girl needs," Sylvia said and smiled. "There's nothing more important than your hair."

"Your hair and your shoes," Momma said.

"Now that's true, isn't it?" Sylvia took Momma by the arm and led her to the shampoo bowl. "Just sit here, Mrs. Groves."

Momma was making conversation. Over and over she was saying the right things.

"Momma plays piano!" I said. "She's played piano since she was five years old."

"I love the piano," Sylvia said. "What's your favorite song, Mrs. Groves?"

There was a long silence and then Momma said, "I'm stroked."

"Well, Momma's had a stroke," I explained. "But she's making a good come back. People get over strokes," I said.

"They sure do," Sylvia said.

Sylvia didn't need to know about the Alzheimers, I decided. We were going to live like Momma was well.

Things went smooth all afternoon. So when Sylvia started to comb out Momma's hair, I thought I could run to Lushbaugh's grocery and pick up a quart of milk. Lushbaugh's is only one block from the beauty shop. I'd be back in just a few minutes.

But when I got back, Momma wasn't sitting in Sylvia's chair.

"Where's Momma?" I asked.

Sylvia was bent over the shampoo bowl with a new customer.

"Why she was just here. Oh, she said something about her Momma in the car."

Momma was looking for Grandma Poinselot! I told myself she couldn't have gone far. But I couldn't find her anywhere. Only Momma could have mistaken Luther Merbaum's black Mercedes for my old Ford. She had opened the door and climbed right into the back seat. Luther came out of the bank, started his car, and never even noticed Momma. He drove half way home before Momma thought of something to say. He had no idea who she was, and that's how Momma wound up at the Cotton Rock Police Station.

The whole thing took only about twenty minutes. But in that twenty minutes, I ate a whole pound of wet corn. I knew I'd have to line up with the truth, soon as I found Momma. I called the police station from Sylvia's. They told me that Luther Merbaum was just bringing Momma through the door.

I went right down to the police station, got Momma and took her home. I settled her at the kitchen table and got her a drink of water. She was still shaking. I put my arms around her. "Momma, I'm so sorry about today."

"I was arrested," Momma said.

"Oh no, Momma. You didn't do anything wrong. You just got lost. It was my fault." I tried to get her mind on something else. "Momma, your hair's so nice. You look beautiful, just like Leah's picture." I looked around for the watercolor. It was still on Leah's easel. The paper hadn't been tacked to a frame, yet. I took it to Momma. She held the picture in her hand.

"You made me nice," she said.

The phone rang. It was Sylvia, calling from the beauty shop. I walked out of ear shot, so I could tell her what had happened. I turned back to check on Momma. She had picked up the scissors and was cutting coupons from a magazine. I kept talking to Sylvia and checking on Momma. But Momma was still pretty upset—picking up the scissors and laying them down, picking them up and laying them down. She took up a whole hand full of coupons and cut across them without even looking.

"Wait, Momma," I called. "I'll have to call you back, Sylvia. Wait, Momma, let me see what you're cutting."

But it was too late. She had picked up the watercolor and cut a deep gash across the face.

"You cut Leah's picture! It's ruined!" I said.

"Should we call Zoe?" Momma asked.

"No. We don't need Zoe! Damn it!"

"My Momma never. . ."

"I know. Your Momma never swore. Well Dade swore, Momma. How bout that? Dade swore all the time!"

"Dade tried …"

"How do you know, Momma? You were always in bed! You just left me and Zoe with Dade. Just 'cause Zoe did all right, I didn't. I didn't do all right, Momma!"

Momma looked terrible. I had to get hold of myself. I turned away from her and began washing up the dishes. Momma was far too sick and old for me to have a showdown now. I just kept washing dishes. Slamming them a little too hard into the drainer.

"I… sizzled the picture," Momma said.

"You cut the picture, Momma," I said. "It's not sizzled. It's cut."

"I sizzled the picture," Momma said again.

"Make up the word, Momma. Make up any word you want," I said, and I didn't say it nice.

"I cut the picture," Momma said.

I didn't answer. Didn't brag on her for getting the word right.

"I cut the picture," she repeated, and then she said, "Anna cut me."

Well, those words stepped right into my soul.

I went to her and put my arms around her old, thin shoulders. "I'm so sorry, Momma."

Her sweet hand patted my back.

"I was awful, Momma."

"You were awful," she repeated.

I sat down at the table beside her. She picked up the slashed water color. "You can fix me."

"No, Momma. No more fixing."

You'd think when someone else is wearing your same mistake, you'd recognize it. I guess I was too busy proving the differences between Momma and me, I never thought to see the resemblance. Momma's heart was broken when Daddy died. Mine was broken when Jake left. Neither of us did too well with a broken heart. Momma married Dade, and I married Willis. Not much difference, really. Willis was just Dade with an education.

Later as I put Momma to bed, I told her again how sorry I was. I slid the sleeping vest over her head.

"I hate this," Momma said.

"I know," I said, tying the straps of the jacket to the bed. "It keeps you from getting up in the night. Wandering around. Those stairs could really hurt you."

I gave her another hug. "I love you, Momma." I went back to the kitchen and sat looking at the watercolor, studying Momma's face. I was surprised to find my own face there. I had always thought I looked like Daddy—-or at least like the pictures of Daddy. But I saw from the painting that I was Daddy's features, draped over Momma's bones. What is a child, after all, but love-making turned flesh and blood, the smile of the man, or the eyes of the woman, pooling like paints in the water glass, pooled and permanent, no matter what becomes of the marriage.

I reckon I've pooled things in my heart: Momma's life and Leah's, little Harlo's and now Sam's, like paints in a glass. Everybody's broken dreams are mixed up in my own. Sometimes when I think I'm fixing Momma's pain, maybe I'm fixing my own.

I can't separate the colors anymore. I see it in Dorothy's face. She would like to tell me something, but can't. I see it in Leah's eyes after we've had words. I see it in Tom Ferguson's eyes when I say that Sam's got to be set free. I guess I always have a little river of fear, running just below the dishes I'm washing or the clothes I'm folding, fear that I'll never be able to fix all the broken dreams. That night I came to know that I can't fix my Momma. It's her life, and she's just trying to live out Alzheimers the best she can.

Momma had decided to stand her ground. And she hadn't forgotten the next morning. When I opened the door to her bedroom, she was standing at the window looking out.

"How did you get out of bed?" I asked. Then I saw that the straps to the sleeping jacket had been cut. The jacket lay on the floor and the scissors on the night stand. She must have slipped them into her pocket when she was cutting out coupons the night before.

"Well, I guess this is what you call, cutting the apron strings, huh Momma?"

"I dressed myself," Momma said.

I looked at her, standing there so proud and tall for all the world to see, wearing her slip on the outside of her dress. All day Momma wore the slip. I didn't correct her mistake, either. I didn't say a word.

Lucy's Angel Gossip

The McCrackens was the first family in town to have a toilet in the house. Jim McCracken ran the post office for half the county. Had the only regular paycheck in Cotton Rock at the time.

A number of us was invited down to see the new toilet. (There wasn't a whole lot to do in the hills, so you never passed up an invitation.) I never seen a porcelain toilet. We stood around saying how shiny it was and comfortable looking. After giving it proper regard, the men took off for the front porch, and the women sat round the kitchen table. Little Rosie served us tea.

Rosie McCracken had a new tea set with real little china cups. Got it from the Sears and Roebuck Catalog. She took to bringing us each a cup a tea. It was only water, but we pretended, cause she's only in Kindergarten, and we didn't want to spoil her play. When all the women drank their little cups, Rosie took to serving the men out on the porch. Rosie was takin' orders for seconds when it come to her momma to ask her where she's getting the water. Turns out it was out of the new toilet bowl.

Mrs. McCracken turned bright as a sumac leaf. She's quick to tell us they hadn't used that new toilet hardly at all. She said they was in such a habit they'd be halfway down the path to the outhouse 'fore it come to them that they had a toilet in the house. So the water in that bowl was almost clean as the well. But, most of us was feeling yeller as a summer squash. Ever body went home pretty quick after that.

Next day the McCrackens come bringing their sorghum to be ground. My daddy owned a cane mill. All the neighbors brought their cane to Daddy. It was my job to ride the horse round and round the grinding stone. That poor horse walked his whole life and never got twenty feet from where he started. I don't know as I got much further.

After we got a load of cane ground up, Daddy'd build a hickory fire. He'd put a pan of cane juice on to cook. It'd start out white and cook up to red-gold molasses. We called it long sweetning.

Short sweetning was the name for store-bought sugar. But we really didn't need to know it cause we couldn't afford it no way. Most folks ate long sweetning, and they paid for the grinding by swapping side meat or pecans or something needful.

Anyway, the McCrackens come bringing their cane to Daddy to be ground. When it was cooked to molasses, McCracken went to pay. He had side meat and head cheese in the wagon. But Daddy just couldn't forget the new toilet. To Daddy the toilet in the house was like a mouse in the cornmeal—no johnnycake was safe.

I don't know what Daddy said, but McCracken left with the side meat and head cheese still in the wagon. Directly McCracken come back with a load of field hay for Daddy's horse. Said he figured the horse didn't have much opinion on toilet bowls.

After a few years most everybody got an indoor toilet. Daddy had to reconsider his opinions of toilets or go outta the molasses business all together.

Yes sir! Rosie's angel must have followed behind all those teacups of toilet water with a grin spreading from one wing to the other. I reckon she called for an angel huddle soon as she hit the playground next morning.

Thoughts from the Back Porch   August 1996

The first time I saw Emmett on the riverbank, he looked like Paddington Bear with fishing boots. He was in his late fifties, and his graying hair was usually stuffed under a battered, canvas fishing hat. He was a big, round man. When he laughed his grin took in his whole face, pushed his cheeks into round balls that shut his eyes and opened his mouth to a row of teeth the color of chewing tobacco.

He often hung around after class to talk about fishing, and I was happy to get his advice on bait or the best places to find browns or walleye. He usually sat at a back table, his big hands clamped around his notebook, which sometimes gave off the scent of fish when I read its pages.

Today, when I passed him, he was sitting on a slab of cotton rock at the river's edge. The only thing that made Emmett happier than fishing was talking about fishing. I pulled in alongside him, cut the motor on the *Rosalee* and prepared to hear his latest fishing story.

"How's fishing today, Emmett?"

"Haven't done any yet. Just sittin' here in the sun dryin' out."

"Get baptized?" I asked.

"There's always some ole boy, just hooked a fish when the horn blows, and he can't let go. He's sure he's got a trophy fish, and he just won't let go."

"Sounds like a story to me," I said.

"Get out of that boat of yours and take a place on the throne." Emmett patted the rock where he was sitting, and then stretched his arms out as though blessing the water. "You're in the presence of trout."

By the time I took a seat beside Emmett, he'd dug a thermos from his backpack and poured us each a cup of coffee. His clothes were truly soaked; his wet shirt clung to the curve of his round belly, and water dripped from the legs of his jeans.

"It happened a few minutes ago. The river was rising up around an ole boy from Texas. Down here fishing for browns. The current was shoving down hard from the dam. He was leaning like a drunk tree, and still he wasn't giving up. Reel was down to the bare spool. Must of had a hundred-and-eighty feet of line out. But once that fifty-degree water hit him where the sun don't shine, he started to come around." Emmett snorted and his eyes shut tight with his laughter.

"It isn't easy to wrestle a man that's stuck to a fishing pole," Emmett continued. "Thing is a fella can get knocked off his footing and ride right off like a cork." Emmett stopped to take a drink of his coffee. "That ole boy just thought he had a fish. It was the other way round, and that fish would a taken him all the way to Little Rock before he would have come to himself. You got to know when to let go of a thing! So I got baptized convincing him of the fact." Emmett chuckled. "You drink another cup?" he asked.

I held out my cup, and he poured each of us more coffee.

We sat in silence for a while, sipping coffee and watching the river.

"See that rock over there, just sticking up?" He pointed a finger toward the far bank. "There's a beautiful brown sitting there. You can bet on it. I try to tell beginners how important it is to put your plug right close to the sweet spot. Not sort of by, but right beside it. You don't ask a pretty girl for a date from across the room. If you're serious, you sit down right beside her."

I nodded.

"You got a pretty girl in your life?" Emmett asked.

"Not exactly…what kind of bait would you use for the brown you pointed out?"

"Beetle spins, pork frogs and crankbaits are all good this time of year," he answered. "But like I said, you can't be wishy-washy about placing the bait. You got to mean business."

"Fish or get out of the boat," my Granddad always said.

"That's it all right," Emmett said. "Now you take that pretty girl that's not exactly in your life. Two bits says you're not serious about catching her. There's something you need to let go of first. Most of life's about knowing what to let go of and when."

The idea of letting go reminded Emmett of his recent dunking, and he inspected his clothes once again. They had stopped dripping water.

"Yes sir, you got to know when to let go. My daddy had a pack of blue-tick hound dogs, four of them. Kept them chained up in the yard. When Daddy was ready to go hunting, he'd come out and loop all four chains onto one ring. Those dogs knew they's going out after a coon, and they'd be yelping and pulling on that ring. Took a strong man to hold them in check.

"My brothers thought it'd be a good laugh to hand the ring to me. I was only six or seven. One minute I was standing upright. Next minute I was on my belly, stretched out like a buckskin hide, hands over my head, hanging on to that ring like I was welded on. Couldn't have laid me out any flatter. I slid along, raking off every tulip and tomater vine between me and the back door. If that yard hadn't been fenced, I might have been drug clear to Canada. Cause it just never come to me to let go."

All my brothers were yelling, "Let go! Let go!" But once the mind is set on a wrong idea, it's just not open to suggestion. There's nothing left to do but tackle the body. That's just what my brother, Ned, did. He met me coming around the house and fell on the dogs with a full body slam. Slowed them dogs to a halt. He had to pry my fingers off that ring." Emmett was laughing again, his eyes disappearing into his cheeks.

"I was just laying in a moan," Emmett said. "I'd filed off every knob and ridge on my body. My daddy come on the scene then and give my brothers the what for. Then he turned to me and says, 'Son, you got to learn the difference between letting go without a try, and letting go before you die.' Anyway there was nothing to do today, but to tackle that old boy and baptize him in fifty degree water. It come to him pretty quick, then, that he'd like to get outta the river."

I handed my empty coffee cup back to Emmett and ordered him to get his story into his notebook.

"Yes, sir, I will. And you might think about putting the bait closer to that pretty girl."

"Now, Emmett, what makes you so sure there's a pretty girl in my life?"

"My wife Lottie knows everything that goes on in Cotton Rock. You sit by a pretty gal on a picnic blanket in the park, she'll start embroidering dishtowels for your wedding."

"Thanks for the warning."

Emmett chuckled.

"My wife died—little over a year ago," I ventured.

"Heard about that."

"I don't know…maybe there's something I need to let go of—like you said."

A big brown leaped from the water, in the very spot Emmett had predicted.

"Better get your pole, Emmett."

I climbed back into the *Rosalee*, and left Emmett casting from the rock. That big brown would be sitting on Emmett's dinner plate tonight.

Anna's Eleventh Notebook

Today the sun is shining warm on my blue cabinet doors, and I am cooking soup and making bread. Making bread busies the hands, allows the mind to rummage. Knead, fold, turn the dough. Knead, fold, turn the dough. I am thinking how to remind Leah about the job at the gallery.

I add more flour to the dough. I showed her the newspaper ad a few days ago. I tried to do it friendly-like. She just glanced at it and laid it on the table.

The dough is sticky. It takes practice to get the dough right. Too much flour means a heavy loaf. Not enough means a dough with no substance. I hear Leah behind me, pouring coffee. So I say offhand, "The ad said they're taking applications through Friday. That's today."

"If I wanted to call, Momma, I would have."

I can tell by her voice, I've made her mad. The easy feeling's gone out of the room. I figure I may as well say what I think. "You need to get out of the house—meet people."

"Stop trying to fix me, Momma!" She's raising her voice.

"I'm not trying to fix you." Now I'm raising my voice.

She takes her coffee and leaves the kitchen. Then she comes back, 'cause she's thought of something. "Notice the word fix, Momma. Fixing me is your fix!"

"My fix," I say. "So now I'm an addict." I smack the ball of dough down on the cabinet. Knead and turn. I hear the back door slam. Leah is going to the yard. Harlo is there, swinging.

I think how Harlo loves the bread when it's warm from the oven. She will spread it with butter and fill her little mouth with its goodness. I think how the bread and a cup of tea will bring a sweet moment to my Momma's life. The bread is one moment I can fix. A little fix. I add more flour, knead and fold.

"A food fix," I say aloud. An ancient woman habit, passed down. I think about holding Sam to the breast for the first time, his little mouth searching, knowing how to nurse without being taught. My body answers, without being taught, making milk from an ancient recipe. I fill his little tummy, little baby eyes nearly crossed with the heavy sweetness of sleep—milk drunk we called it. Feeding—an ancient fix.

I know Leah is too old for me to mother her. But what am I to do? I talk to God about it. I knead the dough and talk to God, and my table of flour is an altar. I'm a high-priest Momma. "God, you see Leah sitting and watching life slide by like the river outside. You see her paint those lost girls in the dark shadows, little Marys who all died the day Leah was supposed to be in charge. You see Leah sitting and staring while life goes on down the road. Cause Leah is afraid to try again."

Lingo Henegar who cuts my grass, wrecked his jeep last year. I saw it parked in front of his house on Maple Street. You knew it was a jeep, because you could still see the canvas top and the squatty body, but no one had to tell you it had been in a wreck. If we could see each other's souls, we'd know at a glance who's had a crash and how serious it is. Lingo spent a lot of time and money trying to fix that old jeep. He once gave me a ride to town. That jeep rides pretty good on the level. But Lingo says when he takes it up Buckeye Hill, even the paint job starts to cry.

I stop and stir the soup on the stove. I watch it simmer. I add the vegetables. I peel the carrots that Harlo loves, and I talk to God about Harlo. I add potatoes for Momma, and I talk to God about Momma. I add the herbs I know Leah likes, and I tell God how Leah needs to get her courage back. I stir the soup, and I check on the bread.

The dough is growing elastic. Knead and fold. The dough has a spring of its own now—it's pushing back against my hands. That means it's ready. I put the ball of dough in a clean bowl, cover it with a towel. It'll take time to rise. I take up a broom to sweep the flour, but I stop. I've had a thought so heavy I need a chair to help me hold its weight. I sit for awhile.

It's come to me that Leah's problem is just the backside of my own. In fact, it's Momma's problem hived off in a forked stick. Momma went to bed and quit. Leah quit standing up, and I can't quit. Can't try, can't quit trying, both are forks hooked up on the same stick. Leah is afraid to try, and I am afraid to quit trying. And that's our fix.

I turn the soup down to a low simmer.

I get my purse and drive to town. I sit down in the Library with the Oxford English Dictionary, cause Leah says that's got the history of every word. I look up the work "fix." I read what the word was doing in the year 1590: "To set one's eyes upon an object." A few centuries later its meaning is, "To unwaveringly set one's affections." Like a pointing dog set on a bird, I reckon. My nose is set on fixing things.

"Fastened, permanent," the Oxford says. Leah and Momma and I are all fastened. Momma laid down when Daddy died, Leah, stands and stares off, and I keep busy. Momma's slipping off her fix with Alzheimer. But I figure it's going to take some kind of blow to knock Leah and me loose from ours.

I figure the blow might come through Willis. I met him in the hallway at the police station. Cora Eckert was hanging on his arm—limping from her bunions. Anyway, Cora hasn't had a date since her husband died, and not because she wasn't trying.

You can bet Willis is up to no good. I'm nervous about my notebooks. Even though I've been careful what I read aloud in class, it's been enough to let Cora know I'm writing about my life. Anyway I told Willis, "Wasn't enough that you made the boy miserable the whole time he was under your roof. You had to spend the last fifteen years trackin' him down for more."

"Truth needs to be told," Willis said.

"I reckon you'll be the first in line to tell it," I said.

"I'll be talking to the Grand Jury first of the week," Willis said.

"And just what will you tell them, Willis?"

"That I found his duffel bag by the river, myself. Gave it to the sheriff fifteen years ago. You won't like what they found in that bag. It's been locked up in the evidence room all these years. Till they found Sam's body, the case was never closed. Sam's alive, and this case is going to trial."

Looks like Willis's fix is finding a scapegoat—and Sam is ripe for the sacrifice. I visit Sam every day. Today, I met Phil Hutchins as I was leaving the jail. He renewed an old friendship with Sam the weekend Phil spent in jail. Little too much to drink, I reckon.

His visits help pass the days for Sam. I figure anybody who will visit you in jail must be more than a strawberry friend—somebody who just shows up 'cause it's the season and shortcake's likely.

Thoughts from the Back Porch   August 1996

I'm sitting on the back porch with my morning coffee reviewing Hawthorne's *Scarlet Letter* for my fall class. I've been intrigued with the parallels between Hester Prynn's life and Anna's. The little society of Puritans fastened the ignominious "A" to Hester's breast to signify adultery. Anna, with her own hand, has fastened shame to nearly the whole of her life.

However, in Hester's case it was not the birthing of a baby out of wedlock or the loss of acceptance that proved unbearable. It was the realization that she had betrayed herself in her marriage. Hawthorne writes that she "deemed it her crime most to be repented of that she had ever endured the lukewarm grasp" of Chillingworth's hand.

Here the parallel abruptly ceases. Anna's anguish doesn't seem to be occupied with "the lukewarm grasp of Willis's hand." Instead, her anguish is that Willis has harmed her children.

It is as if Anna doesn't allow personal dreams—ones that do not include her children. It is as though the young Anna, like her town of Sugar Gum, lies buried at the bottom of Marble Head Lake. Or as Anna wrote of herself, "I'm laying low under an unnamed swamp." Whoever married Willis and raised three children is someone who lives only for the lives of others: her mother, little Harlo, and Leah. But her mother has Alzheimer, and Harlo is a child, so most of Anna's energy seems focused on Leah's life. I was thinking about the pressure this must bring to Leah, when a telephone call confirmed my speculation.

"Would you be willing to get me out of the house for awhile?" Leah asked.

"Sure," I said.

"I'd just as soon keep this from Momma," she said. "Can you come in your boat? I'll be at the blackberry patch—where you found Harlo."

It felt good that Leah had called me for help. Our date had gone well, but I hadn't seen her for over a week. On my way to the dock I realized that the sky was turning gray in a hurry. Rain seemed certain. I went back to the house, grabbed two raincoats and a blanket and rolled the blanket inside one of raincoats.

Leah was pacing the shore when I reached her.

"I hate boats," she said absently, as she climbed in. She realized her mistake and added, "Because of the drowning. But I appreciate being out of the house."

"House getting too small?"

"I need to cool down," she said. "Momma means well. It's her Argus eyes."

"Argus from *Odysseus* or the one turned into a peacock by the gods?"

"They both kept close watch didn't they?"

"Oh."

"I shouldn't be living at home," she added.

We headed downstream for a mile or so. I had in mind finding a quiet cove, maybe sitting on the blanket and talking. Raindrops sprinkled across the water. I was about to suggest we go upstream to my cabin when the storm broke loose.

Leah called out something, but the rain on the water drowned the sound of her voice. "We'd better find some shelter," I yelled and tossed her one of the raincoats. I turned the motor on high and headed for the little stream Alex and I had fished.

The rain tore down in sheets. We reached the sandy beach and jumped out, pulling the boat ashore. "I know a place—a fraidy hole," I yelled through the pounding rain.

I grabbed the other raincoat with the blanket rolled inside and caught Leah's hand. We hurried down the path together.

We reached the fraidy hole and entered the momentary darkness. I unrolled the raincoat and took out the blanket. We spread it on the mossy floor, and dropped down wet and laughing.

"We're soaked," she said.

"You said you need to cool down."

She grinned and nodded. The light from the open door filtered softly through the shadowed interior. Outside, the rain drummed on the hillside around us. The sweet fragrance of mint hung heavy in the damp air.

"Wild mint," I said, nodding toward the leaves growing around the entrance.

"Smells yummy," she said.

There were raindrops on her face. I touched her cheek lightly and smoothed them away.

"Your hands are spacious," she said. "I noticed—when you held my hand."

"Spacious?" I asked.

"Roomy—lots of room for my hand."

It's strange the way people will keep talking, even when they hardly know what they're saying—about the rain, or the soft moss around the blanket. Because what they are thinking is how they are finally going to kiss someone they've known for some time they were going to kiss.

I had known that I would kiss her when I rolled up the blanket and put it into the boat, though I had promised myself I wouldn't. I kissed her again, and again, as one might hurry to eat before the vow to diet has time to overrule, allowing the sweet goodness of the food to suspend all reason.

I kept thinking I'd lose her any moment, that she would be leaving the way she always left. Yet I was no less tormented with the possibility that she might stay—worse, I hated facing the reckless hunger of my own body. I didn't want to get in over my head.

As though on cue, she pulled back.

"What?" I asked. "Let me guess. It's time for a cigarette or time for you to leave or maybe both?" The disdain in my voice was unmistakable.

"I was just going to take off this wet rain coat," she said. And now there was an equal edge in her voice, "Actually, I was just thinking it was time for you to be caustic."

A fight is an easy thing, if two people need one, need an exit. It meant Leah could say, "The storm has passed—I'd like to go."

And I could say, "Whatever you want," as though it was her problem. I could roll up the blanket roughly and head back to the boat, as though I hadn't really wanted to go.

She walked in front of me—rapid strides—heels digging into the sand. When she reached the boat, she peeled off the raincoat as though it were my unwanted representative and flung it onto the seat. She climbed into the boat and stood in the bow, breathing hard. Her blouse, wet from the rain, clung to her breasts. She traced my stare, and turned sharply away, pulling at her blouse, and dropping onto the seat.

To hell with her and her breasts. To hell with her drinking problem and her chain smoking and her abrupt departures.

We reached the blackberry patch, and I angled the boat toward shore. She stood, even before the boat had reached her dock and climbed out into the shallow water. "Thanks for the boat ride." She flung the words over her shoulder, striding up the bank.

"You hate boat rides," I called after her.

I sat, watching her go.

When she'd reached the path, she turned and called down, "You chose the right spot—a fraidy hole."

"Look, I came down here to do a little fishing and—"

"By all means, catch every gill-bearing idiot in the idiot river," she said cutting me off. This time she kept going.

She phoned later. Her voice was calm, careful. "Look—I was upset with Momma. I should have taken a long walk by myself. Let's stop the war. I've been thinking. . .the timing is all wrong. You need to write, and I need to be looking for a job in town. Pick up more hours."

I agreed.

We said all the courteous things people say when they don't expect to be around one another again. I felt relieved. I was free of the entanglement. Free to sit in an empty cabin, watching the gray afternoon sky turn to dusk, admitting that the summer was nearly over.

Anna's Twelfth Notebook

I wasn't surprised to receive a subpoena from the Grand Jury. With Willis involved and Cora on his arm, it was only a matter of time. I didn't figure the hearing would amount to much. I was wrong.

Sometimes a single word can change things forever. The thing is, once you hear a word, you can't unhear it. Some words burn a deep hole in the mind. I knew a burning word was coming at me when the Grand Jury said, "Mrs. McKerry, were you aware…"

There's a certain smell to the truth before you see it standing out in the open. You get little whiffs of it for years, and you move the bed and look or pull open a drawer, but you can't see what the thing might be. I once had a grass snake come in the house. Crawled up the hinge side of the door casing. Lined itself along the crack just as I shut the door. Wasn't a week before I was hunting everywhere for something dead, but it takes light to see a hidden thing. One afternoon, when the door was standing wide, the sun caught a sparkle of the snake scales.

I've been trying to make sense of the drowning for the last fifteen years. Sam was swimming in ten different creeks when he was in grade school. He was a fine swimmer. I guess a Momma will welcome a hundred excuses before she's ready for the truth, if that truth is against her child.

Now I'm sitting here trying to take little glimpses at the noonday sun. "Cocaine," that's what they said down at the courthouse. "Mrs. McKerry, were you aware that your son was using cocaine—that he was selling cocaine?" My mind got caught on that word and couldn't take the next step.

I know they saw that I wasn't trying to dodge the question. I believe they saw that my mind had just gone blind. I wished I was wearing Grandma Poinselot's apron. When she pulled her apron over her face, we knew not to disturb her, because she was praying. But there was no hiding place in the courtroom, no way to get hold of God. I had to sit there in full stare of everybody and try to make sense of what I'd just heard. I said no to the question. "No, I didn't know about the cocaine." I wasn't much help to the Grand Jury after that. They could see I was lost. They excused me pretty quick.

Maggie Johnson was our neighbor back in Sugar Gum. She was born nearly blind, could only see shadows of light and dark. She was thirty-six years old when her husband turned over in his sleep and hit her square in the eye with his elbow. The pain set her to crying like a child. Next day, she was out in her back shed when her sight came back. First thing she saw was the head of a mop. She had no earthly idea what it was, till she reached out and touched it. "Mop!" she said to herself. From that moment on, she had to relearn the world. Nothing made sense, till she touched it and tied up the present to the past. That's what I'm doing now. Tying up fifteen years of thinking things were what they seemed. It's amazing how much sense things make in the dark. Once you think you know what a thing is, everything seems to bear it out. A lie can seem to have all kinds of proof.

I've been sitting at my desk all afternoon, trying to understand the truth. The words blistering through my mind wrote themselves into a little poem:

The mind when caught
cannot escape
the growing light
and forming shape,
which turns full glare,
and states its name,
and nothing more
remains the same.

I've filled twelve of these notebooks with my life. Like I said in the first one, I'm writing to figure things out, my part and God's part. The first glimmer of light is clear: Mary's death might not have anything to do with Rayley Larkin drinking too much. It may not have anything to do with the alarm failing to sound. Maybe Sam just made the worst decision of his life. I figure that the cocaine will be the reason Sam didn't or couldn't rescue Mary. And I'm trying to get myself ready to know the truth.

When you spend years climbing up a long-time commitment, revving your engine most of the way, sometimes getting out and pushing, telling yourself it's all gonna be worth it, believing it the whole way up the hill, there better be something good waiting at the top. Not a bridge that somebody washed out fifteen years before you got there.

The day Sheriff Milby came to tell me that Sam and Mary were drowned was the day I reached the top of the hill and saw there was nowhere to go. It was like I stood outside myself, watching myself—searching around like a crazy woman. Fifteen years of trying just washed out and gone.

And the thing I'm trying to see, right in the middle of the ball of light is this: Maybe God didn't shoot the hole in my heart after all. Maybe I'm the one holding the gun. Maybe that's why I've been working so hard to fix things—'cause if I can't, it feels like I'll be sitting on a hot seat way worse than Dade's and there won't be a way off. I've got a son locked up for manslaughter. I've got a daughter who carries such a weight of guilt she might never climb out of the wine bottle. I've got a granddaughter who gets an angel momma one day and a lost momma the next and has no daddy at all.

My guilt has found me. Like an old, blue-tick hound whose unfailing nose has been trailing me for years, he's treed my shame. And I'm remembering how my son was in the field with Willis, and I was in the kitchen canning a hundred jars of beans, and there were rows of corn and beets waiting in a garden row, long as the river, and my son was in the field with Willis, and I was washing baskets of clothes that cycled back to be folded or washed and folded again, and my son was in the field with Willis, and I was busy tending two more babies in the house. So, I'm sitting here, and the old, blue-tick hound is throwing back his head and howling.

Leah's just come in. She asked about the trial, and I have to tell her about the cocaine. I don't think she was as surprised as I was.

"I think maybe the cocaine is the reason Sam couldn't save Mary," I said.

Leah didn't say anything. I was feeling pretty low, so I kept picking at things. "I thought if I was a good mother, everything would work out," I said. "I was determined not to go to bed like Momma."

"That's a pretty low standard for your life," Leah said. She went to the cupboard and took out a bottle of wine.

"What are you saying, Leah?"

"Your goal as a mother was to simply stay out of bed!" she answered.

"Feels like I'm on Dade's hot seat," I said.

"I've heard this all before, Momma," Leah said. She poured her glass full of wine. "How you had to say you were wrong and sorry before you could get off the chair."

"And?" I asked.

"Saying you're wrong so you could get free, doesn't mean you believed it. Doesn't mean you grew up understanding guilt—what was redemptive guilt and what was destructive." She took a long drink from her glass.

"You haven't done too well with your own guilt," I said. "The only difference between us is your guilt makes you afraid to try, and mine makes me afraid to quit trying." I felt good about those words. I'd been rehearsing them ever since the last notebook. "Tell me I didn't work hard at being your Momma!" I demanded.

Leah turned so she could see me. "Nobody said you didn't work, Momma. But whether you went to bed or canned a hundred jars of beans, it didn't matter much to Sam. Either way you left him alone with Willis."

There was nothing to say to that. So, I'm sitting here in my room, and the old, blue-tick hound has thrown his head back, and he's howling. I've laid down my writing pen. I have nothing more to say. Instead, I washed my hair and changed my dress. I'm going down to the jailhouse, and I'm gonna tell Sam I was wrong to leave him alone with Willis. I'm going to ask him to forgive me if he can.

Emmett's Fishing Report

It's August. Dog days on the river. Temperature's staying in the high nineties, and the fish are going for cold water. You got to do likewise. Sink your hook down one of those sudden drop-offs into the deep. You'll feel the strike and pull of waiting fish!

Yes sir the sun is hot! Best fishing is dark fishing: nights and early mornings. Channel cat are hitting night crawlers. Walleye are slow, holding at twenty-five to thirty feet. If you're fishing bass, try plastic worms or soft jerk bait lures. Bass can't stand it if they think their dinner's getting away. Use slow drops and easy pulls. Gotta keep 'em worried till you set the hook.

But the best fishing's over for a spell. Things pick up in September. Meantime, the eagles have gone off to better fishing waters, and so have the tourists. Course the tourists will come back in the fall to see the leaves turn. The eagles come back, too, They come back to eat the shad. Water temperature drops to low forties, and the shad start dying. Easy pickings for the eagles. Limping prey's easy to bag. And eagles are top of the heap when it comes to bagging. Eagles don't mind eating the dead, for that matter.

Some folks don't think much of eagles. They're just cousin to a vulture. But Lottie and me, we got our own pair of eagles. Eagles mate for life, you know. Our eagles got a nest in the old tulip tree at the side of the house. That tree's only reached half its height, and it's already a hundred feet. Our eagles (we named 'em Herb and Maggie), been nesting in that tree for several years now. An eagle's nest is made with good sized limbs, and it's big. Five or six feet across.

Every spring, Lottie and I watch our eagles spruce up their nest. It's the best entertainment in Cotton Rock. They start adding limbs, and the fun begins. Lottie and I moved our chairs right under the living room window. We got a ring-side seat. Maybe you've never watched an eagle adding limbs to its nest. It comes swooping down as only an eagle can, full speed, claws open to snap the limb off a near-by tree. Never misses a flap of a wing. Just snaps off a limb in-flight and sails right on to the nest. Adds another limb. But every once in a while, Herb guesses wrong on the size of a limb. He hits the limb at full speed, locks those big claws on, and that limb doesn't move. Herb never seems to get over the surprise of it! Goes flinging off, claws over feathers, through the branches! Lottie and me have ourselves a good laugh.

Course, eagles argue more than a married couple. Soon as Herb shows up with a new limb, Maggie starts disagreeing. Herb sets that limb in place, and Maggie goes to moving it. Herb moves it back. They fuss over every limb.

It got so bad that Lottie and I got to fussing about the fuss. I took up for Herb, naturally, and Lottie went for Maggie. Lottie says that Herb lays the branch on the first easy spot, just like a man. Like throwin' socks at the floor stead of the hamper.

I say Maggie's good at finding fault—just like a woman.

Things got a little hot after that. I stood my ground. So did Lottie. Me saying how Maggie's just fault-finding, and Lottie saying she isn't. We kept up that fight till it got serious enough for me to find myself sleeping on the couch. That couch has a bad spring, too. After a night on that couch, I reckoned it was time to make up. I built Lottie a first-rate trellis for her sweet peas, and she softened up. We kissed and sat on the front porch swing holding hands.

I say, "Now we've been pretty silly."

Lottie says, "We sure over-egged the pudding."

I say, "We sure did. Fighting like that over something so silly—just cause Maggie has to find fault."

And Lottie says, "Maggie doesn't find fault!"

And we're at it again!

Thoughts from the Back Porch   September 1996

I'm sitting up on Chinquapin Knob, an outcropping of cotton rock at the top of a ridge overlooking the White River. I've only a few months left of my sabbatical. If I holed up in the cabin starting tomorrow and wrote diligently from now till Christmas, I might finish the novel, might have it ready to submit for publication. The operative words: if I wrote diligently.

Writer's block—a fitting cliché, for the mystery that blocks the flow of words, from wherever it is that they come. In the past, hard work—deliberate and intense seeking—always served to advance my plot. Ring Lardner said that you stare at the blank paper until little drops of blood appear on your forehead. And after the blood, the words are born. I suppose they're spawned by the muse or the gods, or some little clerk in the brain who fingers through trays of possibilities and brings forth a forgotten image. And when it comes this way—after the blood—it's worth putting on paper.

But I'm not even willing to be willing to badger the little clerk, nor to entice the muse. Even my sense of urgency has stagnated. So I have hiked up to Chinquapin Knob, to contemplate the White River once more, because the flow of the river is tireless and unceasing,

Yet this river bed was once solid rock, deposited in the past solitary creases of time by a retreating sea, which laid down blanket on blanket of dolomitic limestone to form a swollen breast of bedrock. Through timeless risings and settings of the sun, as the glaciers came down to scour and level the surrounding land and the sea swept in again, this plate of bedrock remained, a dome of the oldest exposed land in North America—the Ozarks—spreading out before me as far as my eye could see.

The southern edge of this ancient Ozark plate heaved and shoved upward to form the igneous shoulders of the Boston Mountains, and somewhere high on those peaks, a spring bubbled up from the ground. It gathered itself to other little streams washing down the mountain sides, swelling, deepening, surging ever downward to its river birth and its christening: *La Riviere au Blanc*, the White River.

And this young river undaunted and unswerving, began forging its way across the formidable dome of rock, leaving in its wake rock walls, flanking the river bed, sometimes three-hundred feet high. It scraped back trees and scratched off the wilderness to journey as a bird in migration, instinctively, relentlessly, to mate with the sea, sparkling under long, sunshine days and sliding into dark nights under stars where it traced out gravel bars white in the moonlight.

Seven-hundred-and-twenty miles of tireless forging—relentless flow—sculpting overhanging pinnacles, great domes and innumerable pebbled rocks, producing its own infinite library of stone publications, to be read by subsequent generations. Flow.

I unpacked my lunch and poured water into the thermos cup—cold and satisfying. I sat eating my sandwich, watching an eagle soaring in the thermal up-draft, black wings spread, white head and tail against the blue sky. I watched it for several minutes before it dropped, "like a thunderbolt," as Tennyson wrote, hit the river's surface and came up with a fish in its talons. It perched on a rocky ledge across the river, tenting its wings to protect its catch, stepping around, hob-legged on its yellow feet in its ritualistic dance.

A small chipmunk crept tentatively from the stand of chinquapin trees that surrounded the rock where I ate. It sat upright on its little, russet haunches, black beaded eyes contemplating my sandwich. "Smell the salami?" I asked. I tore the crust from my bread and tossed it to a nearby tree root. The chipmunk dashed across the sand-colored rock and grasped the bread in its mouth, then ran to the safety of the tree root and sat once again on its haunches, its little jaws chewing earnestly. The eagle on his ledge across the river still hunched over the fish held fast under its claws, its fierce beak tearing at its prey, as I chewed my salami and cheese: lunchtime on the White River.

In time the eagle spread its wide dark wings and lifted off the rock. I watched as it circled and joined itself to several others circling above the river, watched them lift high into the sky, grow smaller and disappear over the mountain ridge behind me. They were migrating—seeking better fishing waters. They would soon be catching fish off some beach in Florida. The little chipmunk beside me would gather nuts from the chinquapin trees and stock its little home under the rocks for its extended winter stay. I was the only creature in the scene not working to store against the future.

I put away my lunch things, strapped on my pack and began the hike home, walking along the bank of the river, listening to its forward push. Water meeting land—each shaping the other. I stopped to retrieve a piece of marble from the edge of the river and squatted to wash the dirt from its surface, admiring its chalk-white beauty. Michelangelo thought a block of marble contained potential for every creative thought of the sculptor, but cautioned that only the yielded hand could penetrate the stone and realize the image. The yielding of the land to the river and the river to the land—only the yielded hand allowed the sculpting.

I saw all the parallels—could finish the walk home, berating my own failure to acquiesce to the severe work required to carve a story from the waiting page. I placed the rock into my backpack and thought of Leah, of my life apart from my career. The truth was, the only small changes brought by my coming to Cotton Rock resulted from my encounters with Leah. She was a force strong enough to fracture my unwitting hiatus. I missed her.

As I neared town the sun hung low in the sky. I'd be home in another hour. I reached a dirt road and cut across a field. Ducking under a stretch of barbed wire, I straightened to see an old man in bibbed overalls running with a crow-bar and an undeniable urgency. When he saw me, he stopped and called out, "Can you lend a hand?" Then he turned and continued running.

I threw down my pack and ran after him toward a barn with its door flung open. Once inside I saw a cow standing in a milking stall, wild-eyed and bawling. She had caught her head between two rails. She must have first angled her head sideways through the slats to forage a bite of food, just out of reach, then righted her head to find herself unable to escape. In her panic she had tugged backward, again and again, until her mouth foamed white, and her hide was lathered. She was nearing exhaustion.

"The minute she gives up and goes fur her knees, she'll break her neck," the old man said. "If her heart don't give out first." He was trying to pry loose one of the slats. "There's another crow bar up in the loft," he said, nodding toward a ladder.

I scrambled up the rungs and gave a look. I found it propped in a corner. It was no ordinary crow bar. It was at least five feet long and two inches in diameter. Once back with the crow bar, I saw that the old man had made little progress.

"If she goes fur her knees, stick that crow bar in her side—just enough to get her attention. Meantime you could join me on working the board loose."

I jammed the crowbar under a nail on my side of the board.

"Them nails. Tight as bark on a hickory log. Been in here eighty years. Four inches long and squared off," he said.

Using all my strength, I was able to loosen the board just an inch. The old man came over to add his crow bar to mine, and the board gave way. The freed cow sank backwards, her tongue hanging from the side of her mouth.

"She'll have a head-ache, I reckon," the old man said.

For the first time I could give the old man my full attention. He had a full head of white hair, and bushy brows—still remarkably black—which gave him a stern, somewhat owl-like appearance, as though he were always pondering a weighty matter. He had to be in his eighties. I had a new appreciation for the way he was able to run. He was as tall as I, and his back as straight as the crow bar I'd carried down from the loft. He held out a hand, and gave me a solid handshake.

"Eb Freeman. I sure do thank you!"

"John Sinclair—glad I could help."

"Had a feeling 'bout that cow. Heard a kind of scratchin'. Could tell by the rhythm something was caught and rubbin'. Couldn't 'a done it without you."

"You'd have done all right," I said.

"It would'a been a long shot with a bear in the way." he said. He reached into the pocket of his overalls and produced a few nails. He nailed the board in place. He located an extra board which he added to prevent the cow from "goin' fur the greener grass again," as he said.

Then he asked, "You had your supper?"

"No, I haven't," I said.

"Well, Lucy—she's a feeder. She'll insist on you staying."

"Lucy…Freeman? I think she's in my writing class," I said.

"Well, she's been 'a writing down that angels' gossip all summer. Gets awful busy at it. Burned supper more than once." Eb laughed.

Eb pointed toward the direction of the house. It was a typical Ozark cabin—small, unpretentious, and sensible. A number of different materials had been nailed around the foundation, as though anything Eb found that might help insulate—a piece of tin or plywood—had been brought home and nailed over an empty place. I was fairly certain he had never read Thoreau, and yet Eb had followed him more faithfully than most who have endeavored to do so. Eb probably never doubted that the purpose of clothing was simply to keep him warm, or that a house was just an extension of that concept—a place to keep off the wind and rain. He accepted Thoreau's warning—without ever having read it—that when a man "has got his house, he may not be the richer but the poorer for it, that he may find that "the house has got him." I had no doubt each piece of Eb's house was paid for before he nailed it on, and that he knew when to quit nailing and call it home.

There were a number of small sheds between the barn and the house. We neared the chicken house, and Eb picked up two stray hens—"crooked beak" and "sideburns"—dropping them back inside the fence. The harvested remnants of large garden lay next to the chicken house, and beside the garden a number of rose bushes, dried brown by fall, grew side by side with tomato vines. Eb laughed and said, "Ever time I make me a t'mater bed, Lucy puts a flower in it."

We passed a smoke house and a fruit cellar. I knew without looking inside that the walls would be lined with jars of vegetables, jellies and fruits. It wasn't about saving money or forgetting that Lushbaugh's Grocery was less than ten miles away. It was about inheriting a way of life—a lover—that they had no desire to abandon.

"Lucy," Eb called from the doorway, "Come see who I brung for supper." A moment later, Lucy stood in front of us, hands on hips, surprised and laughing.

"Mr. Sinclair! Come on in here!" she said.

Just like that, I was eating dinner at Lucy Freeman's house.

The bowls on her table were filled with her harvest: summer squash, green beans and corn still on the cob.

"You love them maters, she said, watching me devour them. "Here, have some more."

I complimented their garden and their self-sufficient way of living. Once they realized my appreciation for their lifestyle, they were ready to tell me more.

"Cured that ham in the smoke house," Eb said.

Lucy said the cracklings in the cornbread came from the same place.

I spread butter on an ear of corn, and Lucy warned, "That butter's a little soft. Apt to drop right off your knife. Just churned it this afternoon."

"Is this spinach?" I asked.

"No, honey. It's poke-sallet. Just grows wild. But when you go picking, you have to know poke from sour dock or tongue grass."

Their talk was simple—hill-grown and beautiful—like the poke sallet and the tomatoes, talk about how the heavy storm last week had blown a catfish up on the road, how Eb dug post holes all morning, and the crows had followed along to eat the worms. They told stories of hard times, how when their shoes needed polished they had used the black from the bottom of the tea kettle, and how when thread was scarce women had been known to thread their own hair onto needles to mend a dress.

Ozark natives, I thought. They did not view the outdoors as something seen from inside the house, nor as a place to navigate between home and office. The outdoors was more than a lawn that might require mowing or a flower garden to be appreciated. Though Lucy knew beauty when she saw it and had strung a collection of feeders just outside her kitchen window so she could watch the splendor of the hummingbirds, and Eb teased, "Took twenty-five pounds of sugar to feed 'em for a summer."

They understood that life comes from the ground, and they had never thought otherwise. They came from people who cleared fields and built cabins with nothing more than broad ax, cross saw, and a hammer; people who could lance an abscess or deliver a baby; people who had the courage to put a nail against a bad tooth and hit it with a hammer—people who had to be a whole village in one house.

And when they were gone, they would take a nearly extinct way of life with them.

"What brought you here?" Eb asked. "Made you want to teach folks in Cotton Rock?"

I told them about Granddad's cabin, and Eb thought he knew just where it was. "And," I added, "I came down to work on my novel."

"And have you?" Lucy asked. Her eyes had a way of anticipating my answer, an excited anticipation, as though whatever I said would be wonderful. It made it difficult to disappoint her. "No," I had to admit. "But you have to keep it a secret. Might not be good for my students to know."

Lucy nodded.

"Did you think it'd be easier to write down here?" she asked.

"I thought maybe if I got away…"

"Away from what?" she asked. Again her bright eyes waited for my answer.

"I don't know," I said at last.

"That might be a rock worth turning over," she said, and her bright eyes refused to look away from my uneasiness. She just kept smiling and waiting.

"Now, Lucy, that's enough snooping," Eb said. "Let the man eat in peace."

We finished eating, and Eb went out to check on the cow. I helped Lucy clear the table. We talked about the writing class and Cotton Rock, but I was thinking about the things Lucy had said, and about Leah. I was pretty sure Leah knew something about me—something she had perceived with her woman's knowing—something that I needed to know. I would see her again.

Eb returned from the barn. I thanked Lucy for the dinner and told her good-bye. Eb and I located my backpack in the field, and we walked to the road.

"I got a flat boat tied up down on the river," he said, "There's some mighty good places I could show you. Some of them fish are particular friends of mine."

First thing next morning around seven o'clock, Eb knocked on my door, wishing to repay my kindness for saving his cow, and "if I was up for it, he'd show me his favorite fishing hole."

If Granddad had risen from the grave and been granted the morning—to be spent anywhere in the world—he would have been sitting beside me in Eb's flatboat. We fished most of the morning, sitting in quiet coves and filling our boat with a fine catch. We talked about many things, including Eb's report on the cow's recovery.

"She's tucked her prayer bones up and slept mostly." He chuckled. "Like most of us, she wanted what was out of reach."

"Hard to determine what's out of reach sometimes." But I said it with more intensity that I intended.

Eb looked up from his pole.

"I mean the difference between what's unattainable, and what requires hard work." But I didn't intend to be specific, confess that perhaps I didn't have real writing talent, after all.

Eb nodded. "I reckon a fella works hard at certain things his whole life. Expects no more than breaking even. Raising a family, keeping the cellar full. Then, there's things a fella can't have no matter how hard he works at it. The thing just lays out of his reach. Before a fella breaks his neck between the boards, he might want to ask himself what he's really after."

Anna's Thirteenth Notebook

I know saying sorry doesn't give Sam back a lost childhood. Doesn't bring back the roads that passed him by. I don't know what kind of life Sam might have made for himself. There's no reshaping a limb on an Osage tree once it's grown—no undoing the rocks tied to its young limbs, forcing it against its natural bent.

"Willis sure was a son-of-bitch," Sam said, shaking his head. He began to talk about some of the "son-of-a-bitchen" things Willis did—as much as you can talk through a window glass with other people listening. "Remember my broken arm?"

"Lord, yes."

"Fell off the barn roof trying to fly." Sam grinned.

"You ruined my iron, ironing that plastic around conduit to make wings."

"If I hadn't landed on a pile of manure, I'd have broken more than an arm." Then he added, "Willis made me carry those buckets of milk with my broken arm. Tried it with my left, but couldn't get the hang of it."

"I fought hard with him on that one," I said.

"Those buckets held two gallons. I could feel it pulling inside the cast. Sure enough, my arm didn't heal right. Had to have surgery—break it all over again."

"When the doctor came to tell me they were putting you to sleep, I told him how Willis made you carry that milk bucket. Maybe carry a whole lot more I didn't know about." I looked at Sam to see if I was right.

Sam nodded, but didn't fill in the details.

"When you came rolling by me on the hospital cart, you had a cast like I'd never seen before."

Sam laughed out loud. "That was the weirdest cast I ever saw. It was one of a kind."

Sam was right about that. I can still see it in my mind. The doctor made a kind of mitten from a coat hanger, bent part of the long wire into the shape of a hand that outlined Sam's fingers. He put a cotton glove on Sam's hand, and at the tip of each gloved finger, a rubber band knotted and ran up to the wire hanger. It was a fancy web of rubber bands, wires, and a cotton glove."

The doctor said, "Mrs. Sprule, I've engineered a cast that I think will allow his arm to set right this time. I thought up this rig, during surgery. A coat hanger was the best I could find in the operating room."

"That mitt didn't even connect with my fingers," Sam said. "It couldn't have done anything."

"But it did work, son," I said. "I couldn't tell you at the time. The doctor said to tell Willis that mitt wouldn't be coming off till the cast does. Sam won't be able to use that hand for anything. No way to pick up any milk buckets—but he'll be good as new in about six weeks. It came to me then, what the doctor was up to. I asked if he had made many of those coat-hanger casts."

"This is the only one," he said. "But I wouldn't be telling Willis that if I were you."

"I'll be damned," Sam shook his head and laughed. "I never knew."

It was good to laugh at Willis. Took away some of the sting. Gave us back a pinch of the ground that Willis took from us.

It's sad how we sashay round our failures. I must have told Sam a hundred times I was sorry about Willis. But I had never come right out and asked, "Son, will you forgive me for bringing Willis into your life? For keeping you under his meanness all those years?"

But Sam's sitting in a boat that took him into bad water. He must want to take some well-aimed pot shots at me, but he might not be sure of his boat, or how rough the water is or where the shoreline falls. Whatever his reasons, I watched his face for the answer, saw what I knew was a mask, dropping down over his wounds, so he could say, "Sure, Momma. I forgave that a long time ago."

Thoughts from the Back Porch   September 1996

Leah was coming to my cabin for dinner! I had summoned my courage and given her a call, but she had her doubts: "I thought we agreed—it doesn't go well for us," she said.

"Well, yes… we do seem to make the other one want to—"

"Leave?"

"Yes—but," I hurried on to develop my argument, "maybe we're running from something, not from each other." I waited. She hadn't hung up, so I continued, "Somehow we represent the other's pain. And maybe it's time to allow our pain to inform us."

She was silent.

"Leah?"

"So, the pain I bring is helpful?"

"Well… yes."

"Do you want me to bring my thumbscrews or will my presence be enough?"

"I promise to make it a nice evening," I said. "I'll cook us a good meal."

And so she was coming. I carried The Benchmark from the back porch and placed it in front of the fireplace. It was a beautiful evening, too warm to build a fire, but I lit candles on the mantel. I found a tablecloth in a drawer in the kitchen.

I thought about music and realized that I had no idea what she liked. I found a Celtic harp C.D.—fitting for an Ozark evening.

Leah arrived at seven. She wore slacks and a blue, silk blouse, which intensified her blue eyes. I handed her a glass of wine, and went outside to take the trout from the grill.

"We have to eat immediately," I said when I returned. "The fish will be best if we eat them this moment."

We sat down.

"The table is beautiful," she said, tracing the embroidery on the tablecloth.

"My grandmother's work. Granddad said she filled the cabin knee-deep in a woman's kindness. To us," I said, holding up my wine glass for a toast.

She took a bite of the fish and said, "The trout is fantastic."

"Well, it's hard to ruin trout. Isaac Walton wrote a book treasured by fishermen: *Compleat Angler*. He's considered the father of the art of fishing.

I quoted: 'As the old poets say of wine, and the English say of venison, the trout is a generous fish'!"

"I was just thinking that my trout is quite generous!" She was grinning now above her glass of wine.

"Walton said that trout feed clean and purely in the swiftest streams and hardest gravel. Of course," I added, "some people think that trout are just gill-bearing idiots."

"Oh. I did say that, didn't I?"

"Every word."

"So this was your way of making me eat my words," she said, holding up a bite of trout on her fork.

"Absolutely!"

"Hmmm," she said, tapping a finger to her head in mock thought, "I wonder what vengeance there is for making a false accusation?"

"Someone made a false accusation?"

"You seem to have forgotten!" she said, raising an eyebrow. "You took me to a remote cellar, kissed me repeatedly, and then accused me of ruining the moment."

"How unchivalrous!"

"Well, tonight's agenda was pain—you said." She smiled. "I thought I'd start with the kiss."

I was thinking of something clever to say about my "painful kiss," when she set her glass down. "It's empty," she said, and her tone changed. "I could ask for more. I could ask for three more, climb right into my wine glass—but I can do that at home. I think we should do what you invited me to do: allow our pain to inform us. It was your idea, so let's start with you."

The room became uncomfortably silent.

The clock seemed to tick excessively loud—as though hammering out the seconds.

I took a deep breath. "Your mother once wrote in her notebook about pulling the scabs off old wounds. I guess I'm ready to do the same. When I came here, I thought my writing was the problem. I think maybe I'm the problem."

"Didn't you stop writing when your wife died?"

"Yes. But like I told you, the marriage was never really a good one. I managed to write through some pretty strained times—some pretty terrible scenes. We had a vicious fight a few weeks before the accident. Whatever affection remained seemed to end with that fight."

"What did you fight about?"

"She attacked my writing—no—my ability to write. I couldn't seem to recover. I suspected what she said might be true. I wanted to hurt her. I told her I'd been warned about marrying her—her inability to follow through. Susan went crazy. She said she was going to kill herself—get in the car and drive out on the highway. Hit a semi."

"How did you respond?"

I didn't answer.

"She said she was going to hit a semi," Leah repeated. "And what did you say?"

"I said if you're going to kill yourself, be sure to take the old Honda. We only have comprehensive insurance on the new one." I didn't look up now. I didn't want to see Leah's face. "Susan was enraged. But she allowed her rage to carry her past the notion of suicide—thank God. She hurled our wedding picture into the fireplace and screamed what remained to be screamed. I begged her to forgive me for being cruel. But she just waved a wine bottle, said good night and went to bed. When I came in later, she'd polished off a good part of it and was asleep. We never talked about the fight.

"A month later a gravel truck ran a stop sign and hit her broadside. I was at home. I had just mowed the lawn and gone inside to wash up when the phone rang. It was the police, telling me she was dead. They needed me to come down to the morgue and identify her body. There was the terrible thought that maybe, just maybe she'd pulled out in front of that gravel truck on purpose. I hadn't seen her leave—didn't know which car she'd taken. I went out to the garage. I just stood there, my hand on the door knob. I knew if the old Honda wasn't there, I was going to face a hideous truth. I opened the door. The old Honda was gone."

"But you're not God. You don't speak and. . ."

"I'm a writer," I said. "My entire craft is about words. A whole scene turns on the precise word. I know the power of words—the regret. I say, 'I don't want a baby.' Our baby miscarries. I say, 'If you're going to kill yourself, use the old Honda,' and Susan takes the old Honda and collides with a gravel truck."

"It was a month later. The gravel truck ran the stop sign," Leah said.

"It was my wife! You once said that death does something to people like you and me. You said that we don't die, but we're ashamed to live. Sometimes I venture out of the shadows, grab small bites of life, gobble them before old memories become outraged. But inevitably, I return to a kind of suspended death."

"What did Susan say about your writing—in the fight?" Leah asked.

"I don't know. Something about my ability."

"What about your ability?" Leah wasn't going to back down. I suppose I had counted on that when I invited her.

"Like I said, it was a terrible fight. She accused me of being seduced by my own ego. 'You've snookered yourself, Johnnie boy! You've believed you're a writer'"

"And so you've stopped writing," Leah said.

"Apparently."

"Why?"

"Why? What do you mean? I told you. My wife died." I suddenly regretted having invited Leah. I stood up too abruptly. My wine glass tipped over, staining the threads of embroidery.

Leah ignored my agitation. "Why is it useless for you to try to write?"

"I don't know—I don't know."

"Yes…you do." Leah spoke in a near whisper, "You said it yourself. Words are powerful. You know how to wield them—like a sword. You say you don't want a baby, and the baby dies. You say, 'If you're going to kill yourself, use the Old Honda.' Susan takes the old Honda, and she dies. Susan says, you're not a writer. Why do her words have to come true?" She repeated the question slowly, deliberately: "Why do you think Susan's words have to come true?"

"Because… mine did…"

She stood then and walked around the table toward me. This time would not be a stolen fragment, torn in haste and eaten in torture, but a free and generous partaking, a deliberate savoring with the eyes, a slow, pleasuring along the skin, believing that shame would fall away, like the silk blouse from her shoulders, and in tasting her acceptance, I could assent to my own.

Leah's dark hair now spreads across the pillow. Outside the cabin windows, the surging river shapes the yielding of the shore. Downstream in time, the river's passion will be carried out to sea, lost on a distant shore, where things spent, like past regrets, are finally brought to rest.

Lucy's Angel Gossip

Today I's thinking of the Lushbaugh boy. He's all growed up now. But when he was five, we liked to took the skin right off his ears. Some of his scalp too. Little Leonard Lushbaugh never missed Sunday school. Course them Lushbaugh's never came to church with him. If they take time off from the store, they spend it fishing. But sure as they pass the offering plate on Sunday morning, little Leonard was scrubbed and sitting in his place in the Sunday school room. That's 'cause old Granny Lushbaugh brought him. She's been a god-fearing Baptist all her life.

Leonard was as quiet as he was faithful. Never missed a Sunday and never said five words, neither. Everybody knows Dee Lushbaugh and Granny talk as much as magpies. I reckon little Leonard took after his Grandpa. He gave up on talking a long time ago. Might as well, he wasn't gonna find an open slot to stick in a word anyway.

Like I said, Leonard was faithful coming to church, so when we couldn't find him one Sunday morning, we took to looking for him right away. Found him with his head stuck between the posts of the stair railing. "Leonard!" I says, "You got yourself in the stocks for sure!"

They's a long string of steps 'a leading down to the church basement. Two posts to ever step. Leonard was almost down to the bottom when the idea must 'a come to him. He just stopped and stuck his head between the last two posts on the bottom step. He's almost home free when the idea come to him to stop and get hisself in a fix.

We tried to pull him out, but his head was way too big to fit back through them bars. We couldn't figure for the life of us how he ever wiggled his head through in the first place. We pushed and pulled and turned him this way and that. We decided to hold off telling Granny Lushbaugh long as we could. She put a heap of pride on that boy, and we had him looking red as a turkey's wattle.

I tried picking him up. Held him like a log, so that his body was more in agreement with his head. Liddy Bergheart pushed on his head while I held, but we just wedged him in tight as bark on a hickory tree. So we let up for awhile. I sat his body down best I could, but it left him hanging off like a fishing worm from a hook. Looked painful for sure.

That's when I thought of the lard. Liddy found a can in the church kitchen. We greased him up like baked potato. That's how we finally squeezed him through. When Leonard was sitting free and clear I says, "Leonard! Whatever possessed you to stick your head through them posts?"

He says, "I never stuck my head through, Miz Lucy."

I's struck dumb for sure.

Then Leonard just walked around to the outside of them stairs, got down on all fours, poked his feet through the posts and wiggled his body backwards onto the step. Feet first. Never had put his head through them posts! Then he just crawled right out. Same way he got in.

"Leonard!" I says, "How come you didn't say nothing? We could a rubbed an ear off!"

But Leonard used up all his words for the day. Said more words in a morning than he had all year, I reckon. And I was sure glad! Might be a growed man fore he got around to saying anything about it to Granny Lushbaugh.

Liddy and I just sat after church a shaking our heads. I felt as silly as a pig in a silk dress. If angels ever have temptations, I wager Leonard's angel is mighty tempted to speak up for Leonard now and then. I'd sooner be an angel to a rock!

Anna's Fourteenth Notebook

I figured a showdown was going to happen sooner or later, but I wasn't figuring to have it in the aisle of Lushbaugh's grocery. Harlo was sitting in the basket, just getting her coupons spread out, and I was filling a bag with Granny Smith apples when I turned to see Willis standing there looking us over, with those eyes that are chock-full of sure and empty of doubt.

"I reckon you've mortgaged your house to pay for Sam's defense," he said. "My own money working against me."

"The court thinks I earned some of the money, Willis. It's called 'alimony'. And Sam worked. Every morning and night. Every summer vacation."

"That's what family does," Willis said.

"Does family charge its own with grand larceny!"

"Doesn't matter what you think, Anna." His voice was flat and cold as ice on the river. "You always called a weed a rose where that boy was concerned. The law has him now, and the law wasn't raised on a sugar tit."

Things kept going between us, till Willis got red in the face and forgot to hide his rage. He was yelling when he called me, "Packsaddle honey-whore."

That brought folks peeking out from the canned goods and slowing their baskets to a halt. I looked around at the faces. Ever since I got pregnant with Sam, I've been hiding from those faces. I didn't even know what I thought those faces might be looking to see—maybe what it looks like to get caught?

Right there between the Granny Smith apples and the Hodgson Mill flour sacks, I decided to climb out of the swamp. I answered loud enough for all those faces to hear: "Loving someone who runs off to Kalispell, Montana, doesn't make me a whore. Just makes me foolish."

"Got you a shame baby."

"No babies are a shame, Willis. And there's no shame on a flower 'cause it blooms out of season."

I turned my back on Willis then, bagged up my Granny Smith apples, held my head up and pushed my basket down a new aisle. Nobody saw my tears—those little traitors that fall just when you're standing brave. Harlo was the only one that saw, and that sweet little face looking up at me put the starch right back in my backbone.

So, I figure I'm getting close to the end of these notebooks. I've written enough of them to figure out who betrayed me—the one person I may not be able to forgive: myself. After Jake Kenaway, I decided I didn't have any worth. I didn't know when a woman believes she isn't worth much, her children might decide they're not worth much either. If I keep sitting at the bottom of a swamp, my children might decide to stay there too. Yes sir! I'm climbing out!

Thoughts from the Back Porch   September 1996

Leah left about midnight. I sat on the back porch, appreciating the large silver-plated moon. Restored—yes, that was the word. Restored like the river released from the dams that imprisoned its flow.

I went to my desk, slid open the bottom drawer and took out the manuscript. The thin cotyledon of paper I hadn't read through in over a year. It surprised me. Parts of it were okay, maybe even good. I laid the manuscript beside the computer, clicked on the icon labeled novel and began writing! I could feel once again, the flow of the story, released like the river, washing ideas over my mind, surging ahead of my fingers and glimmering in the distance with unexpected turns and little spins of counter plot.

I worked with great energy. "I'm happy!" I shouted at some point, "I am damned happy!" I fleshed out the scenes that were too sparse, confronted the sections which had to be cut, and moved paragraphs, like rocks along the riverbed, till the story moved with smooth, unimpeded flow.

I grappled with the characters, looked them in the face, admitted they were too vague, then birthed them again and again till they stood up from the paper and formed images that moved and spoke and lived within my mind. I wrote until the dawning sun edged pink along the tree line, and feeling great satisfaction, I fell across the bed and went to sleep.

Writing requires the straddling of two worlds: the world of pretend people with fabricated joys and tragedies and the real world with deadlines and telephones, where people have flesh and blood needs and expectations. As I had once failed at maintaining my balance between these two worlds, I immediately failed again.

"I don't want Momma to know I was here," Leah had cautioned me the night before. "I have very little privacy as it is. And it might be awkward for you as her teacher."

"I'll call you," I had promised.

"Only mornings—between ten and eleven. That's when the therapist comes for Mayta. Momma helps with that."

I grabbed up the clock. Noon! The first morning after making love to her, I slept through the designated time to call! There was nothing to do but wait twenty-four hours until the next appointed time. When I reached her, I could hear the hurt and doubt in her voice. She agreed to be in charge of phone calls, but often she called just as I was developing a critical thought. She sensed my agitation—heard it in my voice. Writing is a fussy craft. Thoughts interrupted or postponed, words that are forced after the energy subsides are at best second-rate. Sometimes pivotal ideas are forgotten entirely.

How can you tell the woman who has redeemed your creative muse, perhaps has even become your creative muse, that she has purchased her own neglect? There was no time to nurture our fledging relationship. I'd gotten a good start, but I had a long way to go.

Leah tried to be understanding. But intimacy is achieved, as its name declares, by being intimate, and writing is an isolated, lone occupation. The sweetness we shared that first night faded. I broke promises. Times together were strained, almost forced. The relationship suffered; the novel prospered.

After days of dedicated writing, I mailed several chapters to my agent. He promised to email his reaction. Acquiring the creative writing position at the college seemed approachable. I could still be rescued from a career of teaching freshman composition classes. Maybe Henry wouldn't be the new creative writing professor after all. The thought of watching his condescending swagger parading around the halls was unbearable.

A few days later, my agent called. He'd gotten the chapters and promised to email as soon as he'd read through them. I decided I could afford some time off. I announced the good news to Leah: "Time to celebrate. Let's go out."

"I'm just leaving for a job interview at the gallery. Maybe this evening?"

We made plans, and I hung up the phone. I decided I'd take the boat out and do some fishing. I spent the morning sorting through my tackle box and tying some new flies. I made coffee, filled the thermos and was down on the boat dock when I heard the phone ring in the cabin. I tossed the rope around a piling, noting that I'd have to come back to secure it later and headed for the house.

It was Anna. She began by apologizing. She'd called everyone she could think of, and I was her last hope. She was calling from Ferguson's office and needed to stay to complete some critical matters. "The Grand Jury has indicted Sam." Her voice broke. "For manslaughter." She needed someone to pick up Harlo from preschool. She kept apologizing and saying she didn't know who else to call. I assured her I was glad to help.

I was in town in ten minutes. Weekend tourists lined the sidewalks, their cars filling every parking space. Bumper-to-bumper traffic jammed the streets. People wearing shorts and sunglasses carried shopping bags and strolled casually across the street. I reached Ferguson's office, located Anna's car in front of the office as she'd instructed, and transferred Harlo's car seat to my jeep. I decided it would be easier to walk the two blocks to the play center.

"Mr. Sinclair!" Harlo cried when she saw me. "They said it would be you!" She skipped off to get her doll, Bill.

The teacher handed me a clipboard. "Just sign here," she said, "Mrs. McKerry said you'd be coming."

I wrote my name in the designated box, and Harlo and I were on our way.

"Main Street is full of tourists," I explained to Harlo. "Let's take the back street. We'll make better time." We passed the bakery and the post office, and in the next block, approached the Cotton Rock Mortuary. The building, over a hundred years old, possessed little aesthetic qualities. Its entrance opened directly onto the sidewalk. As we passed by Harlo stopped.

She stood on tip toes trying to see into the window, which had been discreetly covered with thick draperies.

"Mr. Sinclair, this is where they bring you when you die," she said.

"Yes."

She turned toward me. "Mary died. And they brought her here. And when Grandma Mayta dies, they'll bring her here. And when Grandma Anna dies, they'll bring her here. And when Willis Sprule dies, he'll go straight to hell."

I burst out laughing. She dropped my hand at once and hugged Bill to her chest. Her large, serious eyes were filled with disappointment.

"I'm sorry I laughed," I said. "You surprised me. Can you tell me about Willis Sprule while we're walking?"

"He's my grandfather," she said, trying to match her steps with mine. "We don't like him. He was mean to Grandma Anna yesterday."

"Oh," I said.

"He yelled at her the grocery store. She cried."

"Then I don't like him either," I said.

She nodded her head gravely, and slid her hand back into mine. "Charlie told me all about hell."

Who's Charlie?"

"He's at my school. He said bad people go to hell, soon as they die."

"Oh," I said.

She looked up at me with her serious little face as though wondering if I agreed with Charlie. I decided she needed Charlie's kind of justice, and I nodded my head in agreement.

"Right," she said, satisfied with my position. We walked in silence for a time. I watched her little knees lifting and striding bravely forward, following my lead. How did parents find the courage to take such trust by the hand?

We drove home alongside the river, and Harlo immediately thought of a boat ride.

"Oh please, Mr. Sinclair!"

Perhaps we could stop at my house and take the boat down.

My hesitation gave her hope, and she began begging anew, "Please, oh please Mr. Sinclair!"

"Okay," I said. "But your Mother expects you home. It'll be a short boat ride—just down to your house."

She was thrilled. We parked the car in the driveway and headed down to the boat dock, just as the horn blew from the dam. The water would be rising. I should get Harlo a life jacket.

"I have to run up to the cabin," I said. I pointed to the bench in the back yard. "Sit right there on the bench. Stay put. I'll be right back."

I dug the life jacket out from the back of the closet and walked back through the cabin, passing the computer. I was anxious to see if the agent had emailed. I clicked the mail icon, but nothing had come in.

Perhaps it was the horn's second warning sound—warning that the water was rising—that prompted me to remember I hadn't tied up the boat securely that morning. I walked to the window and glanced down at the dock.

I didn't see my boat! It could be on its way down river! I raced to the back yard. Sure enough, the boat was floating free with the current and just nearing the bend. But it was no longer the boat I cared about, because Harlo sat in the back hunched over the gauges. Had she not realized that the boat was moving?

I'd never catch up to the boat on foot. My best chance was to intercept it at the landing. I raced back up the hill to the jeep. I flung the door open, dug the keys from my pocket and jumped inside, jamming the keys into the ignition. I slid the gear shift into reverse and shot backwards up driveway and out onto the road. I slammed into low too quickly, and the engine died. My God, I had to pull it together. I mashed the gas pedal to the floor and ground the ignition. For a horrible moment I thought I'd flooded the engine, but it started at last, and I was moving. I took every curve at top speed. It was only two miles to the landing, but the water could rise nine feet in a few minutes. I'm going faster than the boat, I assured myself. I'll make it there in time.

Thoughts raced through my mind like a phantasmagoric nightmare, playing out above the curving road. I pictured Harlo floating alone in a boat headed down a swelling river! I remembered Leah's face the day she raced across the lawn, tormented because she couldn't find Harlo. Leah could not lose another person to the river. Anna could not lose another person to the river. How could I have neglected a child entrusted to my care? I gripped the wheel, increasing my speed as much as the road allowed. I wasn't far from the landing. By now Harlo must have realized her plight. What if she stood up? I could hear Granddad saying, "A bear could stand up in a johnboat without turning it over." Thank God it wasn't a canoe.

I reached the landing at last and slammed the jeep into park, then I was running, peeling off my shirt, running, sliding, jumping up, and running again. I reached the river and searched upstream. The sun's glare on the water was blinding. I shaded my eyes and stared into the light. I could see the dim outline of a boat, edging around the bend. I was too far away to determine if Harlo was in the boat. I kicked off my shoes and pulled off my tee shirt. I could get to the boat in time, I was sure of it. The water was ice cold and the current strong, but the river had only risen a couple of feet. I'd seen it rise as much as ten feet when the generators were all running. I'd never have been able to fight the current with that much swell. I stopped a moment, treading water. The boat was coming right to me. I was within a hundred yards of it.

I couldn't see Harlo, but she could be huddled down in the hull. I swam long hard strokes, pulling myself through the icy water till I felt the sweet wood of the boat under my hands and lifted my body up over the side. Then indescribable anguish—the boat was empty. Harlo's doll lay on the seat, arms stretched out, glass eyes staring. I thought of Mrs. Lushbaugh's words: "They found little Mary laid out like an angel on a gravel bar."

I crawled to the back of the boat and started the motor. I'd find her! I'd find her. She had to be between here and my boat dock. I'd back-track.

Look for her all along the way. The search was agonized guessing. Every foot upstream could be the wrong way. What if I had just passed over her? What if the current had already taken her down river? Upstream a woman ran wildly along the river bank. As I got closer, I saw that it was Leah in a business suit, running like a puppet on a string in a surreal nightmare, running along the river's edge stumbling, clamoring over boulders in a skirt far too narrow for climbing. She fell momentarily going down on one knee, getting up to run again. I fought to overcome the mounting terror. I should stop for Leah.

I drove the boat up onto the soft sand and jumped out.

Leah saw me and screamed, "Where's Harlo!"

"Hurry! We'll find her."

"What do you mean?" She stopped dead in her tracks. "She was in the boat! I saw her. I saw her!"

"We'll find her!" I helped Leah into the boat. My god! She was wearing heels! She looked around wildly. She spied Bill and held him out as evidence. "She's in the river!" Her face twisted in anguish and she sank down into the boat. "She's in the river!"

"No! No she's not. We'll find her."

I pushed off, wading out to gain the deeper water, pulled myself over the side, and fired up the motor.

Leah sat clutching the doll and moaning.

I headed upriver. "Leah, listen to me," I shouted over the motor. "I need your help. Where were you when you saw Harlo?"

"On the patio. She was crying! Calling me!" Leah broke into sobs.

"We've got to focus! I'll check the banks. You check midstream."

Leah turned back toward the bow and leaned over the edge, peering down into the water. She moved first to one side of the bow and then the other, searching the water, the doll still clutched in her hand. I could hear her moaning over the sound of the motor. Sometimes she called Harlo's name, and once I thought she called Mary's.

I searched along the shorelines, scanning up river as far as I could see. We only had minutes. How long had Harlo been in the water? Leah's house was no more than a mile from the landing.

Time dilation—that's what Einstein called it—the slowing of time. Time occupying different realities. In the river a small girl's time dissipated at what seemed the speed of light, racing against the decreasing supply of oxygen. In the boat, time slowed to a heavy, oppressive inflation, like a nightmare where you desperately need to run, but your legs are great weights that cannot be lifted—two worlds of excruciating contrast. The river had to be twelve feet deep now. But once water covers your head a foot is as good as forty.

Leah had a sudden thought and whirled around, "Life jacket," she yelled. "Did she have a life jacket?"

"No—I…"

"What? What? Were you writing?"

"I just checked my email…I…"

"I hate you! I hate you!" She, turned, moaning, and hung over the edge of the boat, searching the water.

We were nearly back to Leah's dock. I knew by the way she gripped the side of the bow that once we reached her house and hadn't found Harlo, there would be no holding her together.

And then we were there at the dock, and there was nothing to do but turn the boat around and retrace our search. Leah leaped up, screaming, "She's in the river!" You killed her!"

"No! We'll find her! We'll find her!"

But the black thought filling the boat was swallowing both of us so that we couldn't hear anything. Dee Lushbaugh had had to march the length of Leah's dock, with her hands cupped around her mouth, her bright orange hair blowing in the wind—had to nearly get into our boat before we could hear her. "Leah—John! Over here!"

I stared at the orange hair and tried to make sense of her words then make sense of Harlo running across the grass and onto the dock, running in normal time—our time—perfectly whole and waving to us. I grasped Leah by the shoulders and forced her to turn to see her daughter. I felt her body sag against me, felt the cry, come up from deep inside her—a long, terrible howl like an animal. A second later she tore from my grasp, climbed onto the dock and ran to Harlo, catching her up into her arms then collapsing to the ground, holding her, rocking her back and forth sobbing—deep, wrenching sobs.

I sat in the boat watching the two of them, trying to believe that everything was okay—that the world really had rolled back into its orbit. I tied up the boat and dropped down on the dock.

After a time Harlow wriggled free and stood pulling on Leah's hand. "I want to go home," she said.

Leah might have contained the rage had the heel on one of her shoes not caught on the dock and snapped beneath her—the heels with which she had waded the river and scraped over a hundred rocks. She stumbled. I went to her side and tried to take her arm, but she pulled away violently, "Stay away from us!" she screamed. "Stay away from us!" She flung the shoes from her feet, took Harlo by the hand, and walked quickly to the house.

I turned back to face Mrs. Lushbaugh who was shaking her head of orange hair. "You sure stirred up some old fire," she said. "Makes hell look like a lightning bug. I'd give it some time, if I was you."

I nodded my head. "How did you find Harlo?"

"I was out in my boat—going home for bait," she said. "Left Mr. Lushbaugh down at the dam. Anyway I came up river and ran into little Harlo. Standing up in the boat. Crying for dear life! 'Don't that take the rag off the bush!' I says. I came alongside your boat and pulled her into mine. Poor little thing was worried about saving your boat. Never mind the boat, I says. Boats can float. I brought her back here to the house. Nobody was home but the old Grandma. (She pointed to Mayta who was miraculously still sitting on the patio.) Alzheimers has got her. So we just sat on the lawn and waited for somebody to show up."

"Thank you," I said. "Thank you." I might have said it ten more times, but she interrupted me.

"You don't look too good," she said. "I'd say you need a drink or at least a good long sit down."

"I want to make sure they're all right," I said, nodding toward Leah and Harlo. Mrs. Lushbaugh shot me a warning look.

"I'll just check on Mayta," I said and thanked her again.

"Well, I better be getting back to Mr. Lushbaugh." She climbed into her boat, heading down river.

I turned back toward the house. Mayta was still sitting alone on the patio. Leah had forgotten her in the trauma. I walked across the lawn toward her.

She sat quietly, oblivious to the afternoon's events. Her thin hands knotted with veins, rested on the arms of the deck chair. Her white hair, luminous in the bright sun, looked unusually nice, and I remembered that she'd been given a permanent at Sylvia's salon.

I dropped down into a lawn chair beside her. "I'm John. Do you remember me?"

"Yes," she said. "You came from the ship."

"Yes," I said.

"My…my…. " She looked at me with her sad eyes. I suddenly knew what it was she wanted to say. What she had wanted to tell me the first time I met her.

"Your husband was on a ship," I said.

"Yes!" She smiled, grateful that I'd found the words.

"He died," she said.

I nodded. "Pearl Harbor."

"Yes," she said. She laid her head back in the lawn chair and closed her eyes. Perhaps she was thinking of her beloved sailor. We sat side by side in our lawn chairs, in the warm sunshine. After a time she opened her eyes, turned toward me and said, "I lost."

I reached out and took her hand. She closed her eyes and after a time fell asleep. I was still holding her hand when Anna returned from town and found us. She stood looking down on us, purse and keys in hand.

"Mr. Sinclair?" she asked, clearly amazed.

"I think your mother would probably like to go inside," I said. "It's been a pretty eventful day. Leah will tell you about it. I have to go down to the landing and see about my car. Please have Leah call me if I can do anything."

Anna watched me as I crossed the lawn to my boat. She was still staring after me as I started the motor and headed down river. It didn't take long at the landing to find my shoes. I checked on the car. It was parked remarkably well under the circumstances. I would walk down for it later. I climbed back into the boat and headed home.

"Yes Mayta," I said when I passed Leah's house. "I lost, too."

Anna's Fifteenth Notebook

Harlo stood on a chair drying the spoons. She wore one of my aprons. The waist was tied up under her arms, but the apron was still as long as her night gown. She held a dish towel in one hand and a spoon in the other. She rubbed on the bowl of a spoon, held it up close, studied on it and then rubbed it some more. When it was dry enough to suit her, she laid it in the drawer—exact laying—lining it up on top the stack of spoons beneath. Her determination spoke with the clink of every spoon.

Order matters to Harlo. Not just order, perfect order. I've told her that nature isn't big on perfect. I've shown her the stars at night, pointed out how God didn't line them up in rows. But there's something in her that's desperate for straight lines and even rows.

She wore tennis shoes under her apron gown, one with a tie that was coming loose, a rankle that would send her into action soon as she saw it. She would take to the floor and work at the bow till it matched the other shoe. Perfect match.

I figure that if children live in a house where hope has sat down on the sidelines, they might find comfort in spoons that line up and shoe strings that match. I figure that Harlo knows her momma is sitting on the side of the road watching life go by, and a child is not good at watching life go by.

Harlo knows her Momma doesn't even care where the road is leading. So Harlo tires to see down the road as far as she can. She spends time with the calendar and the clock. She wants to know what time or what day a thing is going to happen. Today, she's mapping out school—Kindergarten, which is a week away.

"When will school start?" She wants to know.

I tell her how many days.

"What time will the school bus come? What time will I have to get up?" On and on the questions go. I'm not surprised that Harlo wound up sitting in the back of your boat, trying to read the direction of the compass. Lord knows she'd wear one around her neck if she knew where to find one.

I don't tell her that a compass is a kind of counterfeit. I don't tell her we have no idea where north is in the universe. We don't even know what day it is. Somebody just started counting one day, and we kept it up. Leah says we don't even know the hour of day. Someone declared the time on an imaginary line, and the rest of us set our clocks. But it wouldn't do to tell Harlo this.

I figure Harlo worries about all kinds of things. Maybe even feels like things are her fault. I looked at her standing there on the chair on her own little feet. And I think how a child has to carry the weight of their little world on their little feet, a world shaped mostly by us.

Harlo climbed off the chair, took off her apron and sure enough, noticed her shoe was untied. She sat right down on the kitchen floor fixed on her task. Leah came in from the patio carrying a paint brush. Together we watched the worried little hands tearing at the knot again and again. She didn't stop till the tears threatened and the bows lined up square on the money.

"My child eats the bread of my sorrows," Leah said. "It's hard to watch." She was pouring herself a drink.

"But you don't watch," I said. "That's why you pour that drink, so you won't have to watch." I expected a hot answer. I backed up to the cabinet and hung on for some serious words. But Leah didn't say a single one. She just stood for a long time holding the glass.

Then she walked to the sink, poured out the wine and returned to her canvas on the patio.

When I went to bed that night, I found a little note on my pillow:

> Dear Momma,
>   Several months ago I woke up to find Harlo missing. It wasn't early morning. She hadn't slipped out of her bed. It was mid-day, and I was passed out—drunk. A missing child and a near-by river can send you into a kind of free-fall toward insanity. Once she'd been found, I made an appointment with a therapist and began confronting my alcohol problem. I didn't tell anyone.
>   The shame and guilt of Mary's death was unbearable. Sometimes I could shove the weight of it into God's lap—could be mad at God for being God, or mad at God for not being God. Mary was a victim of the river; I made myself a victim of guilt.
>   Guilt can produce a variety of bitter fruits. One of them can be used as an insidious bribe—a kind of penance:

feeling sorry, wretchedly sorry, can earn forgiveness for the next drink. The therapist and I agreed that I would know when I was ready to stop drinking—that I should decide the time. I decided it would be tonight.

I love you Momma,

Leah

I sat for a long time reading that little note over and over again. I figure Leah's got her courage back.

Emmett's Fishing Report

Fall's in full bloom. Large-mouth bass love the cooler temperatures. They're showing up around the banks early mornings. Browns are collecting in some bends of the river. They'll begin moving upstream to spawn. School's started, and the tourists have thinned out. If you're using artificial bait, power eggs, yellow or orange are filling stringers, and lures are always good for stirring up interest. But the White is running low so use a light, green line. Trout can spot a heavy line pulling a lure.

Leaves are turning red and gold, and it's fall on the White River. If you're a live-bait man nature makes a mighty fine fishing worm and no slouch of a draw. Fly fishermen are busy tying up midge #20s. Course, the midge is so small folks call 'em "no-see-ums." So, the fly-tie boys need a magnifying glass and tweezers.

Thought I'd write a little about night fishing. If you haven't tried fishing in the dark you aren't serious yet. Course seeing in the dark's like separating fly specks from black pepper! Which is why there's mostly fly-fishermen out there stumbling round. But live-bait fellars like it too. It's worth all the surprises. You might get introduced to a stand of barb wire, or measure a sink hole with your knee cap. But there's nothing wrong with falling on your back bumper now and then. Keeps you humble and fit to be around.

Night fishing's the measure of a sure-enough fisherman. Just when other fellas are drifting off to sleep, a down-to-the-bona-fide fisherman's worrying about the big ones that might be nosing around the bank. A true, honest fisherman's got a heart shaped pretty near like a fish.

The darker the night, the bigger the fish. At least a night fisherman thinks so, and there's not much chance he'll prove himself wrong. Anyway you got to do some serious planning when you go out at night. Flash lights, car keys that whistle, things like that.

Familiar trails get twisted around in the dark. Fact is, they get downright spooky. Takes you right back to being a kid, when all the dark corners of your room were hiding bears.

You hear sounds you never noticed when the sun's shining. Some of them sounds is rich with suggestions. Wouldn't do to take off running, neither. The ground will come up to meet you mighty fast. Kiss you flat on the nose.

Truth is, I had to give up on night fishing when I started courting Lottie. I used to come home on a dark night, go creeping up the stairs, trying not to wake up my daddy for two reasons: I'd just as soon him not know how late it was, and I didn't care to face him after I'd gotten him out of a deep sleep.

My brother and I shared a room. The light was just a light bulb hanging in the middle of the room. You turned it on by pullin' a string. One dark night just as I reached out for that string, my brother was just reaching out from his side. Meetin' another hand in the dark will burn a new groove right down the middle of your soft tissue. I haven't been a bit good at reaching out in the dark since then.

I'd be out night fishing and just as I's reaching out to feel for the barb wire, or to part the cattails along the river, the thought of another hand would come to me. That just put the spook on me. Fact is you might not want to think too hard on it yourself, if you got a hankering for night fishing.

But even if I'm laying in my bed, I'm not sleeping easy. My heart is on the river, knowing that somewhere a big trout is rising up out of the water, listening to some lucky fisherman stumble around in the dark.

Thoughts from the Back Porch   October 1996

    I've come to the end of the notebooks. I've retraced my days in Cotton Rock, and I'm more convinced than ever that I've lost the woman I'd like to spend my life with. Why do we sabotage love? Are we so afraid of losing the very thing we swear we want, that we kill it before it has a chance to prove us wrong? I don't know if it's possible for her to forgive me or to trust me again. I didn't think she would agree to see me. I decided to risk an unannounced visit.

    I phoned Anna. "I know you planned to pick up your notebooks, but I'm taking my boat down river. I could save you a trip."

    "That would be fine," she said.

    Ten minutes later, I tied my boat to Anna's dock.

    She invited me in and offered me a chair near her writing desk. "This is a great view," I said, looking out one of the six windows she'd described in her notebook.

    "I forgot you've never been in my house," Anna said.

    Actually I had been to the house the day I returned Harlo from the blackberry patch, but I thought perhaps it was best not to discuss that day with Anna.

    "I saw the sign out on the lawn," I said.

    She nodded. "The trial's been set for the last of March. I'm sure it was Cora Eckert that told Willis about the notebooks," Anna said. "Convinced him they might contain something that could be used against Sam. No telling what Willis has to do to repay her." She thought a moment and said, "Probably had to massage her bunions."

    We laughed.

    "About the notebooks," I said, handing them to her, "I've never told you how much they meant to me. They inspired me to write some of my own. It was the first time I had written since my wife's death."

    "That's a mighty sweet thing to know," she said.

    We talked some about writing and about the class, and I finally ventured a question. "Your house is so quiet—everyone must be gone?"

    "Yes—except for Grandma Mayta. She's resting."

I should ask when Leah would be home—say something that might let Leah know I was hoping to see her. Instead I said, "Well, I'd best be going. Stay in touch."

Anna nodded.

Okay, I told myself as I walked toward the dock. *You have less backbone than a fishing worm!* I'd have to think of a new plan.

A couple days later I took the boat out early and caught three nice trout. Back at the cabin I cleaned them carefully, zipped them into a plastic bag and headed back down river to Anna's.

"Mr. Sinclair?" Anna was clearly surprised by my second visit.

"I've brought you some fish," I said, and explained that my own freezer was full. But I was careful not to extend the package, hoping she'd ask me inside, which she did. I passed one of Leah's paintings and seized my opportunity, "That must be Leah's work," I said.

Anna nodded. We stood looking at the painting.

"The same young girl keeps appearing in her work," I said.

"I didn't know you'd seen her paintings." Anna was curious and waited for me to explain. When I didn't, she said, "Leah's started a new painting. It's different from the others."

"I'd love to see it," I said.

"It's not really finished," Anna said. "Not likely to be for awhile. With her up in Springville."

"Springville! For how long?" I asked.

Anna turned to look at me as though by seeing me more closely she might make sense of me.

"Leah's in Springville for a month of training. She's taken a job at the gallery. Here in Cotton Rock."

"So she'll be back," I said. The sound of relief in my voice didn't go unnoticed.

Anna raised her eyebrows, expecting me to explain.

"Well, I'd better get back to my writing," I said.

At the door, Anna asked, "Mr. Sinclair? Did you want me to have those fish in your hand?"

Good grief! The fish. "Absolutely," I said, holding them out.

Thoughts from the Back Porch   October 1996

In an attempt to maintain its historical image, Cotton Rock had forbidden the use of neon signs. All the shops, particularly those along the riverfront, had wooden signs which hung above their doors from wrought-iron brackets. I stopped beneath the wooden sign which read Cotton Rock Gallery. I hoped to see Leah, to receive her forgiveness.

The gallery was a suite of three large rooms whose walls were lined with paintings, handsomely framed. Everywhere, aspects of the rustic combined with the sophisticatedly smart—including the refinished pine floor and the old tin ceiling. Celtic harp music played softly, and the scent of jasmine drifted with the smoke from of an incense burner. A striking, well-dressed man about my own age emerged from behind a counter. "Welcome to our gallery."

"Thank you. Is Leah Gatewood in?" I asked.

She's working in the back. May I give her your name?"

Before I could answer, a door in the back of the room opened, and Leah entered, brush in hand. She looked younger somehow. Her dark hair was tied back in a ribbon, and she wore jeans and a paint smock. She saw me, and it was clear she hadn't expected me.

"Hello, Leah."

"John."

"I was hoping to see you before I returned to Springville."

She nodded. "We can talk in the studio," she said, and pointed her brush toward the door through which she'd just come.

The room was sunny and spacious. An easel stood beneath a sky-light. Canvases, some in progress and others wrapped for shipping, lined one of the walls.

Leah laid her brush on the easel and nodded toward a small seating area. "Let's sit."

I sat in one of the leather chairs.

"I made fresh coffee." She poured us each a cup, setting them on the glass-topped table between us. She sat in the chair opposite mine.

"So, you're the new director at the gallery." I said.

"Yes. I'm excited about it!"

"And you're painting something," I said. "May I look?"

She nodded.

"A still life—it's quite different from your former work," I said, looking over the painting.

"I'm experimenting with positive space. I worked primarily with negative space before. Used whole tubes of umber and cobalt. Subjects were only present where—or if—the shadows acquiesced. But then, negative space defines the positive."

"The light falling on the window is compelling. Is the light departing or approaching?"

"Those kinds of rays—crepuscular—could be either."

"How's your novel?" she asked when I returned to my chair.

"Nearly finished."

But I hadn't come for polite talk. I had to try to make things right. "I've wanted to talk with you ever since that day—I know it must have been horrific."

"You're not a parent." She flashed a look that warned me not to disagree. "You can't know the agony. Thinking your child might have drowned."

"I should never have left her alone—that near the boat."

"I hated you."

We sat in silence for a moment before she said. "The Grand Jury's questioning stirred some of the old memories of the drowning. Made me talk about things I'd wanted to forget. They just kept hammering at me. What did you see? You must have seen something. They implied I was purposely withholding. I told them about the duffel bag—that I remembered seeing Sam throw it from the rock. But I didn't know where Mary was. Didn't know what happened after that. I kept explaining I had fainted, or so I thought.

"A few days after Harlo went floating away in your boat, the memory of Mary's drowning began to play back in my mind. A sort of flashback. I remembered standing on the bridge above Sleeping Rock. I wanted to check on Mary. I remembered seeing Sam standing up on Sleeping Rock, holding a duffel bag. Mary was playing nearby in one of those pockets of water, left in the riverbed when the engines are not running. As I watched, I realized that the water was rising. Swelling all around Mary. Sam should have seen it too—but he wasn't watching her. He was distracted by something up on the hillside. I think he was trying to decide where to throw that bag. I yelled down, but neither of them could hear me." Her voice broke, and she waited till she could speak. "I don't need to tell you all of it. I just wanted to say that I think Sam's distraction kept him from saving Mary."

"That knowledge must be unbearable," I said.

"Exactly. My realization brought outrage. How could Sam could be so distracted that he couldn't see a child was drowning? My anger consumed me for days. In my pain, I lashed out at Harlo one afternoon. Later, I went to ask her forgiveness. I asked her, '"Will you forgive me?"'

"'Yes,' she said. 'I always do.'"

"That was funny—for a moment. I actually laughed. But I've had to face the truth of it. There must have been countless times she'd had to forgive me. I've spent years consumed with the past. So preoccupied that I executed a thousand small drownings of Harlo's life. Moments missed—gone forever. Moments drowned in alcohol."

A light rap came on the door. It opened and the man from the gallery looked in. "It's almost time for us to go, darling."

"I'll be there in a moment," she answered.

"You're seeing someone?" I asked, trying to sound casual.

"Yes."

I stood. "Thank you for talking with me. I hope that you'll be able to forgive me."

"You're forgiven." She smiled and rose to give me a brief hug.

"Is your painting for sale?" I asked as I passed the easel.

"Yes—when it's finished."

"I'd like to buy it. The approaching light. . .. but you said the light might be departing? I suppose a departing light imparts the greater illumination. Isn't it Dickinson's lines …"

" 'By a departing light…' " she began.

" 'We see acuter, quite,' " I finished the line.

"Yes," she said.

I located the poem when I returned to the cabin, and sitting on the back porch I read the last lines out loud to the sunset: " 'There's something in the flight, that clarifies the sight, and decks the rays.' " The sun's rays, which had been present all day long, were only now visible in the decked lines of pink and gold—visible only because they were departing.

Thoughts from the Back Porch   November 1996

It's November. The moon stays through the day now, a pale ghost behind dark bare branches, and the daylight fades early. An unexpected skiff of snow along the riverbanks makes the water shine turquoise. I've closed up the cabin. I'll be heading back to Springville. I won't return until the college dismisses for spring break. I've made the rounds, saying my good-byes. I hiked down to Lucy and Eb's.

Lucy tells me her chickens are sleepy from the sudden chill, and Eb says the turkey and deer have made off with all the persimmons. I stopped at the dam to see Emmett. He talked about the secrets of catching bass in cold water. He was going home early because Lottie was making dumplings for lunch. Yesterday I returned all my books to the library and ran into Anna. I gave her my college address and asked her to stay in touch. There's no need to say goodbye to Leah. A rather final good bye seems to have taken place the day I visited her at the gallery. The *Rosalee* is stowed away in the boat house, and I've closed up the cabin for winter. I left an extra key with Tom who was adding logs to a fire when I stopped by.

"Take a seat and warm yourself." He pointed to one of two chairs that faced the fireplace. The fragrance of pine filled the room. A black coon dog pulled itself up from its warm place by the fire and padded over to greet me.

"Nice dog," I said, rubbing its long, soft ears. It took in my scent with is big tawny nose, offered me an immense paw, and sauntered back to its place by the fire.

"That's John Paul Jones," Tom said, nodding toward the dog.

"The one who said, 'I've only begun to fight?'"

Tom nodded.

"Let me guess. He must have been a Scotch-Irishman."

"Yep."

"Well the dog seems more like an English gentleman. Quite reserved."

"You know anything about coon dogs?"

"Only a little," I said, remembering Emmett's account of being drug across the lawn.

"Well, they may be Englishmen indoors, but outside they are full Scotch-Irish. Independent and stubborn, if not impossible to turn once they've got a scent. Can run for miles tracking down game."

"An Ozark dog," I said.

"Exactly. Two hundred years of Ozark."

Tom added a final log to the flames and sat down in the chair beside me. The low round table between our two chairs looked like Tom's office desk—piles of papers, files and law books.

"Any word on Sam's case?"

"Trial's been set for March."

"Anna wrote in one of her notebooks that they found cocaine in Sam's duffel bag."

"Willis Sprule made sure that duffel bag of cocaine got in the hands of the police." Tom shook his head. "It's a sick bird that fouls its own nest."

I thanked him for keeping an eye on my cabin. Told him I'd see him in the spring, and walked back through the woods to my car. I drove to the college with a sense of loss and unexpected loneliness. I wondered if it was simply my life without writing—my life without obsession, my life without balance.

The road in front of me traced the meandering curves of the river. "Now see here, John," I could hear Granddad say. "See how on this bend of the river the outside curve is the faster water, cutting away at its bank, and the inside water is slower, losing its energy and dropping some of its load? Then it rounds the bend, and the sides swap jobs. Inside water takes the outside bank; outside bank takes the inside. River shapes its whole course by knowing when to carry the load and when to drop it."

That's balance!

Thoughts from Springville   January 1997

I'm sitting in my office at the college; the semester is underway. I brought my notebooks with me, and I've taken the last one down from the shelf because Anna wrote me a letter, and I think it belongs in my notebook:

>Dear Mr. Sinclair,
>
>The river is covered with patches of ice and snow, and the water's running slow and dark. A man is putting a "sold" sign in my yard. I'll be moving to Leah's apartment.
>
>Thank you for your nice card and letter about Momma's death. She didn't talk much toward the end. Her words seemed to boil down like broth in the skillet. But that makes a rich gravy. On one of her last days she came to me just as I was leaving for town. She put her hand into mine and wanted to go along.
>
>"Oh Momma," I said. "I can't take you with me."
>
>"Then I'll just walk with you as far as I can," she said.
>
>I guess that's all we can ever do with the people we love—just walk with them as far as we can.
>
>Momma had another stroke in January. She died in the hospital. There was no heartbeat by the time I got there, just doctors and nurses pushing buttons and checking monitors. I rushed into the room and called, "Momma!"
>
>As soon as Momma heard my voice, the nurse yelled, "We're getting a pulse." It was like the final flicker of Momma flamed back to be with me, one last time. She opened her eyes, saw me, and then she was gone.
>
>I buried her beside Grandma and Grandpa Poinselot, under the shade of a nice sugar gum tree. It's a pretty place. I like sitting there. There are so many feelings to sort out looking down at the grave of your Momma.
>
>Our Momma is the only door into this world. When we discover the disappointments of this place into which we've been born, we take our disappointments back to Momma, lay them, like blame, at her doorstep. If we're lucky, we live long enough to back off on blaming her, allow ourselves to love her before she dies.

Anyway, I've done considerable thinking out there under the sugar gum tree, and I've come to believe that I gave out as much pain as I inherited.

Momma's pretty French eyes are closed now. I figure those eyes saw more than I knew—understood more than I ever believed."

Anna

Thoughts from the Back Porch   March 1997

It's spring break at the college, and I'm once again back at the cabin, sitting at The Benchmark with my coffee. I plan to fish and enjoy the river for a couple weeks and do some serious writing. My agent had a few favorable comments from a publishing house, but they recommended considerable re-writes. There's the promise of a contract, if the revision meets their expectations.

A deer and her fawn are having spring beauties for breakfast. Grandma Rowden called them spring beauties, and Granddad always reminded me they were *Claytonia*, named after the botanist, John Clayton. Their five petals of soft pink, veined with deep rose spread like a carpet between the porch and the river. They were once eaten by Native Americans, and Grandma always added the petals to her salads.

Brown thrashers are building a nest in the shagbark hickory tree, and from time to time they flute their opinions to one another. The river is running full with spring rains. I took the *Rosalee* out of the boathouse and enjoyed an early morning fishing trip down river. I passed Anna's house. The real estate sign is gone from her yard, and a young man and woman on ladders are giving the bright, blue shutters a fresh coat of paint.

Anna must be lost without her river. However her attentions are surely confined to the courtroom. I dropped by Tom Ferguson's to tell him I was back. He gave me a full report on the trial, which is not expected to last more than a week. Sheriff Milby testified about the presence of the duffel bag and the bag of cocaine. The hearings are recessed for the week-end.

Sunday morning I rose early, took the boat down river, caught two trout and was home by mid-morning. I was busy writing when the phone rang.

"Mr. Sinclair?"

"Anna!"

"Mrs. Lushbaugh said you'd come in for supplies. Said you'd be staying for a couple of weeks."

"Yes."

"Well, I was wondering if you had any extra fish in your refrigerator."

"Fish?"

"Yes—you know—that you might have a mind to be bringing over."

"Well, I did catch two beauties this morning...."

"Well that's certainly thoughtful of you. Would you be coming down right away then?"

"Do you need them right away?"

"Yes, that would be the perfect time. And you do know I'm living with Leah now? Her apartment's above the gallery. You'll see the outside stairs."

She had nothing else to say, except "thanks" and "good-bye."

I placed the receiver in its cradle and stood several seconds without moving, as I ran through a couple scenarios.

All that concerned me as I climbed the stairs above the gallery and lifted the brass knocker on the attractive wooden door was my need to understand Anna's strange phone call.

The door opened, and it was not Anna who stood looking at me, but Leah.

I finally managed to say, "I brought your mother's fish."

"Fish?"

"She phoned."

"Mother's in Springville. She's taken Harlo there to stay with Aunt Zoe. Because of the trial."

"She said she needed the fish right away."

Leah was obviously as confused as I. "Come in. I'll give her a call."

I took a chair in the large, sunny room—almost a gallery itself. The furniture was modern and sparse, and large paintings of bright primary colors filled the walls. A low glass-top coffee table held a single unopened bottle of wine. Leah had said she'd quit drinking. Perhaps it belonged to her new friend from the gallery.

Leah returned in a few minutes to say, "That was a strange phone call. Momma said to tell you that one good fish story calls for another?"

"Oh," I said, finally realizing. "I'm afraid I once used fish as a ruse to visit your mother." I held up the bag of fish. "These might have been an excuse to get me here."

For the first time Leah seemed to understand that I was actually holding a bag of fish. She stood looking at me and my fish, and I at her—at her disheveled hair and her eyes that looked as though she hadn't slept. She took the bag from my hand and carried it to the refrigerator. When she returned, she sat on the sofa behind the bottle of wine. She looked terrible, like a forgotten plant bereft of its turgor, stems drooping and leaves wilted. "I'm in a bit of a crisis," she said. "Up to now Momma's done quite well on her promise to stop trying to fix me. Looks like she's fallen off the wagon. She's certainly afraid I might."

"Is that a valid fear?"

"You are now the only thing that stands between me and this bottle of wine," she admitted.

"I'm here for as long as you need me," I said.

"Are you through with your book?"

"Not exactly. I have the promise of publication—based on some serious re-writing."

"You should be writing then."

"I should be here; I want to be here."

She didn't comment. Instead, she said, "I have to take the stand tomorrow. Testify against my own brother. Admit that he might have been able to save Mary. I have to watch my father's hatred triumph over us. I haven't had a drink since I stopped at the end of the summer," she said. She sat staring at the bottle.

"Have you eaten anything today," I asked.

She shook her head.

"I haven't either. Let's go out and get a good meal."

She looked interested for a moment and then said, "I'm a mess. I need a shower."

"Okay—you shower, and I'll guard the wine," I said.

She was reluctant, but agreed. Several minutes later she appeared in front of me, looking much better. She wore the same yellow dress she'd worn the day I met her in the park with Harlo. She let her hair fall around her shoulders—the way I liked it.

"Do you have a favorite restaurant?" I asked.

She named one along the River Walk.

We arrived at the restaurant, and she nodded at the no smoking sign. "I stopped smoking too," she said. "Smoking—drinking. For me one seemed to call for the other. So, I stopped both."

"That's near celibacy," I said.

"That too," she said.

"Does that include the good-looking guy at the gallery?"

"Things never got that far. "

"Shall I feign disappointment?" I joked.

"He had never experienced a child as part of his life. Harlo didn't seem to fit his priorities," she said.

We finished our lunch and took a walk along the river, eventually sitting on one of the benches near the water.

"Thank you," she said. "I was in trouble. They say that whatever possesses you, ultimately defines you. 'Alcoholic' is a caustic definition. I think I moved away from life to a very narrow place, stayed there more often—longer—till the narrow place was my life."

I understood. I confessed how my writing, flowing or blocked, had removed me from important moments—some of them critical like the day Harlo had floated down the river. We talked about the difficulty of maintaining equilibrium. I told her how trout balance themselves within the ever-changing forces of the river. How they fold back their fins and streamline their bodies when tough swimming is required, or relax—nearly limp—conserving their energy in stormy turbulence.

We talked until afternoon shadows edged across the water—talked easily and perhaps even a little foolishly, as people do when they are immensely grateful for the return of hope.

On the drive home Leah related some of the court proceedings that had occurred the previous week. Sheriff Milby had testified that following the drownings, he had accompanied Willis to the river bank and retrieved Sam's duffel bag. It had contained a half-kilo of pure cocaine, which hadn't yet been parceled into packets and diluted with quinine or milk sugar. Its street value had been estimated at several thousand dollars.

Sam could have been charged with possession of an illegal substance and sentenced to over twenty years in prison, but thankfully, the statute of limitations had run out. However, the charge of involuntary manslaughter had no such limitation, and the cocaine was still pivotal evidence in the case.

"I'm all right," she assured me when I stopped in front of her apartment. I promise to put away the bottle of wine."

"Would you like me to go with you to the courthouse tomorrow?"

"Yes, I would."

"I don't like leaving you alone," I said.

"Mamma's back by now."

"I assume she'll know you've been with me?"

"You can bet the first thing she did was check the refrigerator for those fish!"

Thoughts from the Courthouse   March 1997

The old Cotton Rock Prison located high on a ridge, hovers over the town and the courthouse like a silent apparition from the past. It's a disquieting and unexpected piece of history. The remnant of a buttressed wall, reminiscent of the French Bastille, flanks one side of the prison. The walls are built from formidable blocks of cotton rock, some seven feet long and over two feet thick.

The roof and doors have long ago rotted away, and the walls once the color of white sand, have darkened with age. Visitors are allowed to tour its tomb-like cells and its stone floors, still pierced by iron rings which once chained the legs of prisoners.

I could only hope as I entered the present courtroom of modern, paneled wainscoting that its sense of justice had kept pace with the progression of its architecture. The judge's bench, a raised dais on the far wall, extended to include the witness box. The court reporter and county clerk sat directly in front of the judge's bench, and the counsel tables centered between the clerk and the public rail.

It was nearly nine when I arrived and located Anna and Leah on the front row behind the defense table. I had been writing since daybreak. In order to arrive at the courthouse on time, I had stopped crafting an important scene. For a brief moment I considered arriving late—telling myself that the proceedings would probably not start at the stroke of nine. But I remembered my newly pledged commitment to balance, closed my lap top mid-sentence and walked out the door. I was rewarded by the grateful look on Leah's face when I sat down on the bench beside her.

Anna leaned forward and nodded hello. She wore the gray suit that had become her primary wardrobe. Her hair was pulled back as always into its knot at the back of her head, and I speculated that the buckeye still hung beneath her suit jacket.

"We met with Ferguson this morning," Leah said quietly. "Went over my testimony. I told him it had changed since the Grand Jury hearing. I explained about the flashback. The information is technically new evidence. But because the prosecution has the burden of proof, the defense doesn't have to advise them of any new testimony. This might work to Sam's advantage."

I looked around the room and located Willis, seated almost directly across the aisle. He sat stone-like and did not seem to acknowledge any one, including Cora Eckert who sat beside him. Nearly every bench was filled. Cotton Rock probably hadn't had a case of such interest in years. I caught sight of Dee Lushbaugh's orange hair. Lingo Henegar sat beside her. Phil from the coffee shop and his parents sat behind us. Emmett had left his fishing pole long enough to sit on the back row. I recognized a couple more students from the writing class, including Lucy who caught my eye and nodded.

The somber formality that accompanies the power of the law hung over the courtroom, and people waited in silence or whispered discreetly. The bailiff entered from the side door with Sam who had been brought up from the jail, housed in the basement of the courthouse. He wore a new suit, and his hair had been freshly cut. I would have known he was Anna's boy, even removed from the present setting. Anna was right. There was something boyish and unguarded about him, something in his manner that would have stirred my sympathies, irrespective of his present plight. He located Anna and Leah and took his seat at the counsel table beside Tom Ferguson.

Tom Ferguson opened a worn brief case, pulled out a fistful of files, laid them on the table, placed a hand on Sam's shoulder and leaned in to whisper something in his ear.

He told Anna earlier that Sam would not be taking the stand. "He'll plead the fifth. Letting a witness testify in his own defense is unpredictable as the end of a cow's tail when you're milking. Never know when it's going to slap you. Wouldn't do to have Sam cross-examined after running away for fifteen years. A man defending himself for doing wrong, digs himself into a hole quicker than he can dig himself out."

Vince Millford, the prosecuting attorney, was Ferguson's near opposite. A small, thin man considerably younger than Ferguson, he was fastidious in dress. He entered the courtroom, walked briskly to the prosecution table, snapped open his brief case, reached into its meticulous interior, removed several files and aligned them carefully on the table.

The clerk requested that we all rise, announcing that court was now in session with the Honorable Clark O'Connor presiding. The room rustled with the sound of people standing as Judge O'Connor entered from his chambers and took his place at the bench. He appeared the personification of wisdom: black robe, white hair and calm, firm manner. Throughout the trial he often stared thoughtfully, as judges are inclined to do into some vast, ethereal realm of justice, as though precepts of law were written there, as though he were measuring the testimonies of the courtroom against its lofty, unseen standard.

The jury entered and Millford called Willis as his first witness. Willis took his seat in the witness box, and Millford stood at the lectern. Millford had a habit each time he began speaking of drumming his long, thin fingers against the ear piece of his glasses, each finger, rising up and setting down in turn like the legs a tarantula. When he wasn't talking—merely listening to proceedings—he drummed his fingers against a file or the counsel table, placing each finger with slow and artful precision, reinforcing the image of the tarantula again and again.

Anna immediately dubbed him "the spider" and told us over coffee that when people fell feverish in the hills, it was speculated someone had "put a spider in their water bucket." To Anna, Millford brought poison to the courtroom.

"Now Mr. Sprule," Millford began thrumming his fingers, "Why were you at the river on the day of Mary's death?"

Willis answered, staring straight ahead. "I followed Sam there."

"And why were you following him?" Millford continued.

"I wanted to see what he was going to do with his duffel bag."

The duffel bag was identified as exhibit A, and the questioning continued. "Mr. Sprule, why were you concerned about the duffel bag?"

"Sam said he kept a change of clothes in it. Sometimes went fishing after school. That's what he said, anyway. But I noticed he'd begun to carry that bag everywhere."

Millford raised his eyebrows, and nodded, as though to compliment Willis for his astute observation. But the compliment went unappreciated by Willis, who continued to look straight ahead.

"Did you ever look into the bag to examine its contents?" Millford asked.

"Yes, I did."

"Did you look into the bag on more than one occasion?"

"No," Willis answered indifferently. "Once was all I needed."

"Do you remember on what day you looked into the bag?"

"Yes. It was the day Mary drowned."

"And what did you find?" asked Millford, plucking a new file from the prosecution table.

Willis listed it contents: "Jeans and a shirt, some socks—underwear. I dumped them on the floor. Found a compartment in the bottom. Sewed into the lining. Found a zip-lock bag half-full of white powder. Figured it was cocaine."

A murmur swept across the courtroom.

A plastic bag identified as exhibit B was duly noted and Millford asked, "What did you do after you discovered the cocaine?"

"I tried to call Sheriff Milby," Willis said. "I planned to have him come out and see the cocaine for himself. But Milby was out of the office. They said he'd be back in an hour. Sam didn't go to work till late afternoon. Figured I'd have plenty of time. I went on out to the barn to run some feed through the auger. When I came back to the house, Sam was gone. Took little Mary fishing they said. I checked his room. Duffel bag was gone."

"What did you do next, Mr. Sprule?" Millford asked.

"I decided to go to the river myself. I knew Sam liked to fish off Sleeping Rock. I didn't want a drug addict hurting my Mary," Willis added.

I felt Leah's body tense beside me. I had never sat through a trial before, and I would come to see its singular tortures inflicted on Leah and Anna, requiring them to have the people they cherished desecrated by people like Willis and forcing them to have their personal life laid bare to a casual public.

The questioning continued. "Did you drive to the river, Mr. Sprule?"

"Yes. Drove my truck. Stopped up on Lookout Bend above Sleeping Rock. Walked down the hill. About half-way down I stopped on a little knoll, where I could get a good look."

"Tell us what you saw," said Millford, turning an eye toward at the jury.

Willis began his description, reporting word after word in uniform monotone. It was as if his mouth were an unfeeling machine, as if it were possible to sever his head from his body and set it on the dais beside Judge O'Connor, where it would continue to drone on in its indifferent, mechanical tone. "I saw Sam, standing up on Sleeping Rock, holding the duffel bag. Mary was standing up to her waist in water. I stayed on the knoll, cause it's steep there. I yelled down, told him to throw the duffel bag to my side of the river. I could see the water was rising around Sleeping Rock. Mary was trying to wade out, but the current was pushing hard against her. She was fighting, waving her arms. But the river carried her off."

Pain, forced into the rigid and unnatural confines of public exposure, must garrote itself, so that only small, strangled signs of it escape: a slight shudder from Leah or a breath caught and held—Anna's hands that clench and fear to let go. There was nothing I could do, but to stay beside them, and vow to remain there.

Millford stood arms akimbo, his voice edged in sarcasm: "Even though the water was rising and your daughter, Mary, was struggling for her life, Sam chose to hold on to that duffel bag?"

The question brought Ferguson to his feet with an objection. But Judge O'Connor instructed the witness to answer.

Willis answered in his relentless monotone. "Yes. Water came up over the rock—covered his feet. He knew if he threw that bag to me, he was on his way to prison. That's when he heaved the duffel bag hard, over to the far bank—north bank. When he turned back he saw Mary going under. He tried to swim to her. But she was gone before he got there. He just took off swimming down the river."

"What did you do next, Mr. Sprule?" Millford extended a sympathetic voice, but Willis didn't receive sympathy anymore than he gave it. He seemed to hear with the same calloused indifference with which he spoke.

"I ran back up the hill," Willis said. "Got into my truck. I drove down river a ways. Couldn't see either of them. So I turned around and drove back up to the Dobbs's house. Called Sheriff Milby. He met me there at the Dobbs's. I took him on down to the site of the drowning and the duffel bag. He took it back to the station house."

Millford walked to the counsel table. "How far were you, Mr. Sprule, from the river when you first saw Mary and Sam?"

Willis blinked, as though trying to remember. "Maybe fifty feet. But it was steep. I was trying to get down to the river."

Millford, re-aligning his files into an orderly row, asked the next question without looking up. "You've testified that you saw almost immediately that the water was rising?"

"Yes."

Satisfied with the alignment of his files, Millford turned, facing the jury. "Then anyone close to the river should have been able to tell that the water was rising?"

Ferguson objected that Millford was leading the witness to speculate. Judge O'Connor allowed the question.

"Anybody close enough to see the river—and Sleeping Rock's dead center of it— knew the water was rising," Willis answered.

"In your opinion, Mr. Sprule," Millford asked, crossing his arms, "did your stepson, Sam McKerry, have ample time to save Mary, if he hadn't chosen to save his cocaine?"

Ferguson objected, but O'Connor overruled, "I'll allow the question. The witness is instructed to answer."

"If Sam had gone straight for Mary, instead of deciding which way to throw that duffel bag, she'd be here today."

Millford announced that he had no further questions, and Ferguson stood to begin his cross examination. Ferguson had a way of ambling slowly back and forth in front of the bench, his head bent slightly forward, his big feet padding easily along like a gentle old hound. Yes! I thought. Like John Paul Jones. Like his own coon dog, sauntering along through the house in no particular hurry, the patient result of years of familiarity.

"Mr. Sprule, you testified that you saw the water rising around Sleeping Rock, then you looked over at Mary and saw the river carry her off."

"That's right," said Willis.

Ferguson turned and began ambling back. "What was Mary wearing that day?"

"I don't remember."

"Now let's see…you were only fifty feet away, with a clear view. It was the last time you would ever see your daughter alive. You must remember something about her appearance."

Willis shifted in his chair. "I remember some ribbons. She was always wearing some kind of costume thing for dancing. Had some ribbons tied on her."

"Do you remember what color those ribbons were, Mr. Sprule?"

"Red. Some were yellow."

"Where were they tied?"

Willis blinked, trying to remember. "Around her waist, I'd say."

Ferguson stopped, chin in hand, and looked up as though reading his next question from the ceiling. "How were you able to see those ribbons, Mr. Sprule, with the water up to her waist?"

Willis wrinkled his forehead in thought. "They were floating—like spokes on a wheel—floating out from her waist."

"You say you saw the ribbons floating around her," Ferguson said. He had begun to roam once again. He ambled past Judge O'Connor before turning slowly and asking, "Are you saying that the ribbons were floating against the current?"

Willis hesitated.

"Have you ever seen anything float upstream, Mr. Sprule?" Ferguson asked.

Someone snickered. Willis glanced sharply in the direction of the laughter.

"Mr. Sprule, you've testified that as soon as you arrived, almost immediately, the water was covering Sam's feet, and Mary was being swept off by the current. I was just trying to figure how those ribbons could be floating out like spokes on a wheel, when being pulled by the swell of a river."

"I understand physics," Willis said. A definite energy had entered his monotone. "Evidently, I was there a minute or so before the river started to rise—before there was a current."

"So you actually arrived at the river a minute or so before the water started to rise?"

Like a true blood hound, Ferguson had picked up an important scent, and he meant to tree his hunch.

"If you were listening, you'd know that's what I said." Willis's monotone had begun to venture into new heights of pitch.

"Well, you'll have to forgive me, Mr. Sprule," Ferguson said, meandering calmly. "I'm getting old. Now, Mr. Sprule, since you understand and appreciate physics, you would have noticed when the river started rising. 'Cause the current would have grabbed those ribbons, pulled them in the direction of the flow—or possibly sucked them under, altogether. Would you say that you weren't looking at Mary when the water started rising?"

Willis's heavy brows pulled into a scowl. "I might have been looking at Sam at that moment."

"You might have been," said Ferguson congenially. "You very well might have been, because you hadn't actually come there to check on Mary, had you?" Ferguson stopped to read from a tablet on the corner of the defense table. "You told us that you went to the river because, and I quote 'I wanted to see what Sam was going to do with that bag'."

Willis didn't answer, but Ferguson was on to the next question.

"Isn't it possible, between the time you saw Mary with the ribbons floating around her and the time you looked back to see her being carried away by the current, that several minutes might have elapsed?"

Willis ran his hand through his hair, releasing a few sprigs from the hold of his hair oil. "No. It isn't possible," Willis said.

"You're sure?"

"Yes."

"Well, I'm glad you're sure, Mr. Sprule, because I'm a little short on sure, myself. You've got me a trifle mixed up here," Ferguson said. "First," he said, holding out one hand, "You were sure that you arrived at the river just as the water was carrying Mary away. And now," Ferguson held out his other hand, "you're sure it was sometime after you arrived at the river. Which is it, Mr. Sprule?"

"Sam had time to save her. I'm sure of that."

Judge O'Connor instructed Willis to answer the question.

"I must have arrived before the river started to rise—but not long before."

Ferguson resumed his sauntering and asked, "Was Mary on your side of the river, or the north side?"

"My side—south."

"And you testified that you were only about fifty feet up on a knoll—maybe less, because you were trying ever so hard to climb down."

Willis understood the implication of the statement and said, "By the time I saw the situation, it was too late to get down that hill and get to Mary."

"You said you called down to Sam?"

"Yes."

"What did you say?"

"Tried to get him to throw the bag to my side of the river!"

"So you were interested in saving that duffel bag, weren't you?"

"Yes I was! The boy was selling cocaine!"

"Did Sam answer your request to throw the bag?"

"No. He was scared to answer. Knew he was caught. Just stood there looking up at me," Willis said.

But Ferguson was tracking a new scent.

"Mr. Sprule, the court has established that on the day of the drowning, the generators started at exactly two o'clock."

"Well, the horn never sounded," Willis said, crossing his arms firmly.

"As I was saying," Ferguson continued, shuffling past Willis toward the jury box, "the officials at the dam verified in court on Friday, that on the day of the drowning, the generators started at exactly two in the afternoon. Sheriff Milby's office verified that your call from the Dobbs's house came into police dispatch at exactly two-thirty—thirty minutes after the drowning.

"You testified that after the river carried Mary away, you 'ran up the hill to your truck and drove down river a ways' to look for her. Then, because you saw nothing, you turned around and drove back up the road. You crossed the bridge to the north side of the river and drove to the Dobbs's house. Isn't that a short drive? Maybe no more than five minutes?"

"I suppose."

"According to Sheriff Milby, when he accompanied you to the river, he found that you had already marked the location of the duffel bag with a bandana that you tied to a bush. When did you tie on the bandana?"

"Well," Willis's face flushed red. "I tied that bandana on the way to Dobbs's house."

"So, you must have done that before you made the phone call to the sheriff?"

"Yes."

"But you just testified that you went directly to the Dobbs's."

"I forgot about stopping to mark the bag," Willis conceded.

"So you forgot about stopping your truck, walking all the way down to the river, locating the bag, tying your bandana on a bush to mark the spot, then walking back to your truck, before driving on to the Dobbs's house to call the sheriff?"

"Yes, I said I forgot that part," he snapped.

"Is that sort of like forgetting that your daughter had just drowned?" Ferguson asked. "I mean, you saw the river carry your daughter away. You saw Sam swim down river after her. Because Sam still had hope he could save her. Wouldn't you agree, Mr. Sprule, that when you love someone, you don't give up hope?"

Willis leaned forward in the witness box. "My daughter was gone! I was gonna make sure that boy paid! I was—"

But Ferguson cut him off, "I submit to you, Mr. Sprule that any normal, loving father this side of God's sweet heaven, would have driven down to the first bend, or any likely spot a body might snag. He'd have jumped into that water—cold or not—and he'd have looked for his little girl till he couldn't swim another lick, till he was absolutely sure there was no hope of finding her."

"I knew there was no hope—I saw her go." Willis said. "That river's all muscle when they ramp up those generators. A grown man can't even stand up in that kind of water!" But Willis seemed to understand he had boxed himself into a bad corner. He leaned forward in the witness box and sought to interject feeling into his words, shouting them out to the courtroom. "I loved that little girl! I was her father!" But his voice rang hollow—like a school play, where students know their lines, but their delivery is amateur and lacking in persuasion. It was as though he was so unrehearsed in his own passions, when called upon to display them, he knew no coordinates, no reference points.

Ferguson returned to his questioning. "Why didn't you phone from a neighbor's house on the south side of the river where you were? They could have gotten help sooner."

"It was no use, I tell you," Willis said. "There was no sign of her."

Ferguson stopped in front of the witness stand. "Isn't it true that you were more interested in locating that duffel bag, more interested in getting a bandana tied to a bush than getting your little girl out of the river?"

"You're not going to pin this on me!" Willis shouted, rage apparently the one emotion he could deliver with sincerity. "I'm not on trial here!"

Ferguson sauntered back to the counsel table and settled himself into his chair. "I have no further questions," he told Judge O'Connor.

O'Connor declared a fifteen minute recess.

I walked down the hall with Anna and Leah where we located a coffee machine. Both women were glad for a small reprieve from the strain of the courtroom. We drank our coffee in near silence. Anna spoke only once, "The day I opened the *Cotton Rock Herald* and saw Sam's picture with the caption of manslaughter, I had to accept that everyone would see it. People like Cora Eckert could use it to roll up the morning garbage. But that was nothing compared to sitting in that courtroom and hearing Willis speak the names of Mary and Sam—roll them off his tongue like he had a right."

When court had resumed once again, Millford stood, opened a file, and said, "I call Leah Gatewood to the stand."

Leah was sworn in and walked to the witness box, a brave and solitary walk, and it came to me in watching her that I loved her, that I had been falling in love with her for most of the summer.

Millford asked her to state her relationship to Sam and after the characteristic thrumming of his fingers against his temple, began his questioning. "Now, Mrs. Gatewood, why were you at the river the day of the drowning?"

"I went to check on Mary," she said. As soon as she'd said the words, we saw her look of regret.

"Why were you checking on her?" Millford asked.

"To make certain she was all right."

"And why wouldn't she be all right?" Millford asked, turning toward the jury.

"Sam was always good about taking her fishing. They loved to go fishing together."

"Why were you concerned she might not be all right?" Millford repeated. "Please answer the question."

"I didn't think Sam wanted to take her that day."

"He didn't want to take Mary with him that day?" Millford repeated her words.

"It was my day to take care of her," Leah said. "I wanted to go with my girlfriends. I made him take her."

"So neither of you wanted to take your little sister?" Millford asked.

"I chose to be with my friends," Leah said, nodding her head slowly. "It is the greatest regret of my life."

Millford resumed his place at the lectern. "How did you know where to find Mary?"

Leah explained that Sam and Mary often fished off Sleeping Rock, how she had stood on the bridge which she estimated to be about a hundred feet from the rock.

"Where was Mary?"

"She was standing in a pool of water. I saw the ribbons. I tied them around her waist that morning. They were floating out on the water, like petals around her. She held up her arms like a ballerina. She was dancing."

"And she was on the south side of the river, as your father has testified?"

"She was on the south side as Mr. Sprule testified," Leah said.

Millford ignored Leah's correction. "Where was Sam?"

"He was standing up on Sleeping Rock. I was going to leave. Everything seemed all right—even peaceful."

"Did something make you change your mind?" Millford asked.

Leah nodded. "I saw that Mary had stopped dancing. She called to Sam, and pointed to something up on the hillside in front of them. Sam and her both were looking up at something. They were so intent. I was curious. But the hillside is heavy with trees. I couldn't see. They seemed to be talking to someone on the hillside. Then, I saw that the ribbons were pulling downstream. Saw that the water was rising around Sleeping Rock. Sam and Mary didn't seem to notice. They just kept looking up at the hillside. But the water coming down is icy, and Mary must have felt its coldness. She tried to wade out. But she couldn't keep her footing."

"What was Sam doing?"

"He was holding the duffel bag as though he were going to throw it, looking first to one side of the river and then the other. He couldn't seem to decide which way to throw. I yelled, but Sam seemed too distracted to hear me."

Millford emphasized his words, speaking toward the jury, "So Sam had forgotten his little sister entirely?"

Ferguson's objection was sustained by Judge O'Connor, who ordered it stricken from the record.

Millford redirected his question, "Did Sam drop the bag on the rock and go directly to Mary?"

"No."

"What happened next?"

"I saw Sam throw the duffel bag…wildly, desperately. I remember seeing it sail through the air to the north bank. Then the water slid over the rock and covered Sam's feet. It startled him—he jumped. He knew what it meant and whirled around to find Mary. But the river had her in its grip. I jumped down from the bridge and started running toward Mary. There's a tangle of willows and bushes there. I could no longer see the river. I just kept running, kept seeing that image of Mary struggling in the water and Sam going toward her. When I got to Sleeping Rock…" Leah gripped the rail in front of her; her agony was visible. We had seen it rising within her as she talked, saw it spread across her face as she fought for control. "Everything was gone. The pockets of water. The rock. Only the buoy was left—marking the spot."

Judge O'Connor leaned down from his bench to ask her if she was able to continue. She nodded and composed herself in time to hear Millford say, "What did you do next?"

Leah recounted her search, how she'd run along the river's edge. Once she'd seen Sam further down, still diving, still looking for Mary. In the end, she no longer saw Sam. She thought they had both drowned and she'd run to the Dawson's, a nearby neighbor. She was screaming, and Mrs. Dawson had come outside, had promised to phone for help. Then Leah had fainted, there on Mrs. Dawson's porch.

Millford now stood directly in front of the witness box. "In your opinion, Mrs. Gatewood, if Sam had chosen to save Mary—who had been entrusted to his care—instead of standing up on Sleeping Rock trying to save that duffel bag, would he have had time to save her?"

"Sam would never have let her drown, if he had realized in time—"

"Mrs. Gatewood," Millford tried again, "if Sam had gone to her as soon as the water started rising, could he have saved her?"

Leah looked pleadingly down at Sam, sitting at the counsel table.

"Please answer the question, Mrs. Gatewood."

Leah's answer was barely audible: "I think there's a chance Sam could have saved her."

The courtroom buzzed with whispers, and Judge O'Connor rapped his gavel. "The courtroom will remain quiet, or you will all be escorted out," he warned.

"I have no further questions," Millford said and took his seat at the counsel table.

Ferguson began his cross-examination. "Mrs. Gatewood, you testified that you saw the ribbons go under and the water begin to rise around Sleeping Rock?"

"Yes."

"Then you testified that you saw Sam throw the duffel bag, and then you saw the water slide over the rock and cover his feet."

"Yes."

"Then you saw him immediately turn toward Mary and swim to her."

"Yes."

"Mr. Sprule testified that the water first covered Sam's feet, then he threw the duffel bag, and then he turned to swim for Mary. Are you aware that you are in direct disagreement with Mr. Sprule's testimony concerning the sequence of events?"

"Yes."

"You're certain of your testimony?"

"Yes."

"Is it possible that because Sam was up on the rock, and because he was distracted by Mr. Sprule's presence on the knoll, he didn't realize the water was rising until he felt it hit his feet?"

"Yes.."

"And the moment he realized the water was rising, he instantly turned back toward Mary?"

"Objection, your Honor! Counsel is leading the witness to pure speculation!" Millford said.

Judge O'Connor sustained the objection and ordered that the jury to disregard the question. Nevertheless, the possibility hung in the courtroom and the hope of that thought registered clearly on Leah's face.

Ferguson began his familiar stroll. "What was Willis' attitude toward Sam?"

"He didn't like him," Leah said. "The best Sam could hope for from Willis was to be ignored. That was a good day for Sam. Sometimes I believed Willis hated Sam. He made fun of him. Belittled him often—sometimes abused him."

"Can you give us an example of that abuse?"

Leah hesitated a moment. "When my sister Mary was two, she had pneumonia. My mother had gone to the hospital to be with her. It was early morning. Sam was ten. I was seven. Sam must have overslept. I remember waking up, hearing Willis outside cursing. Yelling that Sam had forgotten to feed the pigs. I got out of bed and looked out the window. Sam was lying on the ground by the kitchen door. Willis stood over him.

"Sam must have gotten out of bed, grabbed his trousers in hand and tried to dress on the run. Each time he tried to stand—balance long enough to pull up his trousers; Willis would kick him from behind with the side of his foot. It was as though he wanted to kick Sam just hard enough to knock him to the ground, and still insure he could get up. If Sam's hands had been free, he could have kept from going face first into the dirt, but he would have had to let go of his trousers. He had no way to free himself of the tangle. Each time he got to his feet, Willis's kick brought his face to the ground. Each time Sam fell, Willis screamed for him to get up. This went on all the way to the barn. I could see that Sam was desperate to get away. He finally got the trousers hitched up enough to run inside the barn.

"I got dressed. I found Sam sitting on the barn floor—asked him if he was all right. He said, 'The kicking part didn't hurt so much. It was the other part.' I was only seven, but I understood he meant the humiliation, the pleasure Willis got from shaming him. Sam begged me not to tell Momma. He said Willis had warned him not to go whining to her. Said Willis would make him pay if he told."

Ferguson had long ago stopped strolling. A woman in the jury leaned forward in her chair to seek Willis out of the crowd. Another juror glared openly at him.

Ferguson advised that he had no further questions, and Millford stood to request redirect of the witness. "Mrs. Gatewood," he began. "Would you say that you have intense dislike for your father?"

"Yes."

"And would you say that you have a great deal of sympathy for your brother, Sam?"

"Yes, I think he had a tragic childhood."

"Would you say that your passionate feelings have affected your testimony—perhaps even given you an opportunity to pay Willis back?"

"If you're saying my passions have persuaded me to perjure myself, you are absolutely wrong! The truth about Willis is quite sufficient," Leah said. "I have no need to exaggerate."

"Mrs. Gatewood, can you think of any reason why Sam would be up on that rock, holding the duffel bag, unless it was to save its contents from the river?"

Leah hesitated.

Millford was happy to repeat the question. "Can you think of any other reason Sam would have been standing up on Sleeping Rock with the duffel bag, if it weren't to save it from the rising water?"

"No. But my failure to think of a reason, doesn't preclude there being one."

"Thank you, Mrs. Gatewood. That will be all."

Judge O'Connor announced that court was adjourned till two o'clock that afternoon. The courtroom emptied quickly.

I waited for Leah to return from the witness box. We tried to locate Anna, but she had left the courtroom. Leah looked for her and found her being sick in the ladies' room. We took Anna home, and she went to her bedroom to lie down.

Leah made sandwiches, and we talked quietly in the kitchen, speculating that if Sam had lost that bag of cocaine to the river, it could have been deadly. It was worth a great deal of money. Some drug lord would have made an example of him.

We ate in silence for a moment, and then I asked, "Why do you suppose Willis lied about the sequence of events?"

"His hatred of Sam has always warped his perspective. He's stubborn and resentful. He may truly believe he's right. And he'll never consider he's wrong!"

"It's hard to believe that an educated man could be so narrow in his thinking," I said.

Leah nodded. "That always baffled Momma."

I wanted to ask more about Willis, but the phone rang. It was Ferguson phoning to tell Leah that he'd had a surprise phone call from Phil Hutchins. He was to meet with him in a few minutes. "Don't tell Anna," he said, "in case it's all vine and no melons. I think there's a chance Phil can tell us what happened. It's been enough years that Phil would be granted immunity from any drug charges."

By two o'clock the courtroom was filled with spectators. Millford recalled Willis to the stand. He went over Willis's testimony about the sequence of events. Willis insisted he was not mistaken. The water had first covered Sam's feet, then he threw the duffel bag, and only then, had he tried to save Mary.

When Millford finished his questioning, Ferguson began his cross-examination. He took up his customary saunter, hands clasped behind his back, and asked, "You've been teaching thirty years, Mr. Sprule. Is that correct?"

"Thirty-five years," Willis corrected. "Thirty-five years of perfect attendance."

I thought I glimpsed a flicker of warmth in Willis's cold exterior.

Ferguson glimpsed it too and asked, "You're proud of that accomplishment, aren't you Willis?"

"Yes, I am."

"Were you ever late to school?"

"Never," Willis answered.

"What do you teach?"

"Mathematics and Algebra."

"Very exact disciplines, aren't they?"

"Yes."

"You're a man who's never late—in thirty-five years—who teaches disciplines which allow no mistakes. Would you say, Mr. Sprule, that you pride yourself on being right?"

"Being right is a matter of education and application," Willis said.

"Wouldn't you say it's difficult for you to admit being wrong?"

Millford objected.

Judge O'Connor overruled.

"I'm not a liar," Willis answered calmly.

"Wouldn't you say, Mr. Sprule, that you find it easier to blame Sam for Mary's death than to ask yourself if you might have had the time to descend that hill and save her yourself?"

Millford was on his feet, objecting that Ferguson was again badgering the witness, reminding the judge that Willis was not the one on trial.

Judge O'Connor sustained the objection.

Ferguson, continued to shamble along. "Were you aware, Mr. Sprule, that Sam had made preparations to leave Cotton Rock? That he was planning a new life as a fishing guide in Little Rock?"

"Yes."

"He had learned of the opportunity in Little Rock on the day of Mary's death, hadn't he?"

"Yes."

"He hadn't even had time to tell his mother, had he?"

"No."

"Isn't it correct that he had told you of his plans when he found you in his bedroom, the day of the drowning?"

"Yes."

"Do you think he suspected you had searched his duffel bag?"

"I figure he knew I'd seen the cocaine."

"Did it occur to you that he was trying to tell you he was turning over a new leaf? That he wanted to quit selling drugs?"

"Yes. I figured he was running out—always was a quitter."

"Quitting—on drugs? That would be unfortunate, wouldn't it Mr. Sprule?"

People chuckled, and Ferguson continued, "We've heard from your daughter's testimony that you didn't like Sam. That you maybe hated Sam."

"The boy had faults. I didn't hate him," Willis answered.

"Mr. Sprule, you always suspected Sam was alive. Isn't that true?"

"Stole my rifle, I knew he's alive."

"You hired a detective to find Sam. Isn't that right?"

"Yes."

"Paid a detective off and on for ten years. Isn't that correct?"

"If he was alive, I wanted Sam to be brought back. He killed Mary sure as if he held her under the water himself."

"Is it possible that your dislike for Sam was so paramount, your desire to see him behind bars so great, that you kept your eyes glued on that duffel bag? Because if that bag was swept away under the current, you would have lost your power over your stepson for good. Your chance to hurt him would be gone. Isn't it true that your hatred for Sam might have cost the life of your own daughter!"

"As I said before," Willis said calmly, "I'm not on trial here. I couldn't save Mary!"

"That's right! You were up on the knoll! Nothing could make you get off that knoll! Except something of ultimate importance—going to tie a bandana on a bush and making a phone call to the sheriff so you could destroy Sam. Isn't that correct?"

If Millford hadn't accidentally upended his briefcase and hadn't been clearly discomposed till order had been restored, he might have objected several times before he got around to it. By that time Judge O'Connor was already ordering Ferguson to allow the witness time to answer the questions. But Ferguson had finished his assault and simply stated he had no further questions. Willis stepped down from the witness stand.

Millford stated that he intended to call no further witnesses.

Ferguson announced that he was adding a new witness. "I call Phil Hutchins to the witness stand," he said.

Phil walked to the stand. If his mother had anything to do with his appearance, she was to be commended. Between his new suit and his pony tail, he could have just arrived from a conference on saving the rain forest.

Several members of the jury were probably owners of the exclusive retirement properties up and down the river. Many of them had come down from Kansas City. They would likely be accepting of Phil.

Phil swore in and stated his name.

"Mr. Hutchins," Ferguson said, meandering toward the jury, "do you know the defendant, Sam McKerry?"

"Yes," Phil answered.

"What was your relationship?"

"I went to high school with him. We were good friends."

"Then I would assume you also knew the members of Sam's family?"

"Yes. I was at their house some. I knew all of them."

"Did you know Mr. Sprule, in particular?"

"Yes. He was my teacher in high school algebra."

"How would you describe Mr. Sprule, as a teacher?"

"He was hard-ass—excuse me." He laughed nervously. "He was tough! He gave some swats no one will ever forget."

"Did you ever receive a swat from Mr. Sprule?"

"Yes, sir. He had a wooden paddle—an inch thick. Made you grab your ankles. You had to stand beside his desk. He could hit you hard enough to send you all the way to the door. Never gave less than five. He could make six-foot boys cry." Phil again laughed nervously. Yet in spite of his nervousness and the constant shifting in his chair, Phil came across as believable.

"How did he treat Sam?"

"I always figured he hated Sam. Got off on making Sam squirm. I felt embarrassed for Sam—for being there."

"Did you ever see Sam show any unkindness or disregard toward Mary?"

"No, sir! He was good to Mary. He was always taking her fishing."

"Were you aware that Sam was selling cocaine?"

"Yeah. I knew it. He was trying to get enough money to get away from Willis. Wanted to get a job as a fishing guide, maybe work down in Little Rock."

"Were you mixed up in helping to sell some of those drugs?"

"Yes. For a little while," Phil said, shifting in his chair. "But after the drowning, I was afraid. Scared me good. I got out of it."

"Now, Mr. Hutchins," said Ferguson and he stopped meandering, "were you at Sleeping Rock at the time of the drowning?"

"Yes sir," Phil said.

"Why did you go there?" Ferguson asked.

"Sam called me before he went to Sleeping Rock that day. Said he was scared. Said Willis knew about the bag. Asked me to cover his back. Take the bag for a day or two. I felt sorry for him. If Willis turned that bag over, Sam would go to jail for a long time. If the law didn't get him, the dealers would."

"And where was Sam when you arrived?"

"He was standing on Sleeping Rock. Only he never saw me."

"Could you explain?"

"Yeah. I parked my car on the north side of the bridge. Walked down to the river. I was supposed to meet Sam by Sleeping Rock. There's a lot of bushes—chinquapin and willows on the north side. Nobody saw me, it was a good thing. I didn't expect to see Willis there."

I glanced across the aisle at Willis. He sat stone-like as usual, staring straight ahead.

Ferguson continued, "Where was Mary?"

"Like they said, she was in a pocket of water on Willis's side. She was dancing around with those ribbons."

"What did you do, then?"

"Like I said, nobody saw me. I decided to keep it that way. I knew Sprule would be more than happy to rat on me."

"You said Willis was yelling. What was he yelling?"

"He was telling Sam to throw the bag to him. Kept ordering Sam to throw the bag to his side of the river. Threatened to make him pay if he didn't."

"What happened next?"

"Sam was scared. He was just standing there, holding the bag. Trying to think what to do. I just kept out of sight there in the willows, watching. None of us noticed that the water was rising."

Ferguson turned to face the jury and asked, "Why do you think Sam was up on that rock?"

"That was the plan," Phil said. "Said he'd sit up on the rock with the bag and be watching for me."

"So he was using the rock as a meeting point?"

"Yes. But I was running late—had trouble with my car. I was supposed to be there before the generators started up. I should have been able to walk right out to Sleeping Rock. Sam could of handed that bag off to me easy. Anyway, like I said, Willis was yelling. Ordering him to throw the duffel bag to his side of the river. I don't think Sam had ever disobeyed Willis before. He was scared."

"What happened then?"

"We were all watching Willis. Sam, me, even Mary. We didn't know what Willis was going to do. He just kept yelling at Sam. I guess all Sam could think of was to throw the bag to my side. Away from Willis. Maybe he figured he'd come back later and get it. Maybe he was just buying time. Maybe he was still hoping I'd show. But I wasn't about to risk touching that bag. I knew Willis had seen it hit the ground. Knew right where it was. Soon as he threw that bag, the water slid over the rock and hit his feet. That's the first I knew it was rising. You could see Sam was caught off guard."

"So you agree with Leah that Sam first threw the bag, and then the water reached his feet?"

"Yes," Phil answered. "The minute he felt that water, he started for Mary. I could see she's going to go under. Scared the hell outta me! I stayed where I was. I knew Sam couldn't get to her, and I'd never make it.

"Sam swam hard, but the river just scooped Mary off her feet, and took her under. Sam dived under, looking, then took off down river. He knew the current would sweep her on down. I saw Willis take off up the hill. When I saw him drive off in his pick-up and head east down the river, I hauled-ass—uh ran up to the bridge. I was just about to my car, when I saw Willis coming back up the road. I dropped out of sight. He drove across the bridge and came right up and parked behind my car. Got out and headed down to the river after that bag. I waited till I was sure he couldn't see me. Then, I got in my car and took off."

"Did Willis try to talk to you, later?"

"Yeah. He knew it was my car. Kept tracking me down. Asking me questions. I kept telling him I didn't know where Sam was."

Ferguson stopped in front of the witness box and asked, "Mr. Hutchins, how many minutes passed—would you say—while Willis argued about that bag, before he started climbing down from that knoll?"

"Three, maybe four minutes."

"In that length of time, could Willis have gotten down that knoll to the river?"

Millford objected.

Judge O'Connor sustained the objection and Ferguson redirected his question. "In your opinion, Mr. Hutchins, could a person descend from that knoll to the river in two or three minutes?"

"Sure. Anybody determined could have gotten down," Phil said. "And that's the reason I came here. I saw how things were going. And I ain't gonna let Sprule pin this on Sam. It isn't right!"

Millford jumped from his chair, declaring all manner of illegal sins on behalf of the defense. Judge O'Connor ruled that the remark be stricken from the record. Ferguson had no further questions, and Millford began cross-examination. He tried to discredit Phil as a drug user and party boy with no job. But he couldn't get Phil to back down from his testimony. At last, Millford dismissed Phil from the stand, and Ferguson called his final witness: Anna McKerry.

Every eye followed Anna as she walked to the stand. She was as near as the courtroom would get to hearing from Sam. She was the flesh and blood of the proceedings—the mother of the accused son, and the mother of the drowned child. For some she represented a curious dread, perhaps even a secret relief that life had not asked of them what it had asked of her. For others she evoked a sense of superiority, an assurance that their careful choices prevented such a moment from having arrived in their lives. Whatever the town's beliefs, Anna sat down, looking out at the courtroom.

I thought of the little girl Anna, who had been made to sit on Dade's judgment seat. The witness box must be of particular torment for Anna. She was sworn in, and Ferguson began his question.

He stood near the witness box, asking his questions with great care. "Mrs. McKerry, is there any doubt in your mind that your son would have saved Mary, had he been aware that the water was rising?"

"Anyone who knows Sam knows he'd have done anything in his power to save Mary. She was the spring of the morning to Sam. I think he proved himself. Like Phil said, the moment Sam felt the water rising, he tried to save her."

Millford could have objected, pointed out that Anna was not at the river to know if Phil told the truth. But he had the great good sense not to criticize the mother of a dead child.

"Mrs. McKerry, we've heard testimony of Willis's treatment of Sam. You must have seen some of that ill treatment."

"Yes, I did."

"Would you tell us about it?"

Anna took her time. Her gaze traveled across the courtroom until she located Willis. She spoke, looking directly at him, "I could tell a number of stories—all of them mean. All of them sad. Sam was mighty proud of Willis in the beginning. Like all little boys, Sam wanted a daddy. I saw how he tried to walk like Willis, talk like Willis." She smiled sadly. "Tried his best to make his voice sound flat and washed out. Not an easy thing for a little boy. Got in a fight at school cause he was bragging how his momma was married to one of the teachers. Nobody believed him, and he stood his ground all the way to a black eye.

"Sam had a heart full of love for Willis. Children are mighty humble. They forgive for a long time. Like I said, I could tell lots of mean things about Willis. But I figure the worst thing Willis did was to kill a little boy's love. Sam's love for Willis just faded away—quiet like—along with trust, and hope. Willis never knew what those things were—so he never even noticed that they died."

The courtroom was silent. Ferguson was finished with his questions and Millford declined cross-examination.

The summations were brief. Ferguson reminded the jury that Sam had never been known to treat Mary with disregard. He had been observed by friends and family to exhibit great concern for her welfare and had been trusted for years to take her fishing. In fact, Sam possessed a great love for his little sister. With his final remarks, the old coon dog measured each word. He remembered every hunch he had treed, and now he bagged the game and brought it home. Like Grandma Rowden, he spoke each word as if it were worth a hundred dollars: "Willis Sprule stopped on that knoll, held there by his hate, held by his obsession to destroy. The rage and threats that he rained down upon Sam rendered both Sam and Mary immobile, frozen in fear, so neither of them noticed the swelling river. Actually, Willis's hate blinded him to the danger.

"If there'd been love in the heart of that little girl for her daddy, instead of dread, she would have—as little girls do at the sound of their daddy's voice—run with gladness to meet him, instead of cowering down in a river that swept her to her death."

Ferguson finished his summary, and the trial had ended. We waited for the jury's verdict, which came a full day later. In the end, all of the arguments, all of the labor for mercy was overruled by the cold hard fact of the cocaine. The fact that a little girl had drowned—directly or indirectly—as a result of its presence, forced the jury to conclude their verdict. The foreman rose to read the jury's response to the charge of involuntary manslaughter: "We, the jury, find the defendant, Sam McKerry, guilty."

Thoughts from the Back Porch   May 1997

    I'm sitting once again on the back porch. I drove down from Springville to attend Harlo's Kindergarten graduation. Perhaps only once in a lifetime does every necessary circumstance converge to create a moment of exquisite justice. It's perhaps also true that only once in a lifetime does such an inconsequential item as a doorknob become instrumental in bringing about such a moment. Yet far greater doors have turned on equally small hinges. Some historians have argued that the common stirrup changed the world of mounted combat—fortifying the rider against the blow of a couched lance, ultimately giving rise to Knighthood and the advancement of feudalism in France.

    Ironically the school board decided to bestow three awards during the celebration of Harlo's graduation: the first award would go to the teacher of the year, Miss Judy Simpson, Harlo's Kindergarten teacher; the second, to the high school science teacher, earning state recognition for developing a science curriculum; the third, to Willis Sprule for thirty-five years of teaching with perfect attendance.

    Willis, never late to school in thirty-five years had no doubt risen early that morning. Graduation was scheduled for 10:00 A.M. at the high school auditorium. According to Cora Eckert, it was 9:00 when Willis entered his bathroom to shave. A few minutes later Willis was ready to exit the bathroom, put on his suit, walk to his pickup and drive the ten miles to town with an estimated arrival time of 9:45. According to later accounts, it was exactly 9:05 when Willis laid his hand on the doorknob, gave it a firm turn and found it had wrung right off into his hand. A second later he heard the sound of the exterior knob fall decidedly to the floor.

    A carpenter might have had a tool or two on his belt or even a reserve in a bathroom drawer. Willis had neither. He exhausted himself ransacking the bathroom for any sort of contrived shaft to thread through the small opening and turn the delicate mechanism that stood between him and thirty-five years of recognition. He knew enough to take the door from its hinges but not without the aid of a screwdriver. The only window in the bathroom was unequivocally too small for his girth, though Willis, no doubt, considered it repeatedly and urgently. There was nothing to do in the end but pour his rage fully on the situation and to kick the door down.

Meanwhile the auditorium bustled with activity. I had picked up Leah, Anna and Harlo at 9:15 sharp. The parking lot was nearly filled when we arrived. Grandparents, uncles, aunts and cousins had arrived to share the achievement of Cotton Rock's Kindergarteners. People carried cameras and presents. Anna held a bouquet of pink rosebuds for Harlo who wore a new purple dress, which she twirled with every opportunity. Lushbaugh's Grocery had contributed refreshments, and Dee stood by a line of tables along the wall giving orders to Lingo who carried in boxes of cookies and bags of ice for the punch.

Leah escorted Harlo to a designated room to be fitted with her mortar board. Anna and I found seats, saving one for Leah. Lucy and Eb waved from across the aisle, and Lucy came over to introduce me to her sister, Opal. "Opal taught most of the parents in this room, you know." Lucy chuckled, telling me to keep an eye on Mr. Davis, the Superintendent. "He loves having his picture taken," she whispered. "'Specially to have it show up in the Cotton Rock Times. Got that photographer on the stage for more reasons than taking pictures of little folks."

Lucy and Opal went their way. Emmett caught my eye and gave a big wave. "Yes," Anna told me when I asked about the woman beside Emmett, "that's his wife, Lottie. Nothing happens in town without Lottie's notice. She could write a column of her own in the *Fish Hatchery News.*"

I read over the program and found Harlo's name. I checked the order of events. The students would march down the center aisle and sit in the reserved chairs in front. The pastor from the First Baptist Church would give the invocation. Mr. Davis—ever mindful of the camera—would present awards to the three honored people, followed by the presentation of diplomas.

At precisely ten o'clock the pianist began the familiar strains of "Pomp and Circumstance." Thirty little people began the long walk down the aisle, intent on marching as they had been shown: step wait, step wait. We could see Harlo now. I squeezed Leah's hand. My throat tightened. This was what it felt like to be a parent, to share the sweetness of an important moment! "The picture!" Leah reminded, handing me the camera. It might well have been Harvard or Yale.

When the last child had filed by and taken a reserved seat in the front, the pastor rose to open with prayer, followed by Mr. Davis who stood to present the awards. Miss Judy and the science teacher each took turns standing patiently beside Mr. Davis for a photo.

"And now," Mr. Davis said, "we'd like to present Willis Sprule with this very special plaque acknowledging his thirty-five years of teaching with perfect attendance!"

The auditorium filled with applause. Heads turned locate Willis, but Willis did not come forward. The applause faded. Mr. Davis consulted with the principal. People kept turning round in their chairs, trying to catch sight of Willis.

Anna leaned over and whispered, "He's never been late a day in his life. Hell has surely frozen over." An uncomfortable confusion followed. Miss Judy crossed the stage to have a word with Mr. Davis, who nodded. "Well," Mr. Davis said, "we're not certain where Mr. Sprule is, but we have an excellent replacement."

Miss Judy escorted Harlo to the platform as Mr. Davis announced, "Willis Sprule's little granddaughter, Harlo, is one of our graduates. We're going to have her receive the award for her grandfather." The audience applauded their approval. But Harlo, uncertain what was being asked of her, did not take the plaque Mr. Davis offered.

Willis Sprule was just entering the room as Mr. Davis knelt down, holding the microphone toward Harlo and said, "I'll bet you're proud of your Grandpa."

Harlo, quite confused, looked up at Miss Judy for direction.

Mr. Davis, signaling the photographer to capture the moment, directed the microphone once again to Harlo, "What do you think of your Grandpa Willis?"

Leah had left her chair, making her way to the platform, determined to rescue her daughter from Mr. Davis's thoughtless exploitation, but Harlo, assured by Miss Judy that she was to answer the question, nodded, speaking in an unmistakably clear voice: "My grandpa Willis was mean to my Uncle Sam. He made my Grandma Anna cry. And when he dies, he's going straight to hell."

For what seemed like an eternity, the room froze in silence. Then from the cookie table, Dee Lushbaugh called out, "That's the best graduation speech I've ever heard!" She started clapping. Within seconds, the auditorium filled with applause. Mr. Davis, red-faced and bewildered was still trying to hand the plaque to Harlo, but Leah had reached the platform, taken Harlo by the hand and guided her back to her classmates. Mr. Davis resigned to the loss of a great photo, laid the plaque down on his folding chair and announced that he would proceed with the presentation of diplomas.

When the last little student had crossed the stage to receive a diploma, a celebration followed with pictures, presents and lots of cookies. Harlo twirled her way to the car, and we drove home with everyone singing "Zippity Do Da."

For several days over backyard fences, telephones and store counters, people recited Harlo's graduation speech to one another. Emmett's wife, Lottie was careful to remind everyone, "Out of the mouths of babes, you know, the Lord speaketh."

Willis, who had been quick to exit the auditorium, didn't stay for the graduation or the cookies. Gossip has it that he will be moving up to Osage Bend.

Thoughts from Springville   September 1997

The Fall Semester is underway, and I've returned to Springville. I'm sitting in bed writing the last entry in the notebook by the light from the bedside lamp. My wife's remarkable blue eyes are closed in sleep.

Little Harlo is asleep down the hall. Leah tucked her in beside her doll, Bill, earlier this evening. Harlo has finished her first month in the first grade. She spent the evening reading her new book to Bill. It might be my imagination, but I think Bill's glass-eyed look of apprehension has nearly faded.

Occasionally when I'm writing, I open the window by my computer and listen to Harlo singing with great abandon, swinging back and forth on the swing I hung in the old maple tree. I think she laughs more easily than she once did. However sometimes when she straightens Bill's coat and then straightens it again, or walks a little too quickly to the bus stop, or asks me a second time how many minutes have passed, I think of Anna. I remember that Harlo, like her grandmother, may always hear the same, urgent voice from life.

When Leah gave up her apartment, we convinced Anna to live in my cabin. We assured her I needed her to take care of things. As soon as spring arrives I'm having some rooms added so Leah, Harlo and I can spend the summer in Cotton Rock with Anna.

I knew that sooner or later, Anna would put the trial into words, and I was right. A letter came today. It seems to close this chapter of all our lives, and so it is the final entry.

> Dear Leah and John,
> I reckon that any heart-scabs I had left got pulled off during the trial. I am grateful that the judge showed mercy at the sentencing. Six years. Perhaps less with good behavior. There will always be thoughts that chap the mind, knowing that I helped to lay stones in the path leading to that day on the river. No matter that the stones were laid on other days, no matter that none of us knew where the path was leading. No matter that Sam laid his own stones in fear

and hopelessness, or that Willis laid them in meanness and revenge. No matter that I laid them in cowardice and sad excuses. We all had our reasons. One day, Leah, when little Harlo is fifteen you'll come to know you laid no stone on that path. It was for you a young girl's simple wanting to be with her friends.

In the beginning I said that I thought writing down my life would put it to rest, would free me from thinking till my head was sore, keep me from traveling like a Scotch-Irishman down worn paths that led into old, sad hollows and up to new ridges where there are things I didn't know, and down into sloughs so deep and dark it feels like I'd never find my way out. The trial was the last dark slough. I've put things to rest.

I guess I never figured how much the past walks in today's shoes. That old prison on the hill above the court house, climbed each stair with me on my way to Sam's trial. We're born prisoners of hope, straining forward against those rings in the floor, straining against the things which have chained each of us by the foot.

Those old prison blocks stacked row on row, are cut from cotton rock that was here long before the White River was running a baby stream. Those layers of dolomite and cotton rock, twisting and turning with the hills in some ancient search, twisting and turning with the river, like they inherited something bent a bad direction, so they're trying to go another. Like our lives.

I figure there's God's choices, and there's mine. I didn't choose a momma that went to bed or a daddy that's lying at the bottom of Pearl Harbor. I didn't choose to be born a woman in the Ozarks hills in the forties. On the other hand, I could have been born the man who dropped the bomb on the deck of my daddy's ship.

Leah, you told me once we don't choose our birth intelligence, or health or fairness of face. We don't choose our parents, or the country where we're born. I reckon we're lucky if we can choose what we'll eat for dinner. I figure that God pretty well dealt us the hand we play. Our choice is how we play it out. Some of us, like me, waste our aces before we're twenty years of age, and that makes a good hand mostly lean. And the lean hand I was holding got handed on to Sam. And to you, Leah, and to Mary.

Our lives, like cotton rock stone, are generations in the making. Maybe the decisions Sam made that day on the river started long before he was born. Maybe it started when the armor piercing bullet sliced through the deck of the U.S.S. *Arizona*, and my daddy saw the smoke and fire coming down the hallway to get him. Maybe it was the day Momma married Dade, or the day she went to bed for five years. Maybe it was the day I first saw Jake riding down the Sugar Gum River, or the day I married Willis. Maybe it was all of those days that caused Sam to stand on that rock frozen with fear and looking at Willis instead of looking at the water rising up around him.

The river that took Mary is bigger than itself. It's a part of all the land it drains and sky it gleans of water. It rides on the backs of all the yesterdays.

The ashes of my daddy have left my mouth, and my judgments of Momma have circled back to name my own failures. I've climbed out of the swamp, and met myself sitting on the bank. My search has come full circle, and I think I've finally paid what it is I owe the dead.

It's fall again. The maiden hair and ribbon fern are bedded down. The redbud trees along the river have lost their wine. John, your Grandma Rowden's words have come around again: "The shagbark hickory tree at the corner of the porch has turned—not just yellow, but true gold."

I spent the summer finding all the herbs that Grandma Poinselot taught me. I've picked their leaves and tied them up in strings along the porch. I have enough to cure whatever maladies we might choose to have. I keep busy. And, of course, I drive up to see Sam every visitor's day.

I washed all the windows last week and raked up the first snow of leaves. If there's anything that you'd like done, you know I'll be smiling all the while—a grateful pie crust surely greases its own pan. Anyway, the last of the berries are all in jelly jars, and it's time to rest awhile.

When you come down, chances are you'll find me sitting on the back porch just watching the river slide by.

Love, Anna

CPSIA information can be obtained at www.ICGtesting.com
Printed in the USA
LVOW061427261111

256544LV00005B/1/P

9 780983 252412